# Off the
## Beaten Path®

# connecticut

## Help Us Keep This Guide Up to Date

Every effort has been made by the authors and editors to make this guide as accurate and useful as possible. However, many changes can occur after a guide is published—establishments close, phone numbers change, hiking trails are rerouted, facilities come under new management, etc.

We would love to hear from you concerning your experiences with this guide and how you feel it could be improved and be kept up to date. While we may not be able to respond to all comments and suggestions, we'll take them to heart, and we'll make certain to share them with the authors. Please send your comments and suggestions to the following address:

The Globe Pequot Press
Reader Response/Editorial Department
P.O. Box 480
Guilford, CT 06437

Or you may e-mail us at: editorial@GlobePequot.com

Thanks for your input, and happy travels!

INSIDERS' GUIDE®

OFF THE BEATEN PATH® SERIES

# Off the
SEVENTH EDITION
# Beaten Path®

# connecticut

## A GUIDE TO UNIQUE PLACES

**DAVID AND DEBORAH RITCHIE**

**Revised and updated by
Joan and Tom Bross**

INSIDERS' GUIDE®

GUILFORD, CONNECTICUT
AN IMPRINT OF THE GLOBE PEQUOT PRESS

The prices, rates, and hours listed in this guidebook
were confirmed at press time. We recommend,
however, that you call establishments to obtain
current information before traveling.

**INSIDERS'**GUICE®

Copyright © 1992, 1995, 1998, 2000, 2002 by Deborah Ritchie and David James Ritchie
Revised text © 2005, 2007 Morris Book Publishing, LLC

Text design by Linda Loiewski
Maps by Equator Graphics © Morris Book Publishing, LLC
Illustration credits: pages 11, 55, 69, 155, and 203 drawn from photographs courtesy of
the Connecticut Department of Economic Development; page 79 drawn from photo-
graph courtesy of Deborah Ritchie; page 140 drawn from illustration courtesy of
Chamard Vineyards; page 144 drawn from photograph courtesy of the Griswold Inn;
and page 169 drawn from photograph courtesy of Mashantucket Pequot Museum and
Research Center.
All other text illustrations by Carole Drong
Spot photography throughout © Jon Arnold Images/SuperStock

ISSN: 1539-8641
ISBN-13: 978-0-7627-4197-7
ISBN-10: 0-7627-4197-X

Manufactured in the United States of America
Seventh Edition/First Printing

# Contents

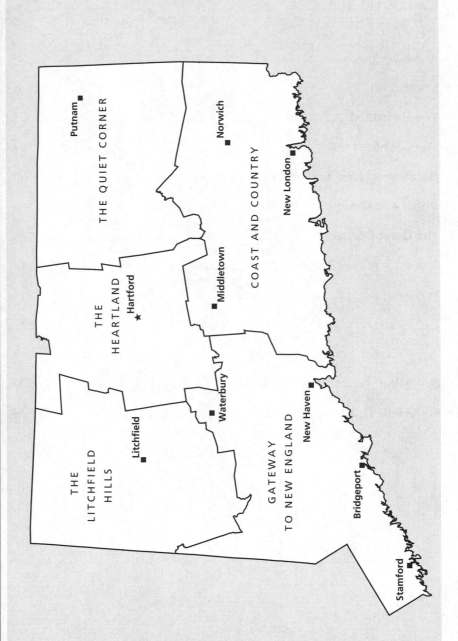

# Acknowledgments

Even a state as small as Connecticut provides many sources of information for those of us who write about its great appeal as a traveler's destination. We feel responsible for keeping ourselves familiar with the full statewide expanse—north to south, east to west—and to do that job we rely upon helpfully knowledgeable people. So our special thanks goes to the always-responsive staffs of the five regional tourism bureaus—and especially to Anne Lee and Diane Moore, representing the Greater Hartford & Connecticut River Valley office.

Barbara Rogers, a longtime colleague and coauthor (with her husband, Stillman Rogers) of the New Hampshire, Massachusetts, and Rhode Island guidebooks in The Globe Pequot series, deserves our sincerest appreciation for advising us of the Connecticut opportunity and recommending us to the appropriate editors.

Working travel writers are like vacationing travelers: They appreciate comfortable, conveniently situated accommodations and pleasurable dining experiences. We were fortunate in those respects, enjoying the hospitality of Hartford's Goodwin Hotel and, in coastal Old Saybrook, the Saybrook Point Inn & Spa. Dinner at downtown Hartford's Trumbull Kitchen was, for both of us, a culinary delight at the end of a long fact-finding day in Connecticut's diverse heartland.

—Joan and Tom Bross

# Introduction

> A good traveler has no fixed plans and is not intent on arriving.
> —*Lao-Tsu* (570–490 B.C.E.)

Nestled between the much larger states of New York and Massachusetts, Connecticut occupies a mere 5,009 square miles along the coast of Long Island Sound. It is, in fact, the third smallest state in the Union. But what a state! Nowhere in America can the traveler find so representative a history, so rich a culture, and so great a physical diversity packed into so small an area.

The Native Americans who lived in the region for millennia before the arrival of the first Europeans called it *Quinnehtukqut* ("Beside the Long Tidal River"). About 20,000 Native Americans lived in the area when the Dutch discovered the Connecticut River in 1614; those who remain now occupy five reservations. English Puritans from Massachusetts began to flood the Connecticut Valley a couple of decades after its discovery by the Dutch, and in 1638–39, the towns of Hartford, Windsor, and Wethersfield adopted the Fundamental Orders of Connecticut, setting up a government for the new Connecticut

## Connecticut River Trivia

The Connecticut River is one of fourteen waterways designated an American Heritage River by former vice president Al Gore.

The Connecticut River is 410 miles long—about 5,551 football fields.

Today's Connecticut River came into being between 10,000 and 13,000 years ago, after the Wisconsin Glacier receded from the New England area.

The Connecticut Valley developed about 220 million years ago in the late Triassic period.

Within the ecosystem of the Connecticut River watershed, you can find ten endangered or threatened species:

Three birds: the piping plover, the peregrine falcon, and the American bald eagle.

One fish: the shortnose sturgeon.

One insect: the Puritan tweed beetle.

One mollusk: the dwarf wedge mussel.

Four plants: the Jesup's milk vetch, small whorled pogonia, Robin's cinquefoil, and the Northern bulrush.

Colony. About the same time, the colony of New Haven was founded farther west along the coast of Long Island Sound. The two colonies were joined in 1662, and the state gained—roughly—its current outline.

Since then the history of Connecticut has largely marched with that of America. During the past 350 years, the state has played a vital role in American experiences, such as the settlement of the frontier, the winning of the Revolutionary War, the adoption of the Constitution, the Union victory in the Civil War, and that vast upheaval known as the Industrial Revolution.

Connecticut's part in the American pageant has left a lasting mark on the state. Its towns have been ravaged by America's wars. Its language and culture have been molded by the nation's immigration policies. Its geography has been altered by the spread of industrialization. Its economy has been shaped by the growth—and demise—of such industries as whaling, railroading, shipbuilding, and textile manufacturing. It has been, in many ways, a microcosm of America.

Sometimes known as the Land of Steady Habits, Connecticut has taken as its official designation the title Constitution State. Washington called it the Provision State, because it fed his army during the darkest days of the Revolution. It is also called the Nutmeg State, a sobriquet just as common as the official designation and perhaps more representative of Connecticut's history and culture; the name Nutmegger was often applied by the residents of neighboring states to Connecticut peddlers, who were famous for selling bogus nutmegs carved from local wood in place of the imported (and more expensive) real thing.

Whatever you call it, Connecticut is a land of odd contrasts and strange delights that have accumulated over centuries. Modern Connecticut has something to excite the whim and tickle the fancy of almost every traveler. Its diverse geography runs the gamut from the sandy beaches and teeming marshlands of its coastal plains and the fertile meadows of its central lowlands to the forested hills of the eastern and western uplands and the craggy granite cliffs that characterize its northwestern reaches. The many eras of its history are enshrined not only in countless museums, galleries, and restorations but in numerous historical structures that are still part of the everyday lives of its people; this is, in fact, one of the few places in America where you can find real Cape Cod saltboxes, Victorian Gothic mansions, and art deco roadside palaces of the early automotive era all happily residing cheek by jowl.

The densely populated cities along Connecticut's southwestern coast and the navigable portions of its major rivers are home to 90 percent of the state's inhabitants and give the state an urban flavor that stands in stark contrast to its rural uplands. This clustering of settlement along coasts and rivers explains why, even though Connecticut is the fourth most densely populated state in the United States (with an overall density of more than 650 persons per square mile), roughly 60 percent of the state is forest land. Most of the trees in these forests are northern hardwoods about sixty to one hundred years old, and they are purely glorious in fall. Another 15 percent of Connecticut is farmland, cultivated by a mere 1 percent of the population. Dairy farming and horse breeding are major Connecticut industries that add their own brand of color to rural areas. So is the cultivation of wrapper tobacco, which is grown under netting and dried in characteristic long wooden sheds that you'll notice dotting the landscape in the northern farming valleys.

In terms of amenities for the traveler, Connecticut has few equals. Though modern accommodations abound, this area, like most of New England, is famous for its quaint inns and bed-and-breakfasts (or B&Bs), many of which are housed in buildings that have been around longer than the state. The state's eclectic cuisine, both cosmopolitan and casual, reflects the cultural and gustatory gifts brought by succeeding waves of immigrants. Its great wealth and emphasis on tourism make it a shopping paradise; establishments range from some of America's largest and most attractive malls to ma-and-pa operations offering only-in-Connecticut crafts to factory outlets that fairly shout bargains.

For the traveler who likes to venture off the beaten path, Connecticut is an especially satisfying venue; one constantly discovers the odd, the interesting, and the truly bizarre tucked away in the most unexpected places. Whether it be a mere whimsy like a roadside rock painted to look like a startlingly realistic giant frog, a truly spine-chilling gothic mystery like the deserted village of Bara-Heck Settlement, or something just plain nutty like the weird and wonderful United House Wrecking, you can never be entirely sure what you will find around the next bend.

We like to think of Connecticut as representing all the best of America in vest-pocket size: gilded beaches that would be the envy of California; rolling hills better than any in Virginia; pastoral farmland that makes you think you're in Indiana; downtown chic that rivals New York; and some of the friendliest people on earth. A truly dedicated traveler (and if you're reading this book, you probably fall into that category) could experience the full diversity of the state in one day. You could jump-start your day with an espresso in West Hartford, drive down to the shore for a few hours of sun and sand capped by a lunch of fried clams at Lenny and Joe's, take an afternoon jaunt up into Litchfield County to browse the antiques shops before driving over to the Quiet Corner for a hayride through its fields and glens, and end your day with one of the best dinners of your life at the Golden Lamb Buttery in Brooklyn.

Geography isn't the only source of variety in Connecticut. Its northerly location and long coastline conspire to produce a multiplicity of seasonal variations in the weather. Each season brings its own wonders and offers its own characteristic activities. Winter means Olde Wethersfield, all dressed up in the spare elegance of a colonial Christmas, pure white candles glowing in many-paned windows, and the faint sounds of Christmas carols wafting across the green. Spring is the season for strolling along one of eastern Connecticut's back roads, watching farmers plow its rolling farmlands, listening to the first few notes of bird song, and sniffing the green tang of growing things in the air. Summer is a time for the shore; for golden beaches, the hiss of the waves, the crunch of fried clams, and the sweet sugary smell of cotton candy. Fall means Litchfield's amber and cinnabar hills, quintessentially New England white clapboard churches posed against the fiery reds of nearby sugar maples, the rush of the Housatonic, and the sweet taste of fresh-pressed cider and cider-glazed doughnuts.

Regardless of the season, traveling in Connecticut is easy, although traffic congestion has become an increasingly prevalent problem, especially during the summer, so you should build in extra time if you are planning to attend an event that has a specific starting time. Interstate highways crisscross the state, with Interstate 95 (formerly the Connecticut Turnpike) running the length of its shore, Interstate 91 bisecting the state from north to south, Interstate 395 winding along its eastern border, and Interstate 84 running from Danbury through Waterbury to Hartford and thence through the northeastern counties to the Massachusetts Pike. The interstate highway system is complemented by an excellent system of state highways. More often than not, this book takes you off the interstates and puts you on the smaller roads that evolved with our state's history from Indian trails to two-lane paved roads. Some of these back roads may seem awfully isolated. But never fear; no matter how far into the outback it feels, you're never more than half an hour from a major highway that will quickly return you to more populated areas.

Clearly, no one book can do justice to Connecticut's 350 years of history or to the diverse delights packed into this one small state. Just as an example, we're pretty certain that there's not a township in the state that doesn't have at least one museum located in a restored seventeenth- or eighteenth-century house and furnished with antiques and artifacts culled from local attics. We could, with some encouragement, write an entire book just on restored buildings.

As in most of life, some judicious editing is necessary. Thus, you won't find herein detailed descriptions of the well-known delights of Mystic or the popular casinos at Foxwoods or Mohegan Sun. Nor do we devote much space to the major attractions in the state's larger cities. These items are well documented in a host of travel books and brochures, many of which are available through Connecticut's tourism division. That office has divided the state into five tourism districts, each with a local office that can provide you with maps and information about the area. For further information on popular attractions and tourism in general, call the Connecticut Commission on Culture & Tourism at (860) 566–3005.

This book does not pretend to compete with the state of Connecticut in offering general travel information or describing nationally famous attractions. Instead, we offer a directory of out-of-the-way places that you might not know to look for if you're not native to the area. Where can you get the best pizza or ice cream or chili dog in the state? Where will you find the most interesting pottery or the neatest antiques or the strangest stores? Where can you experience the uniquely Connecticut and the perfectly New England without having to fight the crowds? We may miss some of the major attractions, but if it's funky, funny, little known, or out of the way, then you'll probably find it here. For convenience, we've divided the state into five sections, matching Connecticut's major geographic, historical, and cultural divisions.

The following state agencies can provide you with other information on travel in Connecticut:

**Connecticut Commission on Culture & Tourism**
One Financial Plaza
755 Main Street
Hartford, CT 06106
(860) 566–3005

**The Museum of Connecticut History**
(860) 757–6535

**The Bureau of National Resources**
CT Department of Environmental Protection
165 Capitol Avenue
Hartford, CT 06106
(860) 424–3000

**The Bureau of Outdoor Recreation**
CT Department of Environmental Protection
165 Capitol Avenue
Hartford, CT 06106
(860) 424–3000

## Area Codes

We've included phone numbers for most attractions. Connecticut has two area codes: Hartford, Litchfield, Middlesex, New London, Tolland, and Windham Counties are in area code 860; Fairfield and New Haven Counties use the 203 area code. Sounds simple? Yep, except that the town of Sherman and the portions of Woodbury with Watertown phone numbers use the 860 area code. The rest of Bethlehem and Woodbury as well as part of Roxbury use the 203 area code. Go figure.

## Tourism Information

The Connecticut Commission on Culture & Tourism publishes a yearly *Connecticut Vacation Guide* and other publications of interest to visitors. These items are available for free by calling (888) CTVISIT (800–282–6863). The commission's Web address is www.ctvisit.com.

Five regional tourism districts around the state provide information, guides, and special event listings targeted to their regions.

How to contact the tourism districts:

**Central**
(860) 244–8181
(800) 793–4480

**South Central**
(203) 777–8550
(800) 332–STAY (7829)

**Eastern**
(860) 444–2206
(800) 863–6569

**Southwestern**
(203) 853–7770
(800) 866–7925

**Northwestern**
(203) 597–9527
(888) 588–7880

A bed-and-breakfast reservation service will help you find the inn that's right for you: www.bbonline.com/ct or www.bnbinns.com.

For a yearly listing of craft shows in Connecticut, call the Trail of Connecticut Craft Centers at (800) 282–6363.

## Fall Foliage

In most of Connecticut, fall foliage hits its peak around Columbus Day. Areas in the north, northwest, and northeast see peak color a little earlier. Starting in late September, you can get a daily fall foliage update by calling (888) CTVISIT (800–282–6863), ext. 88.

## Food in Connecticut

One of our favorite ways to get to know a region is to start with a menu, sampling foods unique to the area. Here in Connecticut, our cuisine is an amalgam of rugged colonial dishes leavened with ethnic foods, the heritage of the immigrants who helped transform our state. It all makes for a diverse and heady cuisine. Try to sample some of these emphatically Connecticut foods when you visit.

**Chowder.** The origins of its name, *chaudière* (large kettle), may be French, but this hearty soup is all New England. You won't find as many fish chowders in Connecticut as in other parts of New England, but we make stellar clam chowders. **New England clam chowder** is a milk- or cream-based soup full of potatoes, onions, whole clams, and salt pork and seasoned with thyme. It's probably the version you think of when someone mentions clam chowder. **Rhode Island clam chowder** is New England clam chowder lightened with just enough pureed tomatoes to turn the soup a rosy pink. **Southern New England clam chowder** is a bracing, briny broth loaded with clams, potatoes, and onions—no milk or cream. **Manhattan clam chowder** is a tomato-based veggie soup with a few clams. To be shunned. Check out the clam chowder offerings at Abbott's Lobster in the Rough in Noank or Lenny and Joe's Fish Tale Restaurants in Westbrook and Madison.

## trivia

The complete title of America's first cookbook was *American Cookery or The Art of Dressing Viands, Fish, Poultry, and Vegetables, and the Best Modes of Making Pastes, Puffs, Pies, Tarts, Puddings, Custards and Preserves, and All Kinds of Cakes, from the Imperial Plumb to Plain Cake. Adapted to This Country and All Grades of Life.*

**Lobster roll.** In some New England states, a lobster roll is lobster salad (cold lobster, mayonnaise, seasonings) served on a toasted hot dog bun. But in Connecticut, a lobster roll is a spiritual experience: fresh, hot lobster meat, dripping with melted butter, served on a sesame-seeded hamburger bun or toasted hot dog bun. Both of Lenny and Joe's Fish Tale Restaurants excel in the art of the lobster roll. Be sure to try one, and don't forget the extra napkins for wiping butter-drenched chins and fingers.

**Grape-Nuts pudding.** Baked custard served in a sweet shell of Grape-Nuts cereal, one version features a swirl of Grape-Nuts throughout the pudding. Much better than it sounds. Check out Zip's Dining Car in Dayville for Zip's recipe for Grape-Nuts pudding.

**Indian pudding.** A robust dessert dating back to colonial times. It's a mix of cornmeal, molasses, and warm spices cooked for hours at a low temperature until thick and amber-colored. Some heretics add raisins or apples. Served with vanilla ice cream or a rivulet of heavy cream. The Griswold Inn in Essex usually has Indian pudding on its fall and winter dessert menu.

**Pizza.** New Haven is the pizza capital of Connecticut, maybe of the United States. New Haven pizza has a thin and crunchy crust and doesn't wallow in toppings. Don't want anyone to know you're a tourist? Call it a tomato pie, not pizza. Pepe's and Sally's are the traditional top choices among New Haven pizza palaces. In Hartford County, the pizza at Harry's in West Hartford Center is glorious.

## Freedom Trail

The Freedom Trail marks locations in Connecticut that were important in the battle to end slavery. For a complete listing of sites, go to www.ctfreedom trail.com.

Among the sites on the trail:

**Harriet Beecher Stowe Center,** Hartford. Home of the author of *Uncle Tom's Cabin.*

**John Brown birthplace,** Torrington. Where the fiery abolitionist began his life.

**First Baptist Church,** Milford. A memorial to the African-Americans who fought in the Revolutionary War.

**Milo Freeland grave,** North Canaan. The grave site of the first African-American to volunteer for service in the Union army during the Civil War. His story was depicted in the movie *Glory.*

**Paul Robeson house,** Enfield. Purchased by the singer and actor at the height of his popularity. His activism on behalf of equal rights resulted in his banishment from the American stage.

## Famous Nutmeggers

**Bill Blass,** designer
**David Bushnell,** inventor of the submarine
**Glenn Close,** actress
**Samuel Colt,** revolver
**Placido Domingo,** opera singer
**Dominick Dunne,** author
**Michael J. Fox** and **Tracey Pollan,** actors
**Peter Goldmark,** long-playing record and color television
**Charles Goodyear,** vulcanization of rubber
**Katharine Hepburn,** actress
**Dustin Hoffman,** actor
**Elias Howe,** sewing machine
**Henry Kissinger,** diplomat
**Larry Kramer,** AIDS activist and author
**Edwin P. Land,** Polaroid camera
**Frank McCourt,** author

**Arthur Miller,** playwright
**Paul Newman** and **Joanne Woodward,** actors
**Jacques Pepin,** chef and author
**Keith Richards,** musician and rock star
**Phillip Roth,** novelist
**Meg Ryan,** actress
**Maurice Sendak,** author and illustrator
**Igor Sikorsky,** helicopter
**Benjamin Spock,** pediatrician
**William Stryon,** author
**Diane von Furstenberg,** designer
**Horace Wells,** nitrous oxide anesthesia
**Eli Whitney,** cotton gin

## State Symbols

- **Official designation:** The Constitution State
- **Indian name:** Quinnehtukqut—"Beside the Long Tidal River"
- **State motto:** He who was transplanted still sustains
- **State flower:** mountain laurel
- **State bird:** robin
- **State tree:** white oak
- **State animal:** sperm whale
- **State insect:** praying mantis
- **State mineral:** garnet
- **State song:** "Yankee Doodle"
- **State ship:** USS *Nautilus*
- **State shellfish:** eastern oyster
- **State composer:** Charles Edward Ives
- **State poet laureate:** Marilyn Nelson
- **State fossil:** *Eubrontes giganteus,* an 18-foot-long carnivore
- **State hero:** Nathan Hale (A captain in the Continental army, Hale crossed enemy lines to gather information about British troop strength and battle plans. He was caught and hanged as a spy and is best remembered for the immortal words, "I only regret that I have but one life to lose for my country.")
- **State heroine:** Prudence Crandall (In 1833 Crandall established the first academy for African-American women in New England. She faced hardship and violence and was placed on trial for breaking a law specifically written to keep the school from opening.)

## Connecticut Firsts

- **1639:** Connecticut adopts the country's first written constitution, the Fundamental Orders of Connecticut.
- **1647:** Hartford hangs the first witch in the colonies at what is now the corner of Albany Avenue and Garden Street.
- **1656:** New Haven creates the first public library from a gift of books from Theophilus Eaton.
- **1660:** Hopkins Grammar School established, the first private secondary school.
- **1727:** Samual Higlley mints the country's first copper coins in Simsbury.
- **1740:** The Pattison brothers (Edward and William) of Berlin make tinware, which they sell door to door. This enterprise inaugurates the tradition of the "Yankee peddler," that slippery Connecticut character responsible for relieving countless residents of neighboring colonies of their excess cash.
- **1764:** Publication of the *Connecticut Courant* (now the *Hartford Courant*), the nation's oldest continuously published newspaper.
- **1771:** The colony forms the Governor's Foot Guard, oldest military unit in America.
- **1775:** David Bushnell launches the first submarine, the *American Turtle*.
- **1776:** Nathan Hale, a Nutmegger and the country's first martyr, is executed in Manhattan.
- **1777:** First trimmed and illuminated Christmas tree in Windsor Locks.
- **1780:** Benedict Arnold of Norwalk becomes the new nation's most famous traitor.
- **1783:** Noah Webster's blue-backed speller printed in Hartford by Hudson & Goodwin.
- Jupiter Hammond of Hartford becomes the first African-American poet to be published.
- **1784:** America's first law school—Tapping Reeve—established in Litchfield.
- **1796:** Hartford's Amelia Simmons, who styled herself "an American Orphan," publishes America's first cookbook, *American Cookery.*
- **1801:** A Mrs. Prout of South Windsor makes America's first cigars, the Long Nines.
- **1803:** Salisbury establishes the first children's library.
- **1806:** Noah Webster publishes America's first dictionary.
- **1809:** Mary Kies receives a patent for weaving silk with straw or thread. She is the first American woman to receive a patent.
- **1814:** Eli Terry patents the first shelf clock in Thomaston.

- **1817:** First school for the hearing impaired—the American School for the Deaf—founded in Hartford.
- **1844:** Charles Goodyear of New Haven receives the patent for vulcanization of rubber.
- **1854:** City of Hartford votes to create Bushnell Park, America's first municipal park.
- **1873:** The first football game is played at Yale.
- **1878:** The world's first telephone exchange and directory opens for business in New Haven.
- **1881:** P. T. Barnum introduces the three-ring circus.
- **1889:** Stamford's George C. Blickensderfer invents the first portable typewriter.
- William Gray of Hartford invents the world's first coin-operated pay telephone.
- **1897:** The automobile industry is born when Albert Pope and Hiram Maxim show off their electric car.
- **1904:** First submarine base established at Groton.
- **1906:** Hartford's Alfred C. Fuller makes the housewife's life a little easier when he starts selling door to door the first twisted-in wire housebrush.
- **1909:** Hiram P. Maxim invents the gun silencer.
- **1917:** John Browning invents the automatic pistol, Browning machine gun, and the Browning automatic rifle, all for Hartford's Colt Firearms.
- **1919:** Homogenized milk first sold in Torrington.
- **1920:** Stamford's Pitney Bowes introduces the first U.S. postage meter.
- **1931:** First electric shaver made in Stamford.
- **1934:** Consumer advocate Ralph Nader born in Winsted.
- **1937:** Margaret Rudkin puts on her apron and bakes the first loaf of Pepperidge Farm bread in Fairfield.
- **1939:** Igor Sikorsky builds the first helicopter in Stratford.
- **1949:** James Wright of New Haven invents Silly Putty, delighting kids and frustrating moms everywhere who find the stuff impossible to remove from the family dog's fur.
- **1954:** First nuclear submarine—the *Nautilus*—launched in Groton.
- **1960:** The world's first two-sided building, also known as the Boat Building, is erected in Hartford. It is the headquarters of the Phoenix Mutual Insurance Company.
- **1965:** Connecticut becomes the first state in the nation to require cities with populations of more than 20,000 to use fluoride in their drinking water.
- **1975:** Ella T. Grasso is the first woman in America to assume the office of governor without inheriting it from her husband.

# The Heartland

The upper Connecticut River Valley is a broad, fertile mead-owland ideal for farming and grazing, and the state's Puritan settlers were naturally drawn to it. It was the first part of Connecticut to be colonized, and those original settlements thrived and expanded until they finally merged to form what is today Greater Hartford, a vibrant metropolitan area of more than 832,000 people at the center of the state's most populous county. Bounding Hartford County's urban and suburban core on the north and west are the rural Farmington and Tobacco Valleys. To the east is pastoral Tolland County. Within these rural boundaries is Connecticut's heartland, the seat of its govern-ment and one of its most important commercial centers. As you might suspect, the majority of the attractions in this area are his-torical and cultural; in addition, you can find the commercial activities and entertainments of a large metropolitan area.

## The Capital

Formerly the site of the old Dutch Fort Good Hope (1633), Hart-ford was the first city in Connecticut. It was famous in the nine-teenth century as a center of the abolitionist movement and the tobacco industry and as the home of the Colt Firearms Factory,

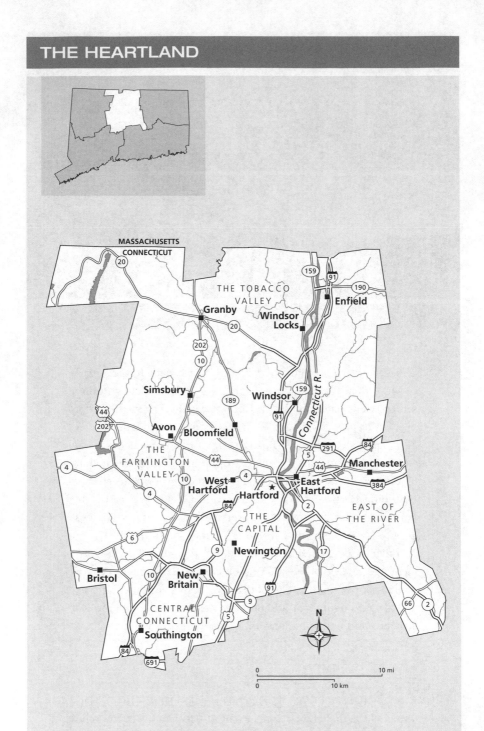

MASSACHUSETTS
CONNECTICUT

20

THE TOBACCO
VALLEY

159
91
190

Granby

Windsor
Locks

Enfield

202

10

Simsbury

189

Windsor

159

91

Connecticut R.

Avon

Bloomfield

84

44
202

THE
FARMINGTON
VALLEY

44

291

Manchester

4

10

West
Hartford

4

5

44

East
Hartford

84

Hartford

2

384

EAST OF
THE RIVER

THE
CAPITAL

6

9

17

Newington

Bristol

10

New
Britain

91

9

5

CENTRAL
CONNECTICUT

Southington

66
2

84

691

N

0                    10 mi
0                    10 km

maker of the Colt Revolver, "the gun that won the West." In more recent times Hartford has grown more tame, and it is now known as the Insurance City.

A pyramid-topped edifice completed in neoclassical style in 1919, the ***Travelers Tower*** looms 527 feet over Hartford for visual prominence—including after nightfall, when its beacon shines. Headquarters for what is now known as The St. Paul Travelers Companies, Inc., this was New England's longtime tallest building, preceding Boston's 1970s skyscraper boom.

For spectacular panoramics from the twenty-seventh-floor observation deck, ride an elevator to the twenty-fourth floor, then climb a seventy-two-step spiral staircase. Open Monday through Friday from 10:00 A.M. to 3:00 P.M., mid-May until the last week of October. Call (860) 277–4208. Viewing spaces are both inside and on an outdoor deck.

Hartford is where the insurance industry was born. The first policies covering shipping were written here way back in 1810. By 1898 the first automobile insurance policy, at the staggering cost of two cents, had been issued by Travelers Insurance Company and the rest, as they say, is history. Today, even with consolidation and downsizing, Connecticut's capital city is still the place to be if you want to live long and prosper with insured security.

Having set a proper mood, head into the center of the city to the traditional starting point for a tour of Hartford. The ***Old State House*** at 800 Main Street was built in 1796 and is the oldest state house in America. After a recent $12 million renovation, it houses a number of exhibits, some inspiring and others just wonderfully silly. It all adds up to great fun in the least stuffy historical site/museum you're likely to come across. For travelers off the beaten path, the big draw is a re-creation of ***Joseph Steward's Hartford Museum*** with its conglomeration of "natural and other curiosities," crammed into an upstairs section since 1791. The wide-ranging diversity from near and far includes "A Calf with Two Complete Heads," African tribal masks, sharks' jaws, a stuffed cobra, giant tortoise shells, artfully impaled tropical insects, a wingspreaded bat-under-glass, a crocodile's head, and drawers full of birds' eggs. For the more serious minded, there are various historical displays and a famous portrait

## AUTHORS' FAVORITES

Bloomfield Seafood

Dinosaur State Park

Governor's Horse Guards

New Britain Museum of American Art

Old New-Gate Prison and Copper Mine

## High Victoriana in Hartford

Its eight-sided gilded cupola gleaming in sunlight, Connecticut's *State Capitol* greets your eyes when you come into Hartford by way of Interstate 84. Designed by Richard M. Upjohn, primarily a cathedral architect, this High Victorian Gothic–style colossus—completed on its hilltop site in 1878—is a marble-and-granite riot of pinnacles, turrets, columns, bas reliefs, statues, heraldic emblems, arches, and porticoes. In addition to state executive offices and legislative chambers, this recently renovated pile of stone contains a variety of historic exhibits, including bullet-riddled battle flags, vintage weaponry, and the Marquis de Lafayette's canvas camp bed. Visitors can take a one-hour guided tour of the premises between 9:15 A.M. and 1:15 P.M. on weekdays year-round (to 2:15 P.M. in July and August) and between 10:15 A.M. and 2:15 P.M. on Saturday from April through October. Go to the League of Women Voters information desk on the first floor by the west entrance (210 Capitol Avenue), although it's best to call ahead: (860) 240–0222. If you prefer self-guided touring, ask for a free, fully detailed booklet.

The State Capitol isn't Hartford's only prominent symbol of nineteenth-century architectural flamboyance. Dominating downtown's Asylum Street/Haynes Street intersection, 1878's *Goodwin Hotel* exemplifies Victorian Queen Anne exuberance with its fancy amber-hued brickwork and molded terra-cotta details. In what was originally a luxury apartment building, Hartford-born financier J. P. Morgan had a private suite on the upper floor. The present-day edifice, with its 135 guest rooms and two epicurean restaurants, is one of heartland Connecticut's most exclusive hotels. One Haynes Street; (860) 246–7500 or (800) 922–5006; www.goodwin hotel.com.

of George Washington by Gilbert Stuart. There's also a gift shop and a fairly extensive tourist information center. The latter is a good place to start a tour of downtown Hartford; you'll find directions to enough museums, homesteads, galleries, and such to keep you busy for at least a week. Call (860) 522–6766.

What looks vaguely like a National Guard armory as you do some sightseeing on Main Street is actually one of Hartford's most distinguished cultural institutions: the **Wadsworth Atheneum,** our nation's oldest continuously operating public art museum, established in 1842. The mock-Gothic "armory appearance" constitutes the central part of an architectural mishmash that includes Renaissance Revival and Tudor-style add-ons. Wadsworth holdings exceed 45,000 works, with the strongest emphasis on all periods of American and European art. Head upstairs to view a couple of world-class attractions—the Nutting collection of Early American furniture and idyllic nineteenth-century landscapes painted by such Hudson River School exponents as Frederic Edwin Church, Thomas Cole, Albert Bierstadt, and Sanford Gifford. A gallery devoted to decorative arts includes eighteenth- and nineteeth-century china crafted in half a dozen countries. And save time to admire large-scale American Colonial canvases turned out by John Trumbull, born in Lebanon, Connecticut, and the son of an early state governor. The museum is closed Monday and Tuesday, otherwise open 11:00 A.M. to 5:00 P.M. Wednesday through Friday, 10:00 A.M. to 5:00 P.M. Saturday. Call (860) 278–2670.

Mentioning painter John Trumbull whisks our thoughts to 150 Trumbull Street, where one of the city's hippest, coolest, contemporary restaurants is a sure-enough indicator of continuing resurgence in the compact downtown district. Namely *Trumbull Kitchen,* an "in" place for lunch or dinner. The chef's fusion cuisine includes Spanish tapas, Oriental dim sum tidbits, and stone-pie thin-crust pizzas. For tasty main courses, patrons can choose pecan-crusted sea scallops, seafood pad thai, hoisin marinated pork chops, all-American meat loaf or New York sirloin, and other such dinnertime goodies. Reservations are a must; call (860) 493–7417.

Art lovers should make a point of seeing two famous pieces of art in the downtown area. Alexander Calder's *Stegosaurus* is a huge steel construction that towers over Burr Mall, a small pocket park between the Wadsworth Atheneum and Hartford City Hall. And watch for Carl Andre's *Stone Field Sculpture* on Gold Street across from the Atheneum and beside the Ancient Burying Ground. This $87,000 sculpture has always been a subject of conversation in Hartford. It consists of thirty-six large rocks arranged in rows on a slope of lawn. Some critics consider it a statement of minimalist art; some witty citizens call it Hartford's Meadow Muffins. You decide what it really is.

After you check out *Stone Field,* walk over to the *Ancient Burying Ground* on Main Street behind Center Church. This cemetery was created in 1640 and holds the bones of some of Hartford's most prominent citizens, including Thomas Hooker. If you're a

## hartfordtrivia

Before he donned his rumpled trench coat and found fame as TV's Inspector Columbo, actor Peter Falk toiled as an efficiency expert for the state's budget bureau, where it would have been very inefficient to ask "just one more question. . . "

Founded in 1764, the *Hartford Courant* (once the *Connecticut Courant*) is our country's oldest continuously published newspaper. The *Courant*'s been around long enough to report the Boston Tea Party as breaking news. In 1796 a Virginia farmer named George Washington advertised in its real estate section.

The Reverend Thomas Hooker is honored as the founding father of Connecticut. These days Hartford celebrates his memory with its laid-back and fabulously flamboyant "Hooker Day" parade, usually held the first weekend in October.

fan of early American art, the tombstones are a treasure trove of colonial death imagery and epitaphs. It's a pleasant place for a lunchtime stroll in downtown. The cemetery is open during daylight hours.

While strolling through the downtown area, look up at the architecture. Hartford has many buildings with some lovely Gothic ornamentation that are certainly worthy of a second look. We've been fans of gargoyles, grotesques, greenmen, and chimeras for a couple of decades, and we always do a gargoyle hunt in every city we visit. In Hartford we particularly like the gargoyles protecting **Christ Church Cathedral,** 45 Church Street, (860) 527–7231, and the winged gargoyle ornamenting the Richardson Building, 942 Main Street.

Next to the State Capitol Building on Jewell Street is **Bushnell Park,** 166 Capitol Avenue, the first plot of land in America taken by eminent domain for use as a park. As you would expect, the park's forty-one acres include manicured lawns, towering shade trees, and the obligatory monuments (including one to Dr. Horace Wells, the man who, in 1844, discovered the anesthetic properties of nitrous oxide); but it is also home to some unusual extras, including the 1914-vintage **Bushnell Carousel,** whose forty-eight antique Stein and Goldstein horses revolve beneath 800 twinkling lights. The band organ is a refurbished 1925 Wurlitzer, and, yes, you really can try to catch a brass ring. The park is open year-round, but the carousel operates only mid-May through September. It is run by the Bristol Carousel Museum. Hours can be erratic, so it's best to call ahead, (860) 585–5411. There's a small charge to ride.

## bushnell park trivia

According to *Yankee* magazine, Bushnell Park is the proud possessor of the largest turkey oak *(Quercus cerris)* in New England. Its trunk is nearly 17 feet around. The tree gets its moniker because the crinkled edges of its leaves remind some of a tom turkey's tail feathers.

Horticulturists may find the half-hour guided Tree Tours of Bushnell Park of interest. The tours explore the rare and native trees in the park and are guided by volunteers. Wear good sturdy walking shoes for the tours. Free self-guided maps of the park and the tree tours are available from the Greater Hartford Convention & Visitors Bureau, located in the Civic Center. Call them at (860) 728–6789 or visit online at www.enjoyhartford.com.

Completed in 1932, the **Trinity College Chapel** on Summit Street boasts stained-glass windows, a cloister, arches, and carved pews in keeping with the best medieval tradition. The chapel's most interesting elements are seventy-eight hand-carved oak pews that face each other across the nave. It took more than thirty years to complete all the carvings. Most of the pews were the work of Gregory Wiggins of Pomfret, who taught Latin, Greek, and German before he decided to become a full-time wood carver. The Charter Oak Pew shows Capt. Joseph Wadsworth hiding the Connecticut Colony's royal charter in an ancient oak tree to prevent its recall by Royal Governor Edmund Andros (not a beloved figure in Connecticut history).

A nifty lunch spot in the vicinity of Trinity College is ***Timothy's*** at 243 Zion Street. This place serves some of the cheapest, best, and most plentiful home cooking in Hartford. The menu, which changes almost daily, features mainly organic food. There is outdoor dining in the garden.

Timothy's is usually knee-deep in students and faculty from nearby Trinity, but it's a congenial crowd, and newcomers are graciously welcomed. As for the food, just try any of the soups or sandwiches. It doesn't matter which— they're all good. Timothy's is known for its desserts, including a highly recommended dense, moist, coffee-kissed Black Magic cake. Portions are humongous, so pace yourself if you want dessert. Open 7:00 A.M. to 8:00 P.M. Monday through Thursday, 7:00 A.M. to 9:00 P.M. Friday, 8:00 A.M. to 9:00 P.M. Saturday, and 9:00 A.M. to 3:00 P.M. for Sunday brunch. Call (860) 728–9822.

After indulging yourself at Timothy's, you may need to walk off a few calories. One of the most pleasant walks in Hartford is through the ***Cedar Hill Cemetery*** on Maple Street down on the Hartford/ Wethersfield town line. Laid out in 1864 by Jacob Weidenmann, who also did the honors for Bushnell Park, Cedar Hill is a classic Victorian city of the dead, full of ostentatious granite monuments, odd carvings, and strange sentiments. The terrain is hilly enough to be interesting, and the grounds are beautifully planted. This is, after all, the final resting place of such captains of industry and commerce as Sam Colt and J. P. Morgan, and also movie-star legend Katharine Hepburn, born in West Hartford. Open during daylight hours.

## morehartfordtrivia

The Phoenix Mutual Life building in downtown Hartford is popularly known as the "boat building" because it reminds many of the locals of a graceful, green-glass boat.

In the mid-1700s the men who lived along the Connecticut River and accumulated vast wealth from the West Indies trade were known as River Gods. You can see a re-creation of a formal parlor belonging to one of the River Gods at the Atheneum. For the 1700s those River God boys lived very well indeed.

Weidenmann also laid out the beautifully landscaped grounds and gardens at the ***Butler-McCook Homestead,*** 394 Main Street. It's the last single-family home on Main Street, and everything in it is original. This lovely house-museum is a terrific place to walk off your worries or sit a spell to restore your spirit and rest your mind. Open 10:00 A.M. to 4:00 P.M. Wednesday to Saturday and 1:00 to 4:00 P.M. Sunday. Call (860) 522–1806 for more information.

The **Connecticut Department of Environmental Protection Bookstore,** 79 Elm Street, may be the most off-the-beaten path attraction in this book. It's a bonanza for hikers, fishers, and armchair geologists. Connecticut's Department of Environmental Protection has produced more than 1,300 publications about the state and its environment, including some dynamite maps for hikers, naturalists, and birders and some publications from not-for-profit and private presses. It's open 9:00 A.M. to 1:00 P.M. and 1:30 to 3:30 P.M. Monday through Thursday. Call (860) 424–3555 for a free catalog and information; http://dep.state.ct.us.

Hartford's **Institute of Living,** 400 Washington Street, the state's first hospital (1822), was one of the first mental health facilities to practice more humane treatment of those afflicted with mental illness. The first lobotomy, then considered a leading-edge procedure, in the country was performed here in 1939. The institute has had its fair share of rich and famous patients, such as Bing Crosby (who used to hop the fence to drink in neighborhood bars), but its permanent exhibit, *Myths, Minds and Medicine,* is a sober look at just how cruelly mentally incapacitated people were once treated. It's strong stuff and includes information on some less-than-humane treatments like cold wet wraps and induced insulin shock, leavened by a bit of nonsense such as movies of "guests" from the 1930s larking about at fashion shows. This is probably not a good place to visit with younger kids.

If you visit the institute, take time to tour the grounds. They were laid out by Frederick Law Olmstead in 1861. Take special note of the trees, some of which are among the largest in New England. A brochure for a self-guided tour of the grounds is available at the guard station at 200 Retreat Avenue. The institute's museum is open 9:00 A.M. to 5:00 P.M. Monday through Friday. Call (860) 545–7000 for more information.

For a taste of Hartford's signature food, head to Franklin Avenue. This is Hartford's Little Italy, and practically any place you wander into will have something to delight your palate. **Mozzicato de Pasquale's Bakery and Pastry Shop** at 329 Franklin Avenue is a warm, dark cafe with a distinctive old-world feel. This is just the right place to spend a rainy Saturday afternoon dawdling over a cappuccino and a pastry or a cup of chocolate hazelnut gelato while entertaining fantasies of Venice. The bakery arm churns out rich pastries and beautiful, traditional Italian cakes, tortes, and cookies. Open every day from 7:00 A.M. to 9:00 P.M. Call (860) 296–0426 for more information.

In the lofty world of culinary accolades, you can't do much better than getting critically acclaimed in *Gourmet* magazine. Jane and Michael Stern heaped praise upon the **Polish National Home,** 60 Charter Oak Avenue. We took them at their word (literally), combining a family visit with a midday meal at this place in an unassuming location on Hartford's east side. When you visit, don't be intimidated by the brick ark in which the restaurant is located, and don't be deterred by the usually locked front door. You'll find the entrance at the back by the parking lot. Once inside, follow your nose. While you will find some familiar American dishes on the menu (fried chicken, turkey, and so forth), the real stars are the Polish dishes like the crunchy, toothsome *placki* (potato pan-

## OTHER ATTRACTIONS WORTH SEEING IN THE HEARTLAND

**Antiq's,**
(American and English furniture)
1839 New Britain Avenue,
Farmington;
(860) 676–2670.

**Behind the Scenes at the Bushnell,**
166 Capitol Avenue,
Hartford;
(860) 987–6000.

**Garden of Light**
(natural food market),
395 West Main Street,
Avon;
(860) 409–2196;
www.gardenoflight.net.

**International Skating Center of Connecticut,**
1375 Hopmeadow Street,
Simsbury;
(860) 651–5400.

**Luddy/Taylor Connecticut Valley Tobacco Museum,**
Northwest Park, 135 Lang Road,
Windsor;
(860) 285–1886.

**New Britain Youth Museum at Hungerford Park,**
191 Farmington Avenue,
Kensington;
(860) 827–9064.

**Rose's Berry Farm,**
295 Matson Hill Road,
South Glastonbury, and
1200 Hebron Avenue,
Glastonbury;
(860) 633–7467.

**Town Farm Dairy,**
73 Wolcott Road,
Simsbury;
(860) 658–5362.

**Tulmeadow Farm & Ice Cream,**
255 Farms Village Road
(Route 309),
West Simsbury;
(860) 658–1430.

**Vintage Radio & Communications Museum of Connecticut,**
1231 Main Street,
East Hartford;
(860) 673–0518.

**The Vintage Shop,**
61 Arch Street,
New Britain;
(860) 224–8567.

**Water Gardens of Eating Greenhouse**
(hydroponic greenhouse),
Hartford Farms,
3 Fowler Place,
Windsor;
(860) 724–3700.

## Hartford's Trashy Museum

If all of us follow our municipalities' recycling schedules and regulations, might we be able to do our part in saving Planet Earth? Well, after a visit to Hartford's own garbageatorium, you'll wind up understanding the benefits of communal recycling. The garbageatorium's real name is the visitor center at the **Connecticut Resource Recovery Authority.** Your tour starts with what is called the Temple of Trash, an area devoted to the cool stuff that people throw out. After goggling at all the neat junk (and wishing you could take some home), you move on to where the real work happens. From a viewing area, you get a bird's-eye view of the ultimate in dumpster diving: watching colossal bins of trash being sorted and then rushed off via conveyor belts to recycling heaven. The wonderful Rube Goldberg silliness appeals to most kids, especially the ones who harbor a secret desire to dig through trash cans. The Connecticut Resource Recovery Authority is located at 211 Murphy Road (exit 27 from Interstate 91). The visitor center is open noon to 4:00 P.M. Wednesday through Friday, September to June, and 10:00 A.M. to 4:00 P.M. Tuesday through Saturday, July and August. (860) 757–7765. No admission charge.

Stratford also has a viewing area where recyclables are sorted. A popular attraction is the Trashasaurus, a large dinosaur model built out of recyclable materials. It's located at 1410 Honeyspot Road Extension. Call (203) 381–9571. Same hours as Hartford.

cakes) and pierogi (half-moon-shaped little dumplings filled with meat, potato and cheese, sauerkraut and mushrooms, or blueberries). For a taste of Poland, try the "Polish plate," which is a mini-buffet including everything from pierogi to *golabki* (stuffed cabbage) to *bigos* (sauerkraut braised with kielbasa and pork). Do we have to mention portions are huge? Don't miss the Saturday polka parties. Full bar. Open 10:00 A.M. to early evening ("about 7:00 or 8:00," later if there's an event scheduled) Monday through Saturday and 11:00 A.M. to 3:00 P.M. Sunday. Call (860) 247–1784 for hours and more information.

The most striking thing about the **Menczer Museum of Medicine and Dentistry** (230 Scarborough Street) is just how far we've come in a couple of centuries. It was not that long ago that doctors were universally known as surgeons, carried their few instruments wrapped in pieces of leather or cloth, and mainly performed amputations. Well into the nineteenth century, doctors were still treating patients by bleeding them, and Louis Pasteur began to work on the germ theory of disease only in 1850.

The museum records the medical profession's progress toward more modern and effective practices in displays of equipment, medications, instruments, and implements of destruction used by doctors and dentists from the eighteenth through the twentieth centuries. There are examining tables and chairs, anesthesia machines, and early X-ray machines. Some rooms contain glass cabinets of instruments; others are set up as period doctors' offices. There are also some gloomy portraits of Hartford's early medical men, a medical library open to researchers, and, of course, a display on the discovery of anesthesia. Open weekdays, 10:00 A.M. to 4:30 P.M. Admission is $2.00 for adults, $1.00 for children. Call (860) 236–5613.

***Elizabeth Park Rose Gardens*** on Prospect Avenue was the first municipally owned rose garden in America. More than 14,000 roses grace the park. There are also perennial gardens, greenhouses, nature walks, and a rock garden. The park offers something special during every season, but it's late June and early July when the roses are at their peak. In those few brief weeks, Elizabeth Park is an experience that overwhelms the senses. The many varieties of roses come in all sizes and hues, and the mingled scents, from the sweetly scented traditional American hybrids to the elegantly fragrant Damask roses, are indescribable. The Pond House on the premises contains a snack bar, lounge, and auditorium. Open daily, dawn to dusk. Call (860) 722–6514.

Back in 1874 the great American humorist and novelist Mark Twain (aka Samuel Langhorne Clemens) began summering in Hartford in a rambling, three-story, nineteen-room Victorian mansion that he had built to his eccentric specifications; in 1881 he had the place redecorated in an even more eccentric style by Louis Comfort Tiffany. For the next quarter-century, this was the Twain family summer home, which he often described as "part house, part steamboat." It was the place where Twain wrote some of his best works, including *Tom Sawyer, Huckleberry Finn, The Prince and the Pauper,* and *A Connecticut Yankee in King Arthur's Court.*

The restored ***Mark Twain House,*** 351 Farmington Avenue, is a museum and storehouse of Twain memorabilia. The unmistakable redbrick building, with

Mark Twain House

its startling three-colored slate roof, its many gables, its monumental chimneys (it has eighteen fireplaces), and its flamboyant exterior walls painted in red and black Chinese stripes and trimmed in dark red, looms over the Farmington Avenue commuter traffic, almost like a lingering sardonic comment from the famous humorist. Inside, each of the mansion's unique rooms has been restored as close to its 1881 condition as possible. About half of the original furnishings remain, including Twain's Venetian bed, whose ornate headboard so intrigued the author that he slept with his head at the foot of the bed so that he could see the intricate carvings. In November 2003, a new museum center was opened, which uses new ideas and technologies to explain the legacy of a literary icon. It includes exhibition galleries, a theater, and classrooms. Open daily 9:30 A.M. to 5:30 P.M., Thursday to 8:00 P.M. Closed Tuesday January through April. Guided tours begin at the visitor center; the last one leaves at 4:00 P.M. Gift shop. Admission. Call (860) 247–0998.

## marktwaintrivia

Twain was fascinated by technology and incorporated many of the day's latest inventions in his home, including central heating and gas lighting fixtures. So it is fitting that the new museum center at the Mark Twain House is the first LEED (leadership in energy and environmental design) certified museum in the country and the first LEED building in Connecticut. Among the many cutting-edge environmental features are the geothermal walls as the predominant cooling source.

Twain's ill-advised investment in a typesetting machine called the Paige Compositor resulted in such a devastating financial loss that he was forced to leave his Farmington Avenue home and move his family to Europe.

*Tom Sawyer* was the first novel in America to be written on a typewriter.

Across the lawn from the Mark Twain House, at 77 Forest Street, is the home where Harriet Beecher Stowe once lived. Today the ***Harriet Beecher Stowe Center*** comprises a museum and library, with the stated purpose of "inspiring visitors to embrace and emulate her commitment to social justice." The complex has a visitor center, a museum shop, and the Katherine Seymour Day House, which offers a vivid glimpse into the life of the woman who helped galvanize the abolitionist cause and contributed to the start of the Civil War with her novel *Uncle Tom's Cabin*. The Day House has magnificent interiors, changing exhibits, a research center, and Victorian gardens. The center is on the Connecticut Freedom Trail and the Connecticut Women's Heritage Trail. It is open 9:30 A.M. to 4:30 P.M. Tuesday through Saturday; noon to 4:30 P.M. Sunday. Open Monday as well Memorial Day through Columbus Day and in December 9:30 A.M. to 4:30 P.M. Call (860) 522–9258.

West Hartford also has a couple of those restored houses that are ubiquitous in Connecticut. The **Sarah Whitman Hooker Homestead** (1237 New Britain Avenue) is a lovely 1720 mansion named for a resident heroine of the American Revolution. Outside there's an herb garden and an antique (heritage) rose garden. Open 1:30 to 3:30 P.M. Monday and Wednesday. Hours may vary so call ahead. Special tours by appointment. Call (860) 523–5887.

The **Noah Webster House,** 227 South Main Street in West Hartford, is the birthplace and childhood home of Noah Webster, author of the first American dictionary. The house is furnished much as it would have been when Webster lived there in the eighteenth century. The delightful thing about this house is that there's always a staff of "interpreters" on hand to answer questions. They dress in colonial garb, and they actually perform tasks such as baking in the kitchen fireplace; you may even get to taste the result. Open September through June daily (except Friday), 1:00 to 4:00 P.M. Open July and August, 11:00 A.M. to 4:00 P.M. Monday, Thursday, and Friday; 1:00 to 4:00 P.M. Saturday and Sunday. The gift shop on the property sells locally created craft items. Admission. Call (860) 521–5362.

Through his dictionary, which he began when he was 43, Webster is credited with Americanizing the English language. He launched the project because Americans in different parts of the country spelled, pronounced, and used words differently. Webster thought that all Americans should speak the same way and that Americans shouldn't speak and spell just like the English. So, for example, his dictionary uses *color* instead of *colour*. He also added some distinctly American words like *skunk* and *squash*. It took him more than

## stowetrivia

Stowe was compelled to write *Uncle Tom's Cabin* by the passage of the Fugitive Slave Act in 1850, which made it a crime for residents of free states to help runaway slaves. The book's power came from the way Stowe humanized enslaved people at a time when they were mostly treated as property. She drew on her own feelings when her eighteen-month-old son Charley died of cholera to convey how a slave mother would feel to lose a child at the auction block.

*Uncle Tom's Cabin* sold over 10,000 copies the first week and was a best seller in its day. Stowe had a prolific career, writing thirty books and countless shorter pieces. She also had seven children.

According to legend, when Abraham Lincoln met Stowe, he said, "So you're the little woman who wrote that book that started this Great War." Stowe herself said, "I wrote what I did because as a woman and a mother, I was oppressed and brokenhearted with the sorrows and injustice I saw, because as a Christian I felt dishonor to Christianity, because as a lover of my country, I trembled at the coming day of wrath."

webstertrivia

In 1774, when he was sixteen years old, Noah Webster attended Yale, Connecticut's only college at that time.

twenty-seven years to finish the dictionary, which contained 70,000 words.

West Hartford is also home to a fine little eatery out of another era. Located at number 319 on Park Road, the **Quaker Diner** is the special labor of love of Harry Bassilakis, whose grandfather built it in 1931. Harry gave up a career with a local insurance company in 1987 to restore the place to its original state, and many of the fittings—the high-backed wooden booths, the counter stools, and the black and white deco tile in the hall leading to the bathrooms—are carefully tended original appointments. Other furnishings are from Harry's personal collection of antiques.

Aside from being a fine restoration, the Quaker offers some of the best diner food in New England. Harry's mom, Agnes, does much of the cooking, including most of the specials and desserts. Just about everything is made from scratch, and some of the recipes, such as Agnes's justly famous meat loaf, are quite elaborate. The breakfasts are also first-rate. We especially like the Hole-in-One: French toast with the center cut out and replaced with a fried egg (the circular section of toast that was removed to make way for the egg goes back on as a hat).

The Quaker is open 6:00 A.M. to 2:30 P.M. Monday through Friday, 6:00 A.M. to 1:30 P.M. Saturday, 7:00 A.M. to 1:30 P.M. Sunday. Saturday and Sunday, breakfast only. Call (860) 232–5523.

The Park Road area is another neighborhood that's pleasant for walking and window shopping. You'll find a couple of good antiques shops, a used book store, and a bakery, **Your Just Desserts,** which specializes in extravagant cakes. Not far from the Quaker, you'll find another equally delicious sampling of Connecticut's melting-pot cuisine. **Pho Tuong Lai** (355 New Park Avenue) is a simple, storefront, family-run place, but we think you'll find some of the best Vietnamese cooking at bargain basement prices in the state. We're big fans of their *cha gio tom,* triangular-shaped, deep-fried shrimp rolls stuffed with shredded carrots, ground pork, and shrimp. Less adventurous palates will feel well fed and well satisfied with any of the ginger dishes, for example, the chicken and ginger with steamed broccoli cooked in a tasty reduction of soy with lots of snappy ginger flavor. Meat and potatoes lovers can chow down on the *bo luc lac* or "shaken beef," which is stir-fried cubes of filet mignon and onion in a savory sauce, served on a bed of cold, crunchy watercress. The "house dish" is *Pho,* the beef and noodle soup that's the national soup of Vietnam. What makes this dish special are the garnishes: lime wedges, bean sprouts, fresh basil, and chilis. Open daily from 9:00 A.M. to 8:00 P.M. Call (860) 523–9134 for more information.

Connecticut residents are passionate about their pizza. Our personal favorite is **Harry's Pizza** (1003 Farmington Avenue). Harry's has one great advantage over most pizza shops: Pizza is all that it does. Oh, you can get a very nice side salad, but you won't find the usual selection of dubious sandwiches and ho-hum pasta to distract the guys in the kitchen. Their eyes are firmly on the pie, and

## Quaker Diner Meat Loaf

1 medium onion, chopped fine

1 carrot, chopped fine

2 stalks celery, chopped fine

½ green pepper, chopped fine

2 tablespoons butter

2 pounds ground beef (for a lower-fat meat loaf, use half lean ground beef and half ground turkey)

⅓ cup ketchup

¼ to ⅓ cup freshly grated Parmesan cheese

2 eggs

½ to ¾ cup flavored dry bread crumbs

salt, pepper, garlic powder to taste

Melt butter in medium skillet over medium heat.

Add chopped celery, carrot, onion, and green pepper. Season to taste with garlic powder.

Sauté for five to seven minutes, stirring frequently, until soft and onion is translucent. Remove from heat; let cool.

Season ground beef with salt, pepper, and garlic powder to taste.

Add ketchup, Parmesan cheese, eggs, bread crumbs, and sautéed vegetables to ground beef.

Mix lightly until all ingredients are combined.

Pat gently into meat loaf shape and place in lightly greased baking dish or pat into lightly greased loaf pan.

Bake at 350 degrees until done. Start checking it after an hour; depending on your oven, total cooking time can vary between one hour and one hour and fifteen minutes. Let cool a little before slicing.

Serve with brown gravy and *real* mashed potatoes.

Serves 6 to 8.

they turn out an excellent one. Harry's standard pie is a traditional tomato and mozzarella number, with a crisp thin crust and an eclectic selection of toppings. Besides the standard sausage, mushrooms, and pepperoni, you can choose from embellishments such as sun-dried tomatoes and the veggie of the day. Harry also makes splendiferous clam pizzas and shrimp pizzas and a surprisingly good Hawaiian pizza with Canadian bacon and pineapple. The shop doesn't exactly serve dessert, but it does deliver complimentary dollops of pink grapefruit or lemon ices as a palate cleanser, an absolutely perfect touch. Open 4:30 to 10:00 P.M. Monday through Wednesday, 11:30 A.M. to 2:00 P.M. and 4:30 to 9:00 P.M. Thursday (till 11:00 P.M. Friday), 12:30 to 11:00 P.M. Saturday, and 2:30 to 9:30 P.M. Sunday. Harry's also has a regular breakfast menu, which is served Friday, Saturday, and Sunday. Call (860) 231–7166.

On the fringe of West Hartford Center at 950 Trout Brook Drive is the ***Science Center of Connecticut,*** one of Connecticut's premier science museums

## A Walk in the Center

People who've developed an attachment to the diversity, energetic buzz, and everything-that's-needed convenience of a centrally situated place to live generally appreciate their urbanite advantages. They can, at their whim, head out for some strolling-while-people-watching, entertainment, window-shopping, and museum-going without having to traipse to a farther-distant city or town. The charming all-American Main Streets of countless New England villages have comparable advantages, even though they exist on a smaller, more intimate scale. Suburbanites—at least in some areas, and those places are increasing—needn't feel neglected. Which brings us to that upscale enclave called West Hartford Center, where Farmington Avenue and LaSalle Road interconnect, about half an hour's driving (or by public transportation) time westward from the capital city's riverfront.

Many metro-Hartford insurance executives choose to raise their families in this privileged neighborhood, with brick sidewalks leading to some 140 shops (ritzy jewelry stores, bookstores, and a dozen designer-label fashion boutiques included), augmented by an abundance of restaurants, coffee shops, and chic cafes in the downtown district and its redeveloped Elmwood Center offshoot.

Although what residents simply refer to as "the Center" has become something of a yuppified Westport clone in recent years, it still offers welcome relief from cookie-cutter mega-malls. In early December, merchants launch the holiday season with a festive walk and (usually in mid-June) the Center celebrates West Hartford Days with some attractive sales. Here are just a few noteworthy neighborhood haunts:

Coffeehouses have proliferated along Farmington Avenue. So if you're hit with a caffeine yen, try *59er's Café, Center Squeeze,* or *Cosi* for a jolt. On LaSalle Road you can do your sipping at the ubiquitous *Starbucks.*

(and we don't say that because The Powers that Be at the museum seem to appreciate dinos as much as we do). Kids can explore the wonders of science and technology close-up and hands-on. Most kids we know like the giant walk-in kaleidoscope and the computer center. The center mounts exhibits throughout the year with lots of hands-on kid activities. Open 10:00 A.M to 5:00 P.M. Tuesday through Saturday, noon to 5:00 P.M. Sunday. Longer hours and open Monday in the summer and during school holidays. Closed major holidays. Admission for adults and children age three or older. Additional admission for the planetarium. Call (860) 231–2824.

South of Hartford is the township of Wethersfield. Once known as Onion Town because the crop grew so well within its confines, Wethersfield boasts the motto of "the most auncient towne in Connecticut." It was an important port on the Connecticut River until the river changed its course and left Old Wethersfield behind. Today *Olde Wethersfield,* the remnants of the original

The *Three Dog Bakery,* 967 Farmington Avenue; (860) 232–6299. Yep, a bakery just for dogs, a sure-enough indication of financial well-being here in the Center. A wonderful bit of silliness, perfect for the local ambience and a zoo during the holiday season, when perfectly sane and civilized people fight over the last doggy gift basket. This is a place to take your favorite pooch for a treat. For instance, how about browsing for something cutely called Snickerpoodles for your pampered canine companion?

*Toast Wines,* 984-B Farmington Avenue; (860) 236–3515. Knowledgeable wine people, tastings on Saturdays.

*Elbow Room,* 986 Farmington Avenue; (860) 236–6195. Even though the menu changes seasonally, a reliable standby is pork tenderloin with Marsala and lemon tea tart with raspberry sorbet. Open for lunch and dinner, seven days a week. Call (860) 236–6195.

*Japanalia Eiko,* 990 Farmington Avenue; (860) 523–7722. West Hartford's home-grown couturier. Joyous, beautifully cut, eminently wearable clothes in lush fabrics and colors for women built like Kate Moss or those somewhat more zaftig.

*Pfau's Hardware,* 982 Farmington Avenue; (860) 523–4201. An old-fashioned, wooden-floored hardware store with all types of cool stuff in every nook and cranny. Kids love the place.

*War & Pieces,* 7 South Main Street; (860) 232–0608. A superior source of hard-to-find military history, strategy, and fantasy role-playing games; models; miniatures; books; and trains for your youngsters.

town, consists of half a dozen eighteenth- and early nineteenth-century homes, a museum, a church, and a seventeenth-century graveyard. Most of these places are on Main Street, and all are within easy walking distance of each other. This small area was the setting for the wonderful young adult book *The Witch of Blackbird Pond* by Elizabeth Speare, as well as for two amusing novels of Gothic horror—*The Other* and *Harvest Home*—written by Wethersfield native Thomas Tryon.

## wethersfieldtrivia

If you're of an architectural bent or just love old houses, you'll love Wethersfield. Wandering through this area, you're sure to spot houses in architectural styles ranging from colonial saltbox to 1950s ranches and everything in between.

The three restored eighteenth-century homes making up the **Webb-Deane-Stevens Museum** (211 Main Street) are the heart of this attraction. Washington stayed in the 1752-vintage *Joseph Webb House* in 1781, and it was there that he and Rochambeau met to plan the Yorktown campaign. The *Silas Deane House* (1766) belonged to a member of the First Continental Congress (and America's first envoy to France). These houses and the *Isaac Stevens House* (1788) contain a collection of furnishings and decorative elements spanning the years 1690 to 1840. There are five acres of open grounds and a couple of herb gardens behind the houses. Open 10:00 A.M. to 4:00 P.M. (last tour at 3:00 P.M.) daily except Tuesdays from May through October; during the winter, open weekends only from 10:00 A.M. to 4:00 P.M. Admission. Call (860) 529–0612.

There are three other restored homes in the neighborhood: the *Captain James Francis House,* about 3 blocks away at 120 Hartford Avenue; the *Buttolph-Williams House* on the corner of Marsh and Broad; and the *Hurlbut-Dunham House* at 212 Main Street. The *Old Academy Museum,* with changing historical exhibits, is across the street from the Webb-Deane-Stevens Museum at 150 Main Street. Also across the street from the museum at 250 Main Street is the *Meetinghouse,* a famous 350-year-old brick church whose congregation of more than 2,000 still worships there each Sunday; you can view the interior with its original hand-carved pulpit on weekdays from 9:00 A.M. to 5:00 P.M. Behind the Meetinghouse are the Old Burying Grounds; thousands of headstones, dating from 1648 onward, record the thoughts, philosophies, and attitudes of generations of local citizens. Call (860) 529–7656 for hours or to schedule an appointment.

It's not normally treated as a historic site, but at 263 Main Street, you'll find *Comstock, Ferre & Company,* the oldest continuously operating seed company in the United States. Since 1820, it's been a source for seeds and plants.

It also stocks specialty craft items and gifts. The chestnut post-and-beam structures date from the late 1700s. Open 9:00 A.M. to 6:00 P.M. Monday through Saturday; Sunday from 10:00 A.M. to 5:00 P.M. Call (860) 571–6590.

In 1966, while clearing ground for the construction of a new state building in Rocky Hill, bulldozer operator Ed McCarthy uncovered some unusual rocks. They had strange markings and scorings on them. It turned out these were the tracks of dinosaurs that prowled the area 185 million years ago. In those days this part of Connecticut was a mud flat on the shore of a huge lake, rich in fish and small crocodilians; good eating for a growing dino.

After covering the initial excavation of 1,500 tracks to preserve them, the state excavated another 500 tracks, enclosed them in a geodesic dome, added an AV facility that offers a neat presentation on dinos, and called the result **Dinosaur State Park** on West Street in Rocky Hill. The inside of the dome is dominated by a full-sized reconstruction of a carnivorous dino called *dilophosaurus,* but the big attraction is tracks. Most of the impressions are three-toed, and they run up to 16 inches long. The park lets visitors make plaster casts of the tracks and posts instructions for doing so; take along a quarter-

## easthartfordtrivia

In 1687 Gov. Edmund Andros, appointed by the British Crown to oversee Connecticut, demanded colonists return the royal charter that made Connecticut a separate colony. Hartford colonists hid the charter in a towering oak tree called the Charter Oak. When the Charter Oak finally toppled in 1856, it was 1,000 years old.

## A Huguenot Haunting

Any Connecticut guidebook will tell you that the **Huguenot House,** in East Hartford's Martin Park (307 Burnside Avenue), is an excellent example of a restored colonial house. They'll talk about the gambrel roof and the vaulted dormer windows. What they won't tell you is that the Huguenot House has ghosts, albeit friendly ones. When the house was moved from its original location to the park, workers started reporting seeing the ghost of a lady in a blue dress. Then, as construction to restore and anchor the house to its new site began, work was frequently disrupted by the loud sounds of crashing, knocking, and hammering, even when the house was empty. The occurrences became so constant, workers dubbed the haunt Benny, and the foreman made out a daily work list for the ghost. Some believe the ghost or ghosts are the original builders of the house. The house was built in 1761 by a family of French Huguenots, a Protestant sect, known for their carpentry. The hours are limited, so call ahead; (860) 568–7645.

cup of cooking oil, about ten pounds of plaster of paris (for casting giant dino tracks, take along twenty pounds of plaster of paris), sticks or paint stirrers for

## rockyhilltrivia

You can see about 500 sets of dinosaur tracks (that's about 2,000 individual dino footprints) at Dinosaur State Park in Rocky Hill.

stirring the plaster of paris, a bucket, and paper towels for each cast. The park also has 2 miles of nature trails and picnic tables. The Exhibit Center is open 9:00 A.M. to 6:00 P.M. Tuesday and Wednesday, to 8:00 P.M. Thursday and Friday, to 6:00 P.M. Saturday, and 10:00 A.M. to 5:00 P.M. Sunday. The grounds are open 9:00 A.M. to 4:30 P.M. Admission. Call (860) 529–8423 or visit www.dinosaurstatepark.org.

When you're in Rocky Hill, you're very close to Cromwell and the site of a family-friendly animal park, *Amy's Udder Joy Exotic Animal Farm Park* at 27 North Road. Animal lovers are habitually very careful about recommending petting zoos and animal parks, but this one gets their enthusiastic approval. The park is licensed by the U.S. Department of Agriculture under the Animal Welfare Act, the Connecticut Department of Environmental Protection, and the state and federal Fish and Game Service, so the animals are well taken care of. You'll find lots of such exotic critters as llamas, peacocks, emus, and Tennessee fainting goats (our favorites). There's a good guided tour, pony rides on Saturday and Sunday, and a picnic area for lunch or snacks. Admission. Open May through Labor Day, 11:00 A.M. to 5:00 P.M. Wednesday through Saturday, and 11:00 A.M. to 4:00 P.M. Labor Day through the end of October (weather permitting). Call (860) 635–3924.

## East of the River

New England's population has swelled from numerous waves of immigrants over the years, and as each ethnic group has been assimilated, it has left behind a host of bakeries, restaurants, and similar establishments. While the people of Manchester may have originated in many different countries, today they share a local history.

Dedicated to preserving the artifacts of the fireman's life, *The Fire Museum* at 230 Pine Street in Manchester has everything having to do with firefighting, from old leather fire buckets and ornate marching hats to wooden water mains and a rare eighteenth-century fire warden's staff. There's even a collection of old prints and lithographs of fires, from the prephotographic era when the artist and lithographer were as important as the reporter to the process of communicating the news. It's all displayed inside a big old firehouse that was built in 1901 to protect the Cheney Brothers silk mills, at the time the main industry of this, the "Silk City."

There's a good deal of large equipment on display, with the emphasis on the hand-operated and horse-drawn. Some of the hand pumpers needed as many as thirty men to operate them. There's also a horse-drawn hose wagon, a steam-operated pumper, and an ornate hand-pulled, four-wheeled hose reel designed mainly for use in parades, a reminder of an age when the local firehouse was a center of social and political activity.

The museum is open mid-April through mid-November, 10:00 A.M. to 5:00 P.M. on Friday and Saturday, and noon to 5:00 P.M. on Sunday. Take exit 60 off I–84 and head east up Center Street to the sixth traffic light. Bear right going up the hill; the museum is about ½ mile from the light. No admission; donations requested. Call (860) 649–9436.

A few blocks away, at 106 Hartford Road, is another museum. This one, the **Cheney Homestead,** is the birthplace of the brothers who launched the silk industry in Manchester (and whose factory the firehouse was designed to protect). The house is filled with eighteenth- and nineteenth-century furnishings, and there's an eighteenth-century schoolhouse on the grounds. Open 1:00 to 5:00 P.M. Friday through Sunday. Adult admission. Call (860) 643–5588.

---

## What's in a Name?

Hartford has been dubbed the "Insurance City," but other Connecticut cities have been nicknamed for the industries that once dominated them. Can you match up the city with its nickname? You'll find answers below.

| | | |
|---|---|---|
| 1. Bristol | A. Research City |
| 2. Meriden | B. Thread City |
| 3. Naugatuck | C. Brass City |
| 4. Stamford | D. Silver City |
| 5. Waterbury | E. Clock City |
| 6. Willimantic | F. Rubber City |

Some Connecticut cities are famous for their flowers. Norwich, for example, is the "Rose City," Bristol is the "Mum City," and Winsted is the "Laurel City." All three cities have festivals that celebrate their city flowers. Call the regional tourism office or the Connecticut Commission on Culture & Tourism office for more information. You'll find these phone numbers in the Introduction.

1. E; 2. D; 3. F; 4. A; 5. C; 6. B.

Far removed in time and space from the Cheney Homestead is the ***New England Jukebox and Amusement Company,*** which operates out of a store-front next to its warehouse at 77 Tolland Turnpike in Manchester. For thirty years this company has been servicing and repairing juke boxes, pinball machines, and other coin-operated amusements. In the mid-1980s the owners decided to augment their service operation with a retail business in nostalgia, with a special emphasis on the coin-operated items that were already the core of their business. Today the New England Jukebox and Amusement Company purchases coin-op amusements and other mechanical devices from all over America, refurbishes them, and sells them to the general public. While the firm is little known locally, coin-op enthusiasts come to Manchester from across the United States to look, listen, and purchase.

For such an unpretentious store, the breadth of merchandise on display here is amazing. There are antique phones, radios, postcards, and ephemera all jumbled up with neon signs and clocks, comics, pinball machines, and old 45 rpm records. There are also all kinds of coin-operated goodies. On one visit, we saw a lovely old popcorn machine; a 1930s-vintage "Flying A Gasoline" pump; an antique bubble gum machine; a 1927 Mills 5-cent slot machine; and half a dozen jukeboxes, not to mention a player piano with neat carved griffin legs. The stars were two original deco-styled Wurlitzer 1015 O.M.T. jukeboxes, complete with working bubble tubes and rotating color cylinders.

The New England Jukebox and Amusement Company is particularly difficult to find unless you know what you're looking for. Take I–84 to exit 63 and get on the Tolland Turnpike heading west. Turn left into the shopping area just past the Acadia Restaurant. Beside the National Speed Center and set back from the road is the New England Jukebox and Amusement Company. Open 10:00 A.M. to 6:00 P.M. weekdays except Monday, 10:00 A.M. to 2:00 P.M. Saturday, or by appointment. If the place seems deserted, ring the bell; they may be in the ware-house. Call (860) 646–1533.

Also in Manchester, you'll find ***Shady Glen,*** 840 East Middle Turnpike. Shady Glen is one of those places that make you think you've walked into a filming of *Happy Days*. It's been around since 1948 and used to sell the milk and ice cream produced on John and Bernice Reig's dairy farm. Today, it's a popular eatery and old-fashioned soda fountain. Besides soaking up the old-fashioned atmosphere, you'll want to try the cheeseburgers. Topped with crispy slabs of fried cheese, they look a little like UFOs. Cheese fanciers can get an order of fried cheese on the side. Then try the ice cream or a soda fountain creation such as a sundae or soda. Every day there are about twenty-five ice cream flavors from which to choose. Popular flavors such as chocolate chip are always on the menu, while flavors such as mincemeat or cranberry sorbet rotate with the seasons. Things get really hectic and crowded at Shady Glen because it's something of a Manchester tradition, but the tables turn over quickly, so be patient and wait. Opens 7:00 A.M. Monday through Saturday, 10:30 A.M. Sunday. Closing hours: 11:00 P.M. nightly, summertime; other times of year: 10:00 P.M. Sunday through Thursday, 11:00 P.M. Friday and Saturday. Call (860) 649–4245. There's a second Shady Glen at 360 West Middle Turnpike; (860) 643–0511.

If you visit Shady Glen with kids, we suggest you let them run off their sugar high with a visit to a museum that's not the least bit staid and gives them lots of wonderful hands-on things to do. The *Lutz Children's Museum,* 247 South Main Street in Manchester, is scaled for and built for children. The emphasis here is on "please touch" science and natural history exhibits including live animals. The museum sponsors several excellent programs throughout the year. Open 9:00 A.M. to 4:00 P.M. Tuesday through Friday, noon to 5:00 P.M. Saturday and Sunday. Closed Monday. Admission. Call (860) 643–0949.

The *Rocky Hill–Glastonbury Ferry,* spanning the Connecticut River and linking one part of Route 160 (Ferry Lane) to the other, has been in operation since 1655. That makes it the oldest continuously operating ferry in America. It's also a good place to cross the river if you want to avoid the usually heavy traffic around Hartford's bridges. Service is provided by a tug called the *Cumberland* and by a three-car barge called the *Hollister.* The ferry operates May 1 to October 31. Hours are 7:00 A.M. to 6:45 P.M. Monday through Friday; 10:30 A.M. to 5:00 P.M. Saturday and Sunday. Prices are almost insignificant. For more information call (860) 443–3856.

## glastonburytrivia

In Connecticut signs commemorating historical events are literally in your face. A while back, just to show they didn't take things too seriously, some wags in South Glastonbury erected a billboard that read 357 YEARS AGO ON THIS SPOT, NOTHING HAPPENED.

## Central Connecticut

New Britain got its manufacturing start making sleigh bells. From these modest beginnings the city gradually branched out after 1800 into the manufacture of other hardware products, until it eventually came to be known as the "Hardware City." With the expansion of industry came waves of new immigrants seeking jobs in the tool works. The Irish came first, then the Germans and Swedes, then the Italians. The biggest waves, though, consisted of Eastern Europeans, including Lithuanians, Ukrainians, and Armenians. Probably the largest group in this wave were the Poles. Even after the hardware industry moved abroad, Polish immigrants continued to come to New Britain. Today the city's population of first- and second-generation Poles is greater than that of many cities in Poland. They have contributed their music, their language, and their food to the city.

The center of the Polish community is a Broad Street business district where Polish is spoken almost as freely as English.

You can taste the wonders of Polish food at *Cracovia* at 60 Broad Street. Our Polish friends swear by its food. The decor here is dominated by the Polish falcon, and announcements about upcoming community events are printed in Polish. Thankfully the menu is in English, and the waitresses are good at explaining menu choices to non-Poles. The food is Central and Eastern European, bounteous, and cheap. The pierogi are excellent. So are the *golombki* (tender, tasty cabbage rolls stuffed with beef and rice, braised in a slightly sweet tomato sauce). Most of the entrees are served with true mashed potatoes, with the happy little lumps that mark them as the real thing instead of the instant variety. The homemade soups are served in bathtub-sized portions; the white borscht and the dill pickle soups get high marks. Open 8:00 A.M. to 8:00 P.M. daily. Call (860) 223–4443.

To create at home some of the Polish specialties you enjoyed at Cracovia, make a stop at *Podlasie,* 188 High Street. It's like visiting a marketplace in Eastern Europe. You'll find Polish mineral water, dark dense bread, newspapers, ingredients for Polish cooking, and some very intriguing Polish chocolates on the shelves. The back of the store is given over to a dairy case (great country butter), a pastry case full of some elegant-looking tortes and cakes, and a case for cheeses, herring, fresh meats, and cold cuts, many made in the store. Most of the shoppers are Polish, so Polish is the common tongue. There's usually at least one English-speaker in the store who is happy to help you translate. If not, we've gotten by quite nicely by pointing, smiling, and nodding. (There is another Podlasie in Bridgeport at 2286 East Main Street; 203–335–0321.) Open Monday through Saturday at 9:00 A.M. Closing hours: 5:00 P.M. Monday and Saturday, 6:00 P.M. Tuesday and Wednesday, 7:00 P.M. Thursday and Friday. Call (860) 224–8467.

You wouldn't expect a community touted as the Hardware City to be home to a nationally recognized art museum, but New Britain is just that. The *New Britain Museum of American Art* (56 Lexington Street), established in 1903, is the oldest museum in the United States devoted solely to American art. Its 3,000 holdings include portraits by Cassatt, Stuart, Copley, and Sargent and the western bronzes of Solon Borglum, as well as works by the likes of O'Keeffe, Noguchi, and Wyeth. Its collection of American impressionists is second to none.

There are landscapes by Hassam, Inness, Bierstadt, Cole, and Church, among others. Most impressive of all are the *Arts of Life in America* murals by Thomas Hart Benton. These murals must have been reproduced in half the American history textbooks published in the past thirty years, and most people are familiar with them, but it's only when you look up at the full-size originals that the power of Benton's work really manifests itself. Open noon to 5:00 P.M. Tuesday, Thursday, Friday, and Sunday; noon to 7:00 P.M. Wednesday; 10:00 A.M. to 5:00 P.M. Saturday. Gift shop. Admission is $6.00 for adults, $5.00 for seniors, $4.00 for students, and free for children under twelve. Free admission on Saturday morning from 10:00 A.M. to noon. Call (860) 229–0257.

New Britain is also home to the **Copernican Observatory and Planetarium,** a small planetarium, observatory, and space museum located on the campus of Central Connecticut State University, 1615 Stanley Street. The planetarium presents programs every Friday and Saturday at 8:30 P.M., and the observatory is open at the same time. The latter facility has several telescopes, including a monster with a 16-inch reflector. You can visit the observatory without visiting the planetarium. There is a modest admission for presentations or for visiting the observatory. Call (860) 832–3399.

**newbritaintrivia**

The Copernican Observatory and Planetarium at Central Connecticut State University in New Britain houses the second largest publicly available telescope in the United States.

Before hardware meant things like CPUs and printers, New Britain was Connecticut's (maybe the world's) Hardware City. That history is commemorated in the **New Britain Industrial Museum,** 185 Main Street. It's a small but choice museum, put together by people who genuinely love New Britain and its industrial past. You can trace New Britain's past and see its future as you view the history of the companies that put New Britain on the map: Stanley Works, Fafnir Bearing, and American Hardware. Open 2:00 to 5:00 P.M. Monday through Friday, noon to 5:00 P.M. Wednesday. Free. Call (860) 832–8654.

Taking the family to see a major-league baseball game is so expensive these days you may feel you face a choice: college tuition or a ball game. For a baseball outing that is more economical and intimate, Connecticut offers four *Bull Durham*-esque options (see sidebar), including one in New Britain, which deliver all the authentic appeal of America's pastime without forcing you to sell your Mickey Mantle rookie card. You can sit close to the action, and chances are good you'll be able to snag a foul ball or a player's autograph. Best of all, you might discover the next Barry Bonds or Derek Jeter before the rest of the world catches on. Check out the **New Britain Rock Cats** (New Britain

# Take Me Out to the Ball Game

Other minor-league teams in the Nutmeg State include:

**Connecticut Defenders** (Dodd Stadium, Norwich Industrial Park, 14 Stott Avenue). The Defenders are an AA professional baseball team affiliated with the San Francisco Giants. Games are played from April through September; tickets range from $5.00 to $10.00. Call (860) 887–7962.

**Bridgeport Bluefish** (Ballpark at Harbor Yard, 500 Main Street). The Bluefish are a professional baseball club not affiliated with a major league team. Their season runs from April through September; tickets range from $3.00 to $18.00. Call (203) 345–4800.

**New Haven County Cutters** (Yale Field, 252 Derby Avenue, West Haven). The Cutters are a professional team affiliated with the independent Northeast League. They play May through September; tickets range from $5.00 to $12.00. Call (203) 777–5636.

Stadium, Willow Brook Park, 230 John Karbonic Way). The Rock Cats are members of the Eastern League, AA professional baseball, affiliated with the Minnesota Twins. They play April through September, with tickets ranging from $4.00 to $10.00. Call (860) 224–8383.

When we made our big move to Boston's Italian North End, we quickly developed a serious fondness for the old waterfront neighborhood's traditional pastry treat: cannoli. So now we can sinfully indulge upon the slightest impulse. But don't be jealous. These ricotta cheese–filled goodies *can* be found in Connecticut. For instance, at **Giovanni's Bakery and Pastry Shop,** 456 New Britain Avenue, Newington. Not only are the cannoli delightful, but the cookies, cakes, and all those other wonderful Italian pastries—the ones with names we can never pronounce—are equally toothsome. Giovanni's also dishes up great Italian ice, making it a refreshing stop on a blistering central Connecticut summer Sunday. Closed Monday. Open 7:30 A.M. to 7:00 P.M. Tuesday through Saturday and 7:30 A.M. to 1:00 P.M. Sunday.

Several "hams" of our acquaintance took us to task for not including the **American Radio Relay League,** 225 Main Street, Newington, in previous editions. To assuage hurt feelings and because we think it's a cool place, here's the skinny on the ARRL. Founded in 1914, the 163,000-member ARRL is not only mecca for ham radio operators but also the official voice of Amateur Radio. In these days of computers, e-mail, telecommunications, and cell phones, you may think of ham radio as merely an interesting hobby. During natural disasters, however, ham radios help rescue people and provide vital information. Our favorite ham operator, Bill Blackwell, once provided a "find shelter now" warning to a lady in the Caribbean during a hurricane that probably saved her life. Beside the administrative offices of the ARRL, you'll find W1AW, the league's amateur radio station. Visitors can tour the station, listen to radio calls, try their hand at tapping out code, or view some of the artifacts of the league's history. By the way, there's no one story as to why operators are called hams. Some people say it's because the radio gives operators a chance to "ham it up," others say it comes from the ham-fisted way early operators pounded their code keys. The most likely story is that "ham" is derived from "am," a contraction of "amateur." Call (860) 594–0200 for information about tours, special programs, or membership in the league, or visit them on the Web at www.arrl.org.

As you drive down Route 9 between New Britain and Farmington, you'll pass a hauntingly familiar sculpture of some American marines raising a flag. This is the ***Iwo Jima Survivors' Memorial Park and Monument.*** It is dedicated to 6,821 Americans who, during World War II, gave their lives in the desperate fight for the Pacific island of Iwo Jima, the place where it was said that "uncommon valour" was a "common virtue." The monument's sculpture re-creates the famous flag-raising by American troops atop Mount Suribachi. On special days, such as Veterans Day, the monument is decorated with an avenue of American flags. Open 24 hours daily.

Back in the eighteenth century, ***Route 10*** was the major thoroughfare passing through Plainville. It was down this road that Rochambeau's French army

## Pop Culture

Midwesterners like us grew up calling that fizzy, sweet stuff that came in bottles "pop"; we didn't learn to call it "soda" until we moved to Connecticut. When we moved farther north to Massachusetts, we'd call it "tonic." Whatever you call it, soda pop was one of the quintessential memories of our youth. About twice a summer, our fathers would load up the kids in the station wagons and drive down to the local bottling plant where we'd pick up a case of pop—clear glass bottles of neon-colored liquid, all nestled nicely in a wooden carrying case. Somehow picking up a six-pack of cans at the convenience store doesn't carry the same aura of romance. That's why we make a pilgrimage each summer to ***Avery's Beverages,*** 520 Corbin Avenue in New Britain. It's the wonderful Aladdin's cave of jewel-colored soda and mysterious Rube Goldberg machinery we remember from childhood. At Avery's they bottle soda the way we remember it, wooden carrying cases and all. The family has been bottling soda in the same red barn since 1904. You can choose from among twenty-six different flavors of soda or go for what we do, the mixed case. If you call ahead, you can arrange a tour of the bottling works. Call (860) 224–0830 for hours and tour information or log on to www.averysoda.com.

marched on its way to join Washington at Yorktown and win the decisive battle of the American Revolution (the location of one of the French campgrounds is marked by a small plaque next to a gas station on Route 6 in Farmington). French armies notwithstanding, the road was less traveled in that century, and trips had to be planned more carefully. To aid the traveler the route was marked with milestones indicating the distance to Hartford. Today, at three places along the east side of Route 10 (at the corner of Betsy Road, at the junction of Route 372, and in front of Woodmore Village), you can still see the old milestones.

Just south of Main Street on Route 10, you can also see the **Old East Street Burying Grounds.** First used in 1766, this cemetery is noted for its remarkable headstones. It is also known for a curious effect of Plainville's geography. The water table lies very near the surface here, so special poles had to be employed to hold the coffins of the departed in their graves. The cemetery went out of use in 1856 and is closed today. Each Memorial Day, however, after the parade, the cemetery holds an open house; you can also get a guided tour by calling (860) 747–6577 for an appointment.

Bristol's **Lake Compounce Theme Park,** 822 Lake Avenue, is the country's oldest continuously running amusement park. The roller coaster, the dreaded Zoomerang, is properly frightening, and the water park is perfect on a hot day. But we like Lake Compounce for its old-fashioned carousel. You'll find horses carved by Looff, Carmel, and Stein & Goldstein. There are forty-nine horses (twenty-seven jumpers and twenty-two standers), a goat, and two chariots. The original Wurlitzer organ still grinds out tunes for riders. Admission. Open daily, except Tuesday, from about Memorial Day until Labor Day and weekends from Labor Day until the end of September. During Halloween, Lake Compounce sponsors a scary haunted house attraction with some way scary admission prices. AAA members get a discount. Call (860) 583–3300 for operating hours and schedule; www.lakecompounce.com.

If you're interested in antiques, shopping at **Dick's Antiques,** 670 Lake Avenue in Bristol, is a must. Proprietor Dick Blaschke, who we've known for years, will entertain you with yarns about his adventures in antiquing. You'll be impressed by the dazzling collection of Victorian, oak, and country furniture; vintage glass; china; clocks; lighting fixtures; and accessories. Dick and his partner, Rick Kuracz, are not only extremely likeable guys, they're also top experts in their field. So you can buy with confidence. Hours: 10:00 A.M. to 5:00 P.M., Monday, Wednesday, Thursday, and Friday; noon to 5:00 P.M. Saturday; July and August: 10:00 A.M. to 5:00 P.M. Monday or by appointment. Best to call ahead: (860) 584–2566.

About the middle of the nineteenth century, Bristol was the center of clock- and watchmaking in the Northeast. At one time the town supported 280 clockmakers, and in 1860 they turned out a total of 200,000 clocks. Today the great clockworks are only a memory preserved in the town's ***American Clock & Watch Museum,*** which is located in a big white clapboard house at 100 Maple Street.

Within the walls of the 1801-vintage Miles Lewis House and two modern additions, the museum manages to display a collection of 3,000 clocks and watches, including many made locally. This vast assemblage is organized by types and eras, so that as you move from room to room, you can observe how the styles of clock cases changed to match furniture styles. Tours are entirely self-guided, but the exhibits are well marked. Among the more interesting items are some oak clock cases from the 1920s and 1930s, which are exhibited together with the metal rollers that pressed the intricate designs into the wood. There are also some lovely "tall" clocks, including some made by Eli Terry. There's even one clock whose workings are carved entirely from wood. The American Clock & Watch Museum is open daily, from April through November 30; 10:00 A.M. to 5:00 P.M. Open during the winter by appointment only. Admission. Call (860) 583–6070.

Clocks and watches aren't the only items collected in Bristol. Housed in a restored turn-of-the-twentieth-century factory building at 95 Riverside Avenue, the ***New England Carousel Museum*** contains some of the best examples of antique carousel art in existence, more than 300 pieces in all. Featured items include a collection of band organs, the entire carousel from Santa's Land, in Putnam, Vermont, and a gorgeous pair of 1915 carved chariots, each encrusted with 1,500 glass jewels. The museum also has two art galleries and a fine history exhibit. This was the first museum of its kind on the East Coast, and many preservationists still consider it the best.

The main museum occupies the building's ground floor. Wood-carvers and painters perform restorations on the second floor, and if you happen to be there while they are working, you can go upstairs and watch. Open 10:00 A.M. to 5:00 P.M. Monday through Saturday, noon to 5:00 P.M. Sunday. You can also reserve the museum for special events, with youth group sleepovers (called Painted Pony Pajama

New England Carousel Museum

Parties) and weddings being hot tickets in this part of the state. Admission. Call (860) 585–5411.

One of the best attractions in Bristol is one that you are unlikely to stumble across unless you're a native Nutmegger and you happen to be around at Halloween time. For many years now, Bristol artist Cortland Hull has been re-

## Halloween Spooktaculars

New England and Halloween go together hand and glove. Maybe it's the scudding clouds posed against a full harvest moon. Maybe it's the whirling wisps of ground fog whipped along by a shuddering wind. Maybe it's the weight of all those years of history. We're not sure what it is, but we enjoy Halloween in New England a lot. While the Witch's Dungeon is our all-time favorite Halloween celebration, Connecticut really goes all out for Halloween.

New England wouldn't be New England without its old, hallowed cemeteries. The headstone inscriptions tell us much about rich and poor families as well as entire social histories. Travelers with proper doses of curiosity can explore these ancient graveyards. Scattered throughout the region, they're touchingly plentiful here in Connecticut.

*Old Norwichtown Burial Ground,* Old Cemetery Lane (off Town Street) in Norwich. Located near the town green, the cemetery is open every day until dusk. Brochures are available at the cemetery entrance for self-guided tours. For more information, call the Norwich Tourism Office at (860) 886–4683.

*Cedar Hill Cemetery,* 453 Fairfield Avenue, Hartford, offers self-guided walking tours with free brochures available at the cemetery and free guided tours on most weekends throughout the summer. For a schedule of tours, call the cemetery office at (860) 956–3311.

*The Wethersfield Historical Society* offers tours of the Ancient Burying Ground at certain times of the year. The tours begin at the cemetery behind the First Church of Christ, 250 Main Street. Admission. The society also sells a booklet for self-guided tours, which is available by calling (860) 529–7656.

The *Middlesex County Historical Society* offers a graveyard tour each year on the Sunday before Halloween. Admission. For more information call (860) 346–0746.

Another Halloween Spook-Fest:

The *Haunted Graveyard at Lyman Orchards* in Middlefield isn't a proper cemetery, but rather a fundraiser (and hair-raiser) for juvenile diabetes. The event consists of several outdoor areas, including haunted castles, bizarre mazes (the scariest part for us), and the pièce de résistance, the graveyard. There's no guide on your tour; just stumble along from site to site, getting the bejeebers scared out of you. This place is so scary we recommend you leave little kids at home. The haunted graveyard usually opens on weekends sometime after Columbus Day and stays open through Halloween. Admission. Call Lyman Orchards at (860) 349–1793 for hours and more information.

creating some of the world's classiest horrors in a museum that he operates only during the first three weekends (Friday through Sunday) in October. This seasonal extravaganza pays loving tribute to Vincent Price, Boris Karloff, Lon Chaney, and Bela Lugosi. Hull's **Witch's Dungeon,** 90 Battle Street, is a labyrinth of room-sized scenes from famous Hollywood chillers, complete in every visual and aural detail. Imagine standing before a realistic Egyptian tomb and seeing Kharis, the mummy, slowly rise from his sarcophagus, or watching Dracula wither to dust after being impaled by Dr. Van Helsing. The Witch's Dungeon is a fine place to celebrate All Hallows' Eve by getting scared out of a few years' growth, but be cautioned, this place is not for younger children. Admission. Open the first three weekends in October, 7:00 to 10:00 P.M. Call (860) 583–8306. For information on special events year-round, go to www.preservehollywood.org.

**Saint's** on Route 10 in Southington has a simple philosophy: Use top-quality ingredients and don't tinker with success. The philosophy must work because the eatery's been dishing up its famous hot dogs to popular acclaim since 1967. Since then, they've used the same mustard, the same relish, and the same chili sauce recipe. *Yankee* magazine gave Saint's an honorable mention when it rated "Best Hot Dogs of New England," and some chili dog connoisseurs swear these dogs are the best in the state. Saint's is something of a local hangout with an easy camaraderie shared with the customers and the staff. Open daily from 6:00 A.M. to 8:30 P.M. Call (860) 747–0566.

# The Tobacco Valley

Located off Route 20 in East Granby, *Old New-Gate Prison and Copper Mine* was originally chartered as the first copper mine in America in 1707. By 1773 further mining proved uneconomical, and in December of that year, the Simsbury copper mine was turned into the Connecticut Colony's chief place of confinement for various classes of thieves and counterfeiters. The new facility was named for London's notorious Newgate prison, whose grisly reputation it eventually came to share. Newgate became the nation's first state prison in 1776, when the colonies severed ties with the British Crown. In 1827 the prison was abandoned, and its inmates were transferred to a new prison in Wethersfield; in keeping with the prison's lurid history, an inmate died the night before the transfer while trying to escape. During its half-century of operation, Newgate was widely known as "the worst hell-hole in North America." While the prison did include a substantial complex of above-ground buildings, the prisoners were confined 50 feet below ground in the dank passageways of the old mine. Disease claimed many. Others committed suicide or went insane.

# Connecticut's Friendliest Antiquing Village

Woodbury may boast of having Connecticut's "Antique Avenue" and Putnam might wear the laurels for being a whole town of antiques shops, but for our money, the prize for the friendliest antiquing destination in the state goes to the Plantsville section of Southington (exit 30 off Interstate 84).

When we first visited Plantsville, we assumed its name came from its proximity to Cheshire, the Bedding Plant Capital of Connecticut. The owners of the Plantsville Station Antique Shoppes quickly set us straight. Plantsville is named for its founder, Robert Plant. (Unfortunately, not the Robert Plant of Led Zep fame.)

Throughout the year Plantsville keeps a busy calendar of special events such as a Halloween festival and a winter holiday celebration. Call the Central Connecticut Tourism District at (860) 244–8181 or (800) 793–4480 for more information. Visit them on the Web at www.centralct.org.

The village is pretty compact; we recommend you park your car on Main Street and just start exploring. To get you started, here are a few of our favorites:

*Plantsville Station Antique Shops,* 75 West Main Street. This group shop carries lots of nice old linens, oak furniture, and collectibles. Owners Robert and Kathleen Celetano are very friendly and helpful—just don't ask them when the next train leaves. The building in which the shop makes its home only looks like a train station. In previous incarnations it housed a machine shop and other light industry—never a train station. Even so, the Celetanos frequently field phone calls from people wanting a train schedule. Open Wednesday through Saturday, 10:00 A.M. to 5:00 P.M., and Sunday from noon to 5:00 P.M. Call (860) 628–8918.

*Victoria Rose,* 35 West Main Street, doesn't sell antiques. It's a charmingly decorated little jewel box of a store brimming with Victoriana. Just about anything you might covet from the pages of *Victoria* magazine, you can find at Victoria Rose— collectibles, cards, wrapping paper and gift bags, decorative items, and wonderful replica, ornate Victorian jewelry. Definitely worth a visit. Open Tuesday to Saturday, 10:00 A.M. to 5:30 P.M. Call (860) 621–0935 for more information.

*Nothing's New,* 69 West Main Street, is a cool place for people who like old vacuum-tube radios. The owners, John and Corrine Watts, specialize in the sale and service of vintage radios. It's a fun shop to poke around in and an interesting experience for kids. Try explaining a vacuum-tube radio to kids raised on computers. Open Wednesday to Saturday, 10:00 A.M. to 4:00 P.M. Call (860) 276–0143 for more information.

One of the prison's most famous inmates was William "Big Bad Bill" Stuart of Wilton, the leader of what was, in the second decade of the nineteenth century, the most infamous criminal gang in New England. From his early teens, when he was expelled from school for (among other things) tarring and feathering the schoolmaster's cow, Bill had been raising Cain; before entering Newgate, he blasted his way out of a seemingly secure stone-walled jail in Albany and had escaped from numerous other jails. Newgate was his greatest challenge; in fact, Stuart made two unsuccessful attempts to escape. The second, in 1817, resulted in a prison riot in which Big Bad Bill was bayonetted three times, shot in the groin, and sabered across the head. Stuart healed and was finally released in 1825 to disappear into the Litchfield Hills. The riot he started, however, sparked an investigation that ended the worst practices at Newgate and ultimately contributed to its being shut down.

The ruins of Newgate are picturesque, the view of the surrounding countryside is magnificent, and there are picnic facilities available outside the walls. The real fun, though, is the underground tour of the mine itself. The gift shop sells some neat replicas of jailers' warrants and "wanted" posters and cute "I Escaped from Old Newgate Prison" T-shirts. Open Wednesday through Sunday, 10:00 A.M. to 4:30 P.M., from mid-May through October. Bring sneakers or walking shoes and a sweater or jacket if you intend to go underground; the mine is damp, and subterranean temperatures average in the forties. Admission. Call (860) 653–3563.

If you are a lover of attractions of the biggest, smallest, first, and oldest variety, take a minute in Granby to visit the 300-year-old **Granby Oak** on Day Street, off Route 20. It's shown prominently on Granby's town seal, which appears on everything from official stationery to town vehicles. In the fall, the oak is especially attractive and worthy of a photograph, as numerous artists and photographers can attest.

Folks with a passion for antiques love to discover "just the right" store, shop, gallery, yard sale, barn, or auction house. One such place—**Salmon Brook Shops,** 563 Salmon Brook Street in Granby—offers that kind of tough-to-find challenge. (Granby itself is what you'd have to politely call remote: a fair distance north of Hartford and close to the Massachusetts state line). But getting there is definitely worth the drive. Salmon Brook Antique is a cozy group shop, with lots of cutie-pie stuff. While you won't find eighteenth-century Newport desks, you will find lots of nice kitchen items and a plethora of ephemera (postcards, movie posters, and advertising art). A frame shop shares quarters with the antiques shop, so when you find the perfect old movie poster, framing it is easy. The people who staff the place are as charming as the objects they sell. Call (860) 653–6587 for hours, information, and directions.

For anyone interested in the history of aviation, the **New England Air Museum** in Windsor Locks is a must. The museum features an extensive collection of aircraft, memorabilia, and exhibits housed in three large display hangars. Some of the larger aircraft are kept outdoors. The oldest of its seventy-five aircraft (a beautiful wood-and-canvas Bleriot XI monoplane) dates from 1909. There is also an extensive collection of World War II vintage fighters and bombers and quite a number of modern jet aircraft.

There are also numerous smaller items of interest, including a variety of engines, some cockpit simulators, and a collection of flight memorabilia. Many of these smaller items were acquired from area aerospace companies and can't be seen anywhere else.

To get to the Air Museum, take exit 40 off Interstate 91. Get on Route 20. Take that to Route 75 North. Follow the signs from that point. Open daily, 10:00 A.M. to 5:00 P.M. Gift shop. Admission. Call (860) 623–3305; www.neam.org.

A few miles up Route 75 from the New England Air Museum is another museum commemorating a quite different era. The restored 1764-vintage home at 232 South Main Street (Route 75) in Suffield is now the *King House Museum.* The building's interesting architectural features include seven original fireplaces (one with a beehive oven) and a unique shell-carved corner cupboard. Among the period furnishings is a four-poster bed that formerly graced the Jonathan Trumbull house in Lebanon. Displays include an assortment of Bennington pottery, a tinware collection, and, appropriately enough for the Tobacco Valley, a collection of cigar and tobacco memorabilia. The King House Museum is open May through September from 11:00 A.M. to 4:00 P.M. Wednesday and Saturday. Admission. Call (860) 668–5256.

The *Connecticut Fire Museum* at 58 North Road (Route 140) in East Windsor is one of two unrelated museums in Hartford County that attempt to trace the history of firefighting. It has a collection of about twenty fire trucks built between 1850 and 1950. It also includes some models and displays on the history of firefighting. Open April through August, 10:00 A.M. to 4:00 P.M. weekdays; noon to 4:00 P.M. Saturday and Sunday. Open September and October 10:00 A.M. to 5:00 P.M. Saturday and noon to 5:00 P.M. Sunday. Admission. Call (860) 623–4732.

The *Connecticut Trolley Museum,* at the same location as the Connecticut Fire Museum, is one of two unrelated trolley museums in the state. This one, run by the nonprofit Connecticut Electric Railway Association, has a collection of more than thirty trolley cars made between 1892 and 1947 plus steam and electrical locomotives and various historic railroad equipment. While most of the trolleys are from New England and Canada, there are some from as far away as Illinois and Ohio and one from Rio de Janeiro. The museum offers a carbarn tour and a 3-mile trolley ride. Special events are held throughout the year including the annual Winterfest in December, which features leisurely rides along a 1½-mile route decorated with twinkling colored lights. Open 10:00 A.M. to 4:00 P.M. Monday, Wednesday, Thursday, and Friday, noon to 4:00 P.M. Sunday. Closed Tuesday. Take exit 41 off I–91 and follow the signs. Call (860) 627–6540.

Once upon a time, every town had a ***Bart's Drive-in,*** 55 Palisado Avenue, Windsor. Today, they are as scarce as hens' teeth. Once you find a place like Bart's, you become a customer for life—it's just that kind of place. Bart's started as a hot dog stand and eventually expanded to include an indoor dining area. One counter serves cold sandwiches—that's the counter in the eat-in area. The walls are lined with newspaper clippings, telegrams, and letters. The grill and ice cream fountain counter is the more popular counter. Even with indoor seating, lots of folks continue to eat in their cars or at the picnic tables that overlook the river. You can usually spot anglers fishing from the shore or in boats, so after a meal it's fun to sit awhile and watch or stroll down the sidewalk that runs along the river. On Wednesday night in the summer, Bart's hosts Cruise Nights. Bart's has customer service that many Fortune 500 companies might adopt: Treat customers like they are your own best friends. That's true whether you're a lifelong customer or a first-time walk-in.

The grill menu features hot dogs, hamburgers, award-winning chili dogs (regular or spicy), French fries, onion rings, fried fish filets, wholebelly clams, etc. The full-meal menu changes daily; offerings include homey dishes like meat loaf, shepherd's pie, yankee pot roast, and pasta dishes. Old-fashioned milk shakes in vanilla, chocolate, coffee, strawberry, and peanut butter (better than it sounds) are available at the fountain. For 25 cents more, you can request an old-fashioned malted milk shake. The staff keeps the eat-in area pretty clean, but sometimes the traffic is so heavy that you may need to brush off a table before you sit down. Open daily 8:00 A.M. to 8:00 P.M. Call (860) 688–9035 for information about special events.

Settled on October 4, 1633, Windsor claims to be the "oldest English settlement in Connecticut," though Wethersfield disputes this claim. Windsor is also home to the annual ***Shad Derby Festival,*** a distinction disputed by absolutely no one.

## windsor trivia

In 1647 Alse Young of Windsor was the first person to be hanged for witchcraft in New England.

Windsor resident Amy Archer-Gilligan was the inspiration for the elderly poisoners in the play and movie *Arsenic and Old Lace.* She ran a boardinghouse on Prospect Street and poisoned some of her pensioner tenants with homemade wine. The great-grandparents of one of our friends knew Amy and described her as "the nicest, most genteel lady you'd ever want to meet." Alas Amy's boardinghouse has been cut up into apartments and is not open to the public for tours.

# Walking and Hiking Hints

Connecticut offers miles of wonderful walking and hiking on state trails and in state and municipal parks. We want you to enjoy your hike and stay in the best of health, so please take a few precautions:

Wear appropriate clothing for the season. Wear footgear that protects your feet and ankles from injury and, even in the hottest weather, don't forget to wear socks.

Bring a hat, sunscreen, insect repellent, and a first-aid kit.

Don't get dehydrated. Bring along extra water, no matter what the season.

If you're hiking in a park with park ranger services, always check in and tell park authorities where you'll be hiking.

Lyme disease is a problem in Connecticut. Symptoms include: rash, flulike symptoms (such as fever, joint aches), headaches, stiffness, stiff neck, and occasional forgetfulness and mental confusion. By taking a few simple precautions you can avoid contracting Lyme disease:

If there are furred animals around, then it's a good bet ticks are around, too. Make it a habit to check your dog for ticks after each walk. Learn how to distinguish the deer ticks from "dog ticks." Deer ticks in the adult form are reddish brown; dog ticks are larger and darker than deer ticks. Dog ticks are not believed to carry Lyme disease.

Wear protective light-colored clothing and brush your clothes carefully before going indoors. Tick repellent spray can be effective, but follow manufacturers' directions carefully. Take a thorough shower after a walk or a hike and check yourself carefully.

If a tick is attached to you, carefully remove it by tugging gently with fine-nosed tweezers. Do not burn it off or cover it with an ointment such as Vaseline because this can increase your risk of infection. When you've removed the tick, save it in a small empty bottle (an empty prescription bottle is ideal) for identification, if needed.

Find out more by talking with your physician or a staffer with the local public health department.

The Connecticut River shad is a fat but bony, blue-green-and-silver relative of the herring. Each spring the shad migrate to northern waters to spawn, and one of their favorite spawning grounds is in the Connecticut River near Windsor. This means Windsor gets the best of the shad world, both fish and roe.

As a comestible shad has both its partisans and its detractors. Some natives feel spring isn't spring in Connecticut without a dish of broiled shad roe with bacon or shad baked on a plank. Others maintain that you should throw away the shad and eat the plank.

In Windsor they've been celebrating the shad as part of the town's annual rite of spring for more than four decades. The shad season lasts for about six weeks, but most of the shad festivities happen during the first two weeks of May. That's when you'll find everything from the Shad Derby (biggest shad caught) to the crowning of the Shad Queen, with a golf tournament and road race thrown in just to make things interesting. On Derby Day Windsor pretty much closes up shop to honor the shad with a townwide festival on Broad Street, where you'll find many food booths featuring the shad and its roe.

Shad mania aside, Windsor is known for a small but interesting museum that documents the early days of European settlement in Connecticut. The Windsor Historical Society's **Wilson Museum** at 96 Palisado Avenue features exhibition galleries, a research laboratory, a learning center, and a gift shop. The society's library includes, among other things, old journals and maps, an 1800 highway survey, and an original payroll list of the Windsor residents who answered the rebel alarm in Boston in spring 1775. The museum also contains a variety of Indian relics and a display of Americana that includes a rare Hadley Chest.

The society offers guided tours. The museum is open Tuesday through Saturday, 10:00 A.M. to 4:00 P.M. Adult admission. Call (860) 688–3813.

In Bloomfield you'll find one of the best places in Hartford County for a leisurely walk: the campus of the CIGNA Corporation at 900 Cottage Grove Road. You can roam more than 280 acres of roads and trails that pass through woodlands and by ponds, and lush plantings as well as sculptures by Isamo Noguchi. Open daily dawn to dusk.

If you've eaten a chocolate mousse cake in an upscale restaurant or have stared longingly at one in a gourmet market, the chances are it's a David Glass Chocolate Mousse Cake, made by Hartford's premier dessertmeister. Few people know that you can buy seconds and irregulars of his desserts at **Desserts by David Glass,** 1280 Blue Hills Avenue, Bloomfield. Here, most of the fabulous David Glass desserts, such as the Passion Fruit Mousse Cake or the Espresso Walnut Cake, are for sale, and seconds and irregulars of the signature chocolate mousse cake are turned into Chocolate Mousse Balls. Savings are excellent, sometimes as much as 50 percent off retail. The cakes available depend on what's being baked, so call ahead. Open 8:00 A.M. to 5:00 P.M. Monday through Friday. Call (860) 769–5570.

Bloomfield is a far piece from the shore, but it's home to one of the best, most underrated seafood restaurants in the state: **Bloomfield Seafood,** 8 Mountain Avenue. In its earliest existence, it was hidden behind an auto repair shop. After that location burned, the owners moved it to its current home, tucked into a very pedestrian shopping center. In fact, the location is so uninspiring you might be tempted to bus right past it. Don't—it offers some of the best and freshest fish and seafood in Hartford County at very good prices. Epicures like the seafood chowders or stews; the oyster stew is especially comforting on a blustery day. We prefer our fish simply prepared, so we love their sautéed sole. You can't go wrong ordering from the regular menu offerings or the daily specials. Don't leave without sampling their key lime pie. The service is knowledgeable, warm, and friendly. You'll find the staff knows how to treat kids well. The servers have the knack of turning the biggest "fish-frowning" kid into a fish-eating fan. Open for lunch, Tuesday through Saturday, 11:00 A.M. to 2:00 P.M.; early bird dinners, Tuesday through Saturday, 4:00 to 5:00 P.M.; dinner, Tuesday through Saturday, 4:00 to 8:00 P.M. Call (860) 242–3474 for more information.

# The Farmington Valley

*Hill-Stead Museum* (35 Mountain Road) is so Farmington that it is almost impossible to imagine it existing anywhere else. Housed in a white clapboard 1901 replica of a neocolonial house built in an eighteenth-century English farm–style is an amazing collection of French impressionist paintings, prints, antique furniture, porcelain, textiles, and clocks.

Hill-Stead was originally home to Cleveland iron mogul Alfred Atmore Pope. In keeping with his wealth and pretensions, Pope made sure that when it was time for daughter Theodate to go away to school, his child was entrusted to a proper Eastern institution: Miss Porter's School in Farmington. Upon graduation Theodate persuaded Daddy to forsake the Buckeye State and move east to the Nutmeg State. She also talked him into springing for a new house designed by then-trendy architect Stanford White with a sunken garden designed by landscape architect Beatrix Farrand. And, since Theodate had an abiding interest in architecture, nothing would do but that the young lady should assist White in designing the new family manse. White was either a very good businessman or he was truly impressed with Theodate's work, because he cut his fee by $25,000 in appreciation of her help. Miss Pope went on to become the first woman licensed to practice architecture in the United States.

Like so many American captains of industry, Pope was a collector. This was an age in which America's newly rich raided the homes and galleries of Europe for furnishings, often buying art and antiques in wholesale lots. The Popes were fairly typical in this regard, and their tastes were certainly eclectic. Chippendale furniture, fine porcelain, contemporary bronzes, and pre-Columbian statuary all jostled for space in the Pope home. On the walls hung a Degas, a Manet, a Cassatt, and no less than three Monets. The piano was a custom-designed Steinway. It was all gloriously excessive. And it is all still there, just as it was when Theodate died, leaving behind fifty pages of instructions for the house to be turned into a museum and maintained just as she left it.

Hill-Stead Museum is open 10:00 A.M. to 5:00 P.M. Tuesday through Sunday, with the last tour leaving at 4:00 P.M. each day. The grounds are open 7:00 A.M. to 5:30 P.M. Hill-Stead has a wonderful gift shop, which includes prints of works exclusive to it, such as Monet's *Haystacks* and Degas' *Dancers in Pink.* Admission. Call (860) 677–4787. For tour information, call (860) 677–9064; www.hill stead.org.

At 37 High Street in Farmington, just around the corner from the Hill-Stead Museum, is the ***Stanley-Whitman House,*** a beautifully restored 1720 colonial homestead. The original house, built to a typical early eighteenth-century standard, has a central chimney flanked by two chambers on each of two floors; it was later expanded by the addition of a lean-to that gives it a saltbox shape. The wood-sided exterior was originally painted with a mixture of ox blood and buttermilk; the restoration has not gone to quite that extreme, but otherwise it seems authentic. Hinged access panels inside the house let you see details of the original construction and restoration. The house is filled with period furnishings and is surrounded by herb and flower gardens. The gift shop sells items of local historical interest. May through October, open Wednesday through Sunday, noon to 4:00 P.M. November through April, open Saturday and Sunday, noon to 4:00 P.M. Admission. Call (860) 677–9222.

The neighborhood around the Stanley-Whitman House includes a large number of eighteenth-century (and some nineteenth-century) homes and buildings, all of them still in use by modern residents. These can be seen to best advantage from Route 10, where, in less than a mile, you can view a 1772 Congregational meeting house, a renovated 1650 gristmill, a colonial-era graveyard, and the remains of the Farmington Canal. Also on Route 10, a couple of hundred yards from the intersection with Route 4, is Miss Porter's School, known for turning out such graduates as Jacqueline Bouvier Kennedy Onassis.

The old saying "can't see the forest for the trees" is particularly well suited to the MDC's (Metropolitan District Commission) ***Demonstration Forest Trail,*** Farmington Avenue (Route 4) on the Farmington–West Hartford border, near MDC Reservoir 1 (the West Hartford Reservoir). On this ¾-mile trail you can find many points of interest that illustrate just how interconnected and complex our ecosystem is—worlds within worlds. At the trailhead pick up a booklet describing the trail's twenty-eight points of interest. As you walk the trail, you'll see the environment not from your point of view but from the point of view of the animals and plants that inhabit the ecosystem. It's a wonderful way to teach kids how trees depend on birds, and how the insects on the forest's floor live in their own little universe. The booklet also includes some interesting tidbits about the plants and animals that make their home in the Demonstration Forest area. This is an excellent field trip for

## The *Amistad* Revolt

Thanks to a couple of recent books and a Spielberg movie (filmed in part at Mystic Seaport), the *Amistad* Revolt now has its rightful place in American history. If you don't know the story, here's a vest-pocket synopsis. In spring 1839 people of the Mendi culture were abducted from their home in Africa by slave traders and transported to Cuba, where they were sold into slavery and boarded the schooner *Amistad*. Once aboard, the Mendi, led by Sengbe Pieh (later called Joseph Cinque), rebelled against their captors and staged a successful mutiny. The Mendi attempted to steer the boat back to Africa, but instead the *Amistad* floated off Long Island Sound and eventually was brought into New London. The Mendi were arrested and tried, spending more than a year in jail in New Haven. Former president John Quincy Adams successfully argued their case for freedom to the United States Supreme Court. But what happened to the Mendi after they won their freedom forever linked Farmington to the *Amistad* story. In March 1841 thirty-eight Mendi traveled to Farmington, where they lived and were educated for nine months while the village raised funds for their passage home. In November 1841 thirty-seven Mendi left Farmington and started the long journey home to Africa, arriving in January 1842.

The Farmington Historical Society, 71 Main Street, (860) 678–1645, publishes a pamphlet featuring a map of *Amistad*-related sites with a short history of each. For more information call or write the Farmington Valley Visitors Association, P.O. Box 1015, Simsbury 06070; (800) 4–WELCOME. For a fee the Farmington Historical Society offers group (ten or more persons preferred) tours of Farmington sites on the Freedom Trail. Call (860) 678–1645 for more information. See the New Haven entry in Gateway to New England to learn more about New Haven's role in the *Amistad* Revolt, and to find out about *Amistad*-related sites you can visit there.

school classes, Cub Scouts, or Brownies, or an Earth Day celebration with your own kids. The MDC demonstration trail is open year-around from 7:00 A.M. to dusk. There's ample free parking. For more details log on to www .themdc.com/demoforest.htm.

Heading into Farmington on Route 4 west, you'll see a small plaza off to your right as you come down the hill. It houses the ***Epicure Market*** (838 Farmington Avenue). We love heading west on Route 4 to the Litchfield Hills, but on some days of the week the whole Litchfield Hills region can feel as though it's wearing a big CLOSED sign. That's why we usually stop at the Epicure, the Farmington Valley's version of Dean and Deluca, for picnic fixings. You'll find wonderful takeout at the deli, from entire meals to hearty sandwiches. The market carries the awesome LaBreu handcrafted breads, perfect with a deli salad sampler or a selection from the cheese case. To wash down your picnic, you can choose from their selection of microbrews or Norwalk's own SoBe soda. Open daily from 8:00 A.M. to around 7:00 P.M.; longer evening hours on Friday and shorter hours on the weekend. Call (860) 677–2824 for hours and information. (There is another Epicure Market in Willington, at 14 Phelpsway Crossing.)

Should you be in Farmington over a weekend and find yourself with a little time on your hands, stay on Route 4 west through Farmington Center, cross the bridge over the Farmington River, and turn right onto Town Farm Road.

## Minigolf

Big-time, headline-making tournament champions and weekend duffers will tell you with equal outspokenness that golf belongs in its lofty niche on the international sports scene. And think about the famous courses, from California to Scotland. But *miniature* golf, with all its goofy charm, is a different story. Statewide, Connecticut has plenty of teeny-weeny putt-putt layouts in settings ranging from pretty and pastoral to outright Disney-ish. Here is a random trio:

*Riverfront Miniature Golf and Ice Cream,* 218 River Road, Farmington, fronts Antiques on the Farmington, so parents can drop the kids off for a round of minigolf while they leisurely browse through the antiques shop. Unlike most minigolf courses, Riverfront doesn't rely on kitsch, but rather has constructed a course with hazards and holes made up of rocks taken from the nearby Farmington River. It's one of the prettiest minigolf courses we've seen and one adult enough that older kids will enjoy it without thinking it's "uncool." A word of warning: The course runs along the Farmington River, so keep an eagle eye on overeager youngsters, who might go on a bender by inventing their own rules involving throwing balls and golf clubs into the rushing stream. There's a cute ice-cream shop attached to the golf course, where parched duffers and their families can refresh themselves. Birthday parties and other special occasions are a specialty. Open daily from around Memorial Day to Labor Day; open weekends from Labor Day through around Halloween. Call (860) 675–4653.

*Safari Golf,* 2340 Berlin Turnpike, Berlin. Safari Golf is probably Connecticut's most famous minigolf course. Playing it is a lot like taking a safari; you'll find lots of life-size jungle animals lying in wait for you, waterfalls to traverse, and lots of waving, ominous junglelike landscaping. The replicas of lions, tigers, and other critters give the course a sense of wonderful silliness, and the water hazards make it difficult enough that older kids and adults won't get bored. Open daily in the summer, with shorter hours in fall and spring. Ice cream and other snack stuff available. The folks at Safari Golf know how to make kids' birthday parties an occasion. Call (860) 828–9800.

*Hidden Valley,* 2060 West Street, Southington. Like Riverfront, Hidden Valley relies on pretty rather than cute. It's a challenging course for older kids and adults with lots of waterfalls and other traps. Batting cages and snack foods available. Available for birthday parties and other special occasions. Open daily in summer, 10:00 A.M. to 9:00 P.M. The batting cages are open 11:00 A.M. to 9:00 P.M., with shorter hours in spring and fall. Call (860) 621–1630 for information.

## Farmington Antiques Weekend

Travel about 1½ miles on Town Farm Road to the verdant pastures of the *Farmington Polo Grounds,* 152 Town Farm Road, (860) 677–8427. Most weekends between Mother's Day and Columbus Day, this spot hops with activity from various shows. In early June and over the Labor Day weekend, the Polo Grounds host the Farmington Antiques Weekend, (860) 677–7862, one of the most prestigious (and colossal) antiques shows in the country. Ralph Lauren, Steven Spielberg, and Barbra Streisand are style-setters who have been spotted here. The quintessential Farmington Antiques Weekend story is the one about the dealer who asked Robert Redford to show his driver's license before accepting his check.

Veteran showgoers know the ins and outs of successful antiquing, so take note of the following rundown. (Other events at the Polo Grounds include: two huge craft fairs, held over Mother's Day and Columbus Day weekends, folk-art shows, chili cook-offs, and horse shows.)

No matter whether you attend in the spring or fall, the Farmington Antiques Weekend is one mammoth show. Here's how to make the most of the show:

Don't dress to kill. Yeah, it's a kind of chi-chi show with an upscale crowd, but wear comfortable clothes and shoes. Don't forget your hat, sunglasses, and sunblock.

Stormy weather. It's more likely the spring show will be washed out, but Labor Day is smack dab in the middle of hurricane season, so be prepared. Umbrellas are OK, but a rain hat and poncho or foldable raincoat is better.

Hands-free. Forget the designer leather bags. Bring a fanny pack or, better yet, a backpack for money and personal things. A folding tote bag for carrying small breakable stuff is also helpful.

Bring folding green. Forget charge cards and even checks. You'll get the best deal if you pay in cash. Many dealers and the food vendors can't break large bills (and many are suspicious of counterfeit $50s and $100s), so bring along small bills.

You'll pass a monster forty-five-hole golf course called *Tunxis Plantation Country Club and Golf Course,* 87 Town Farm Road; (860) 678–7128. How Tunxis Plantation Country Club came into being is something of a local legend. Denied membership in one of Farmington's snootier golf clubs, a local developer simply built his own. Golfers of our acquaintance highly recommend the place, especially for autumn golfing. Tunxis Plantation usually opens around Easter and closes mid-November. Open 7:00 A.M. to 7:00 P.M. weekdays, 6:00 A.M. to 7:00 P.M. weekends. The clubhouse serves food.

About 2 miles past Tunxis Plantation you'll happen upon the *Simmons Family Farm,* 199 Town Farm Road; (860) 679–9388. This was one of the oldest family farms in Connecticut, but in 2001 it was bought by the town of Farm-

Nix the early admission. Unless you're a dealer or have a long or very specific hit list, don't pay the early buyers fee ($20 per person for admission between 7:00 and 10:00 A.M.), but do arrive as close to the 10:00 A.M. general public show opening as you can.

Bring extra water. Various service clubs sell beverages and food at the show, but we usually tote along some extra water. The field gets dusty, so pack some Wash & Dry towelettes or a damp washcloth for mopping up. The food at the show is just OK, so bring a snack and eat elsewhere after the show.

Leave tiny tots and dogs at home. Neither will have a good time. It's hot, crowded, dusty, and full of boring, big-people stuff. And the tents are chockablock with fragile, very expensive pretties that tempt tiny hands and wagging tails.

Use the porters. It doesn't cost much to have them haul your treasures to your car.

It's easy to get lost. Set up a meeting place like the main food tent or the ATM for reunions. Also, it's a good idea to decide who stays put and who hunts if someone wanders off.

Use your program to mark dealers and to take notes. Trust us, by the end of the show, you'll never remember where you saw the perfect Roseville vase at 10:00 A.M.

If you snooze, you lose. When you find the absolutely perfect whatever, snag it. Prices are relatively high at the Farmington show, but if you ask, most dealers will do a little better on the price. Nonetheless, the discounts might not be as generous as you're accustomed to. The closer you get to the end of the show, the easier it is to dicker.

Be prepared. Bring a notepad, pen, and measuring tape. Bring measurements of any space at home you want to fill.

ington. Be sure to see the rolling meadows in this gentle valley. They are marked by glacial mounds left by the last Ice Age. During spring and fall you can often see a rafter of wild turkeys grazing in the fields. Yes, *rafter* is the term for a flock of turkeys. The farm's vegetable stand is open from tomato and corn season through pumpkin season. You'll also find wonderful tiny nubbin new potatoes, squash, some herbs, and colorful bouquets of old-fashioned kitchen garden flowers.

Crossing into Avon, follow Town Farm Road to its end. If you turn left, you travel the narrow, winding roads past *Avon Old Farms School.* This private school for boys was designed by Theodate Pope Riddle of Hill-Stead Museum fame. The buildings are modeled after cottages in Great Britain's

Cotswolds. There are no tours of the campus for the public, but you can drive through the school to look at the buildings. By the way, Old Farms Road can be tricky; it's full of sharp curves, twists, and narrow bridges, so drive carefully and obey the speed limits.

If you had turned right instead of left, you would have quickly happened upon *Fisher Meadows Conservation Area,* a wonderful little park for hiking and walking. The green trail around Spring Lake measures a little over a mile and is a good, flat walk. For a more strenuous hike, take the 2-plus-mile red trail, which follows the Farmington River. The red trail offers lots of up and down walking, so it's not a good walk for small kids or tots in strollers. In the spring and summer, both trails offer great opportunities to spot wildflowers such as the Virginia waterleaf, a declining species numbering less than twelve populations in Connecticut. Due to fallout from the town council's Dog War of 1998, dogs are no longer permitted to run off-leash.

Back out on Route 4 west, you'll encounter, tucked away in a converted trolley barn, a top-flight restaurant called *Apricots,* 1593 Farmington Avenue, that serves an eclectic cuisine based on French, nouvelle American, and country cooking. The downstairs is a comfortable bar and lower-priced pub-style restaurant, popular, noisy, and crowded. Pub food is also served on the patio. Upstairs is an elegant, white-tablecloth eatery, occupying several rambling, windowed rooms overlooking the Farmington River. The service is impeccable. The menu changes throughout the year, but there's always a pasta and chicken dish of the day, as well as several fish and seafood entrees. Among the memorable dishes are pork tenderloin in sour cherry sauce and the apricot dessert sampler full of everything apricot from gelato to chocolate-apricot truffles. Open daily for lunch (11:30 A.M. to 2:30 P.M.) and dinner (6:00 to 10:00 P.M.) and Sunday for dinner (5:30 to 9:00 P.M.). Call (860) 673–5405.

About 5 miles east of the center of Farmington along Route 4 is the Unionville section of the township. During the late eighteenth and early nineteenth centuries, this area was a minor industrial center. It made flints for Washington's army and guns for the War of 1812. It also manufactured the pikes that Torrington native John Brown took with him to Harper's Ferry (and that he intended to use to arm the Southern slaves whom he planned to induce to revolt). The *Unionville Museum* at 87 School Street displays many of these locally made items. The museum is open 2:00 to 4:00 P.M. Wednesday, Saturday, and Sunday. Call (860) 673–2231.

Located in a converted gristmill at 218 River Road in Farmington's Unionville section is *Antiques on the Farmington,* a multidealer shop. The antique furniture and appointments are displayed to advantage in room settings, and considering the quality, prices are quite reasonable. Open 10:00 A.M. to 5:00 P.M. every day but Tuesday. Call (860) 673–9205.

*LaMothe's Sugar House* at 89 Stone Road in Burlington is one of just a handful of real old-fashioned sugar houses left in Connecticut. Here, during February and March, visitors can tour a working house and see the whole process of "sugaring off." There's a big old sap boiler that cooks maple sap into syrup, which you can then see blended with cream and butter and poured into molds to make creamy shaped candies (like Santas or maple leafs), or mixed with other ingredients to make maple taffy. The sugar house sells syrup, maple candy, and maple fudge. Visitors always get a sample of some type of maple sweet. In Connecticut the peak season for sugaring off is late February or early March, but LaMothe's is open year-round. In addition to the sweet treats, LaMothe's also keeps several bunnies and pigs, and their golden retrievers are always around to provide a neighborly escort to the sugar house. Open year-round, 10:00 A.M. to 6:00 P.M. Monday through Thursday, to 5:00 P.M. Friday and Saturday, and noon to 5:00 P.M. Sunday. See syrup made mid-February through mid-March on weekends. Call (860) 675–5043 for more information.

About ¼ mile south on Route 10 (Waterville Road) from Avon Old Farms is the *Avon Cider Mill.* Armando Lattizori built the mill back in 1919, and the present generation of Lattizoris still makes cider the old-fashioned way. When Armando opened his cider mill, he bought a used cider press; today that more-than-200-year-old press is still making cider. During cider season the press runs six or seven days a week and produces 35,000 to 60,000

## connecticut's maplesyrup

It takes forty gallons of sweet sap from the sugar maple tree to make one gallon of maple syrup. Maple syrup comes in grades, with Fancy being the lightest in color and the most delicate. As you move from Grade A Medium Amber to Grade B, the syrup's color gets darker and the flavor stronger. Real maple fanciers might want to check out the Annual Hebron Maple Festival, which is usually held the second weekend in March. It's a good place to enjoy sugar on snow, a taffy-like candy made by pouring boiling hot maple syrup on clean snow. Visit www.hebronmaplefest.com.

## howdoyoulike yourcider?

Early cider is sweet. Mid-season cider is tart. And sweet comes around again with late cider because the apples are riper and have more sugar.

gallons of cider. Avon Cider Mill also sells produce, lots of local apples, crafts, home-baked goods, pumpkins galore, and Christmas trees. Between Columbus Day and Christmas Eve, you can get hot fritters and doughnuts on weekends. The mill shuts down after Christmas and opens again in the spring to sell bedding plants. In season, open daily, 9:00 A.M. to 5:00 P.M. Call (860) 677–0343.

If you continue west on U.S. Highway 44, you'll pass *Old Avon Village* on East Main Street in Avon. Visitors always ask us about the giant rocking chair in the front of the shopping complex. The huge Hitchcock-style rocking chair is something of a local landmark. People give directions based on proximity to the rocker and rival high school students often "chair-nap" it to celebrate a football victory. Unfortunately the story behind the big rocker doesn't exactly sing with romance. When a furniture dealer in New Britain went out of business, managers of the shopping center moved the chair to Old Avon Village as a marketing ploy. For information about Old Avon Village shopping or special events, call (860) 678–0469.

As the theme song for *Cheers* goes, everybody needs a place where they know your name, and for us that place is *Fabiola's Bistro,* 195 West Main Street in Avon. Like many of the places we seem to gravitate to, Fabiola's is a bit hard to find. Look for it in the Tweeter's Plaza, sort of tucked around the corner from The Dormitory. Fabiola's is a no-frills, family-run kind of place. Don't look for decorated plates or tricky dishes. Do look for big bowls of wonderful, from-scratch soups, such as lobster or crab bisque, roasted tomato, or corn chowder. Fabiola's has a knack for making vegetarian sandwiches taste every bit as savory as those with meat. Taste-test the Beatrice Veggie, which consists of heaps of seasonal veggies stir-fried with a lively teriyaki sauce, topped with a rich mix of three cheeses, and served on a crusty grinder roll. On days when we're being bad and eating meat, you can't beat Fabiola's burgers. Portions are generous,

## Seeing Connecticut's Fall Foliage

Here are some of our suggestions for places to see the best and the brightest in Connecticut's fall colors.

*Avon.* A walk, either on the green or red trails, around Spring Lake in Fisher Meadows Conservation Area. See our earlier description of Fisher Meadows.

*Burlington.* A hike along the Blue Trail's Mile of Ledges. Not for the beginning hiker, this rough trail starts off Greer Road, which is off West Chippens Hill Road.

*Farmington.* A ride west on Route 6 is a good starting place for fall foliage.

and prices are low for the quality of food served. Open for lunch only, Monday through Saturday from around 10:30 A.M. to 3:00 P.M. Call (860) 674–9113.

Farther west on US 44, you'll find the ***Avon Congregational Church*** at the intersection with Route 10. The Congregational church in Litchfield may be the most photographed church in New England, but to our mind, this classically simple, 180-year-old white church is one of the most beautiful we've ever seen. From its weathervane to its crisp white curtains, this church exemplifies the religious life of New England. Services and church school are held on Sunday at 10:30 A.M. Call (860) 678–0488.

The ***West Avon Congregational Church,*** 280 Country Club Road, is another picture-perfect, classic New England religious edifice. It's been around since 1751 and gets prettier every year. Call (860) 673–3996.

Heading north past Avon Old Farms along Nod Road, you'll eventually come to the ***Pickin' Patch,*** at number 276. The land here has been farmed since 1666. This family-friendly farm stand and pick-your-own place is one of our favorites in Connecticut. During pick-your-own strawberry season, the Pickin' Patch looks like the Grand Central Station of strawberry patches. Their strawberries are incredibly sweet and fragrant; in fact, on a hot day, just inhaling the concentrated strawberry aroma can be an intoxicating experience. In addition to produce, raspberries, and blueberries, Christmas trees, wreaths, and holiday flowers are sold. The farm stand opens when the pansies start to bloom and stays open until Christmas Eve; open 8:00 A.M. to 6:00 P.M. daily. On October weekends, you can take a hayride with the Pumpkin Lady to the pumpkin patch. Call (860) 677–9552 to find out what's available for picking.

## peachykeen factoid

According to the state's Department of Agriculture, Connecticut orchards produce more varieties of peaches than apples. You can buy them at roadside stands or pick your own at farms. A couple of the best places to PYO are: **Belltown Hill Orchards** in South Glastonbury, (860) 633–2789, and **Starberry Farm** in Washington Depot, (860) 868–2863. Best time to pick peaches? From mid-July for yellow peaches through August for the incredibly fragrant and sweet white peaches.

Just west of the junction of US 44 and Route 10 north is Avon Park North. Turn into this complex on Ensign Drive, then turn onto Bunker Lane. At numbers 25 and 27, in a historic stone-walled building that used to be an explosives plant, is the ***Farmington Valley Arts Center.*** This picturesque structure is home to the Fisher Gallery and Shop and to about twenty artists' studios. Pottery, basket weaving, printing, painting, leather working, and silversmithing

## Praise the Lord and Pass the Doughnuts

Like countless other travelers, we enjoy stumbling upon a locale's lesser-known place that oozes true neighborly folksiness. Which would aptly describe **Luke's Donut Shop,** 305 West Avon Road, a discovery made during some weekend rambling in the Farmington Valley. Luke's is an old-time, unfranchised doughnut shop where everything is made fresh by the owner and his family. In the 1980s, *Yankee* magazine named Luke's one of the top six doughnut places in New England. We like the plain cake and maple doughnuts, but we certainly wouldn't turn down one of Luke's cinnamon rolls, crullers, or cream-filled delights. And Luke's is one of the few places these days you can get what our dads called a "cup of Joe," no fancy flavorings, no special Seattle roast, just fresh-brewed all-American coffee.

Almost more important than the doughnuts and coffee is the sense of community Luke's gives Avon. Avon is basically a bedroom community without a real center or much of an identity, unless you count the town council's silly Dog War of 1998. Regulars have been coming to Luke's for years, and if you want the skinny on what's happening in Avon or what the hot-button issues are, just hop on a stool and listen a while. Be careful where you sit because, depending on the time of day, seating around the counter at Luke's is a hard-won privilege of the regulars. Open 6:00 A.M. to 8:00 P.M. daily. Call (860) 673–0622.

are all represented. Studios are open at the discretion of the individual artists, but Saturday afternoon is when most of the artists are available. The shop and gallery are open Wednesday through Saturday (daily during November and December), 11:00 A.M. to 4:00 P.M.; they are closed for major holidays. Call (860) 678–1867.

The *First Company of the Governor's Horse Guards* (West Avon Road; Route 167) is the oldest cavalry unit in continuous service in the United States, tracing its lineage back to 1658, when the Connecticut Colony founded a troop of mounted guards. In 1788 the Horse Guards were reformed as a company of Light Dragoons, modeled on the Royal Regiment of Horse Guards in England. When Connecticut joined the Revolution against the British Crown, the new state took over the Horse Guards. In those days the unit's main function was to escort and protect visiting dignitaries, and it acted as an honor guard to President Washington when he visited Wethersfield in 1789.

The unit saw somewhat more dangerous service as a mounted unit in the War of 1812 and the Spanish-American War. In 1916 it patrolled the Mexican border during operations against Pancho Villa. Dismounted and reorganized as a machine gun battalion, it served in seven major engagements in France during World War I. At the end of the war, the Horse Guards were remounted as

the 122nd Cavalry Squadron of the Connecticut National Guard; four days after
Pearl Harbor they became the 208th Coast Artillery and served as an antiaircraft
unit in the South Pacific.

Today the Horse Guards' duties are once again mainly ceremonial. The
company makes appearances at presidential and gubernatorial inaugurations. It
consists of thirty riders and thirty-two horses. All horses are donated, and they
include just about every breed except Clydesdales. On Thursday, from 7:00 to
10:00 A.M., the public is invited to watch the unit practice its drills (at which
time you can also tour the stable). These consist of intricate, beautifully chore-
ographed precision maneuvers, often accompanied by music. Call the Governor's Horse Guards at (860) 673–3525 for information on drills. The Horse
Guards host two horse shows each year: one in late June and one in early
October. The Second Company of the Governor's Horse Guards holds its summer practices in Newtown; look under the Danbury entry in Gateway to New
England for details.

Once a large dairy farm, **_Riverdale Farms Shopping_** on Route 10 north
of Avon is now the site of one of the more interesting shopping centers in the
area. This complex occupies several low hills under the eye of the Heublein
Tower, atop Talcott Mountain to the north and east. Eleven renovated farm
buildings along with five new buildings now house around fifty offices, stores,
and boutiques. Most of the stores are crafts, gift, or fashion stores, but Riverdale
Farms is also home to the Farmington Valley outpost of Harry's Pizza of West
Hartford and a sushi bar.

West of Avon is Canton, which like so many Connecticut towns, has a
ghost. This one is supposedly the shape of a Revolutionary War messenger
who disappeared in the vicinity while conveying a payroll from Hartford patri-
ots to French officers aiding the Americans. After a bleached skeleton was

## Talking Turkey

_Gobble, gobble, gobble._ You probably won't be watching the Horse Guards practice
when the winter holidays roll around, so stick a bookmark here to remind you to seek
out the farm next to the Horse Guards headquarters: **_Miller Foods Inc.,_** 308 Arch
Street in Avon. This place grows some of the best gobblers in the region, but fresh
birds are only available during the fall and winter holidays. At Thanksgiving Miller's
pitches its "turkey tent," an outdoor bazaar full of lots of special goodies for your
holiday table. The turkeys sell like hotcakes, so call ahead to order. Outside the
holiday season, Miller Foods sells other meats such as hams and smoked turkeys
plus natural pet food. Call (860) 673–3256; www.choicemall.com/millerfoods.

found under the Canton Tavern, where the man was last seen alive, stories began circulating that the innkeeper had murdered the hapless messenger and stolen the money. Shortly thereafter, people started seeing a headless horseman, presumed to be the ghost of the paymaster, riding west along the Albany Turnpike (US 44) toward Saratoga. They still do. So if you're down by the Canton Golf Course some dark and foggy night, and you notice that your headlights are shining through a ghostly horseman and his steed to illuminate the road beyond, don't pay it any mind. It's just the Headless Horseman of Canton on his perpetual journey.

The headless horseman isn't the only antique in Canton. In fact, from Canton west to the state line, the Albany Turnpike (US 44) is dotted with dozens of antiques shops, flea markets, and just plain junk stores filled with antiques, collectibles, and vintage items. Some of the best are in Canton itself, including **Antiques at Canton Village** in the Canton Village Shopping Center and **Balcony Antiques** at 81 Albany Turnpike. Both are multidealer shops, and Balcony is the oldest such shop in the state. Antiques at Canton Village is open 10:00 A.M. to 5:00 P.M. daily, and noon to 5:00 P.M. Sunday. It is closed on Tuesday. Call (860) 693–2715. Balcony Antiques is open 10:00 A.M. to 5:00 P.M. Monday through Saturday and noon to 5:00 P.M. Sunday. Call (860) 693–6440.

One of the best ways to learn about antiques or to snap up some good furniture at bargain prices is to go to an auction. For our money the best auction is held at **Canton Barn Auction Gallery,** 75 Old Canton Road, Canton. You never know what you'll find—Arts and Crafts one week, Country Victorian the next. Almost as much of a draw as the auction are the homemade pies. We favor the chocolate pecan, which is sinfully delicious, but every flavor has something special. Be warned, however, the pies go at the speed of light. Here's the drill: Grab your pie, reserve your seat (nothing fancy, just slap a Post-it note on your chosen seat), and then preview the auction. Auctions are usually held on Thursday with previews a couple of hours before the 7:00 P.M. start, but call (860) 693–0601 for auction and preview times.

In recent years, US 44 has become Farmington Valley's Restaurant Row. From Avon to Canton, there are more restaurants of different types and ethnicity than we can describe in this book. Here's the lowdown on a couple of our favorites that you might not find on your own.

**The Bamboo Grill** at 50 Albany Turnpike (US 44) in Canton is a wonderful Vietnamese restaurant with tasty, inexpensive, and healthy food. You can't go wrong ordering any of the bun dishes. *Bun* is sort of Vietnam's fast food; it consists of rice noodles topped with grilled meat or chicken, shredded lettuce and carrots, caramelized shallots, chopped peanuts, and a wonderful sweet-hot-tangy sauce. Open for dinner only, Tuesday through Sunday, from 5:00 to

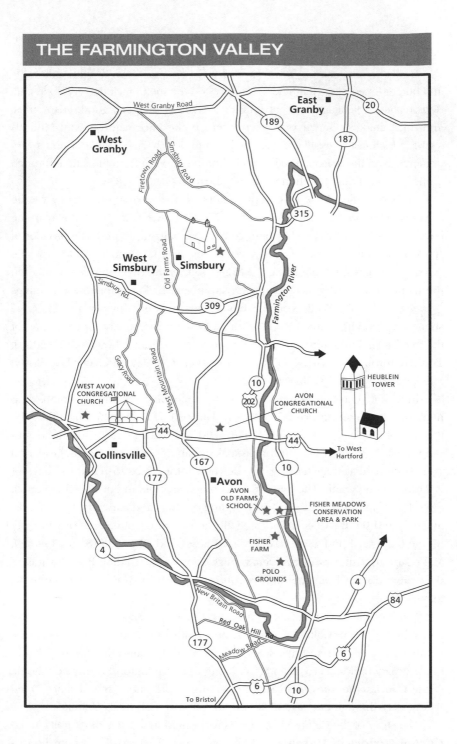

9:00 P.M., later hours on weekends. Call (860) 693–4144 for hours and reservations (a good idea on weekends).

Under various names, *Junior's,* US 44, Canton, has been delighting hot dog and burger lovers since the fifties. Mainstays on the menu include very good chili dogs (called "Michigan dogs" at Junior's); excellent burgers; good, crispy fries; and thick shakes. Our favorite menu item is the chocolate coconut Mounds shake, which tastes just like the candy bar. Junior's is open daily, but hours vary depending on the season. You'll usually find them open from lunchtime through dinner. Winter hours are shorter, so call ahead: (860) 693–8838.

Probably one of the best-kept secrets on the Farmington Valley foodie scene is *Hibachi* at 33 East Main Street (US 44) in Avon. It's nestled way in the back of Old Avon Village shopping center. Specializing in perfectly wonderful "pick-up Japanese cuisine," nearly everything on the menu is cooked on the smoking hot grills that dominate the front room of the two-room restaurant. On the menu you'll find grilled food such as ginger chicken, Japanese dumplings *(gyoza),* and sushi. While you can buy a soda to wash down your lunch, we suggest the soothing green tea. You can take your food away, or eat at one of the two tables in the tiny, austerely elegant dining room. 11:00 A.M. to 7:00 P.M. Tuesday through Thursday, 11:00 A.M. to 8:00 P.M. Friday and Saturday. Closed Sunday and Monday. Call (860) 674–1266.

In recent years, US 44 has taken on the atmosphere of an anonymous strip mall. But the *Trading Post,* 215 Albany Turnpike (US 44), Canton, still sits by the side of the road, looking much like it did way back in the 1970s, the beginning of its "Temple of Cool" promotional slogan. If your coming-of-age period goes back to that freewheeling decade, here's the place to relive the days of your long-gone youth. The interior looks much as it did in our crunchy-granola days, full of imported clothing and dangling earrings and ear cuffs, bedspreads, incense, and tie-dyed T-shirts. Beside all the other accoutrements of latter-day hippie life, you'll find good buys on used tapes and CDs. Call (860) 693–4679. Make sure to visit *Eastern Accents,* next door to the Trading Post, for lots of decorative objects from Asia and beyond. Call (860) 693–4679 for more information.

South of the town of Canton on Route 179 is the village of Collinsville, formerly home of the Collins Company, an eighteenth- and nineteenth-century manufacturer of axes and machetes that were sold around the world. The old brick factory building at 1 Main Street along the Farmington River is now home to the *Collinsville Antiques Co.,* an operation representing fifty dealers. Open Wednesday through Sunday, 10:00 A.M. to 5:00 P.M. Call (860) 693–2658.

The story of the Collins Company is recounted in a series of exhibits in the *Canton Historical Museum* at 11 Front Street. This small museum houses one of the largest collections of Victoriana in the United States. There is also a striking 2,000-square-foot railway diorama accurately showing Collinsville and Canton as they appeared circa 1900. Open April through November, 1:00 to 4:00 P.M. Wednesday through Sunday, 1:00 to 8:00 P.M. Thursday; December through March, 1:00 to 4:00 P.M. Saturday and Sunday. Admission. Call (860) 693–2793 or visit www.cantonmuseum.org.

Simsbury was settled in 1648 by a group of Windsor families who acquired the land from the Massacoe Indians. They called their new settlement Massacoh Plantation, a name that was eventually changed to Simsbury when the town was incorporated by the Connecticut General Court in 1670. In March 1676, when King Philip's War began to heat up, the entire village of about forty dwellings was destroyed by Wampanoag Indians. The Wampanoag uprising was over by August, but it was two years before reconstruction began. Once it did, Simsbury quickly became an important factor in Connecticut's economy and politics. The first copper coins in America were struck here in 1737, and the first steel mill in America was built here in 1744. Hundreds of residents fought in the American Revolution, including Maj. Gen. Noah Phelps, who, as America's first spy (he was just a captain then), entered Fort Ticonderoga in disguise to gather information for Ethan Allen; Allen then proceeded to capture the fort. By the 1820s the town was a major stop on the Farmington Canal, which ran along the route of today's Hopmeadow Street (Route 10).

## simsburytrivia

Simsbury's main avenue, Hopmeadow Street, gets its name from the fields of hops that once grew where the street runs today.

***Pettibone's Tavern,*** junction of Routes 10 and 185, specializes in seafood and steak. The bill of fare isn't fancy or revolutionary, but they do know how to grill a mean steak, and the salads and potato dishes are always good and savory. Berthed in a mellow yellow colonial building, the decor is as fancy as the menu is simple. You'll find lots of lavish wood carvings and vast fireplaces. The big draw, though, is the restaurant's resident ghost who has been known to give diners a friendly pat or poke now and again. Pettibone's ghost is a Farmington Valley tradition, with radio disk jockeys often spending All Hallows' Eve at the restaurant reporting on ghostly doings. Whoever the ghost is, she appears to be friendly, usually making appearances only when the restaurant decides to renovate or redecorate. Open 11:00 A.M. to 2:00 P.M. Monday through Saturday for lunch. Dinner is served daily starting at 5:00 P.M. Call (860) 658–1118.

The ***Phelps Tavern Museum,*** 800 Hopmeadow Street in historic Simsbury, consists of period rooms and interactive exhibition galleries, showing visitors what it was like to be a guest at the Captain Elisha Phelps House when it was an inn between 1786 and 1849. Three successive generations of Phelps tavernkeepers are chronicled, along with the social history of New England taverns. Back then, Connecticut towns were requred by law to have at least one tavern for the accommodation of travelers, who arrived by horse, stage-coach, and canal boat. The museum is part of a two-acre complex operated by the Simsbury Historical Society that also includes a museum store, research center, and award-winning period gardens. Open year-around, except holidays, Tuesday through Saturday from noon to 4:00 P.M. Guided tours at 12:15, 1:15, 2:15, and 3:15 P.M. Admission. For more information call (860) 658–2500.

## simsburytrivia

In 1737 Simsbury's Samuel Higley developed the first copper coinage in America. The Higley copper was worth two and sixpence (42 cents) in paper currency. The coin's motto was: "I am good Copper."

The first safety fuse, used for mining and exploration, made in America was made in Simsbury in 1836 by Richard Bacon. Mr. Bacon, who ran the mine at Newgate, entered into a copartnership with the English firm of Bickford, Smith & Davey.

You might be tempted to zip past *One-Way Fare* at 4 Railroad Street, thinking, as we did for years, "former railroad station turned restaurant. Nah, way too cute." One-Way Fare is more than a cutie-pie place full of railroad memorabilia. To us, it seems like an extension of Simsbury's town hall, a place where longtime residents meet to talk about the burning and not-so-burning issues of the day. It's popular, too, with the members of the Thomas the Tank Engine set, who enjoy inspecting all the cool train stuff in the restaurant and the adjoining railroad cars. Big people can take comfort in the eatery's signature burgers: a tower of hamburger patties, Canadian bacon, sautéed onions, and cheese on an English muffin—great with a nice cold beer. As with Luke's in Avon, seating at the bar is a hard-won right. Newcomers who hop up on the bar stools can expect, at the very least, a stern look from the regulars. From May through October, it's pleasant to eat outside on the front porch. Call (860) 658–4477 for hours and information on daily specials.

The rambling, comfortable *Simsbury 1820 House,* 3 blocks down from Massacoh Plantation at 731 Hopmeadow Street, is one of those country inns just made for winter celebration dinners. The house, built in 1820, was the home of Gifford Pinchot, the man who raised America's consciousness about conservation. Today the restored inn looks much like it did in its heyday with shining oak floors and glorious leaded glass windows. All the rooms are comfortably furnished with antiques and high-quality reproductions. The dining room serves a menu that's probably best described as contemporary American, with an emphasis on seasonal foods. The desserts are excellent. Open all year. The dining room serves dinner from 5:00 to 8:00 P.M., Monday through Thursday. Call (860) 658–7658 or (800) TRY–1820.

For much of Simsbury's early history, **Talcott Mountain** cut the region off from the meadowlands of the Connecticut River Valley to the east. This isolation ended when the Albany Turnpike was hacked across the mountain, but the state of mind engendered by that knife-edge of rock looming dramatically over the landscape remains. Though separated by only a mile from the towns of Hartford's meadowlands, Simsbury, Avon, and even Farmington, to the south, have far more in common with the small towns to their west than they do with the suburbs east of the mountain.

There has been a tower atop Talcott Mountain for most of the past 190 years. The first was built in 1810 and was the inspiration for John Greenleaf Whittier's poem "Monte Video." It was blown down in a windstorm in 1840. Others followed until finally, in 1914, businessman Gilbert Heublein built a fourth tower atop the mountain, a grand white 165-foot-high edifice of steel and concrete anchored in the rock. For twenty years this so-called Heublein Tower was a summer home for the Heublein family. Today the mountain and its tower are all part of **Talcott Mountain State Park.** Four states are visible from the top of the tower, but first you have to get there. The main public access route is off Route 185. A road leads partway up the mountain to a parking area, from which you can hike the 1¼-mile trail to the top. The early part of the climb is fairly steep, but there are benches for resting. Once you reach the tower, you'll have to make another climb up the stairs to the top; there are no elevators.

The park is open year-round. Heublein Tower is open Thursday through Sunday, 10:00 A.M. to 5:00 P.M., April 1 through Labor Day, and daily, 10:00 A.M. to 5:00 P.M., Labor Day through October. Call (860) 242–1158.

When leaving Talcott Mountain, turn left on Route 185 and drive west toward Route 10. A mile or so west of the access road, you'll come to an old iron bridge. On your right is a huge, bare, witchy-looking tree whose branches loom over the road like some spectral presence. This is the Pinchot Sycamore, reputedly the

Heublein Tower,
Talcott Mountain State Park

oldest tree in Connecticut. The small meadow in which it grows is open to the public and has some picnic tables and benches if you care to sit a spell.

Cyber-travelers might want to check out other tall trees in Connecticut. The *Connecticut Notable Trees Project* maintains a Web site that lists the tallest and biggest trees in the state. Besides a city-by-city list of notable trees, you'll find information on how to measure and report the big trees you spot on your travels or in your front yard. http://notabletrees.conncoll.edu/.

*Merrywood,* a cozy B&B, located at 100 Hartford Road (Route 185) in Simsbury, has some notable trees of its own. Set off among tall pines on five secluded acres, it's hard to believe this quiet and elegant colonial revival B&B is just minutes away from US 44 and some of the Farmington Valley's best shops and restaurants. The interior of the house is furnished with what the owners, Mike and Gerlinde Marti, call "an eclectic mix of period antiques, oriental carpets, and original artwork." Many of the decorative elements are souvenirs from the couple's world travels. Merrywood sleeps six, with two double rooms and one suite, all with private baths. Unlike many B&Bs where decorating is more important than the guest's comfort, the beautifully decorated guest rooms contain lots of amenities targeted for maximum comfort. Afternoon tea is served for guests. Merrywood's breakfast menu is one of the most ambitious we've seen at a B&B, with offerings like eggs Benedict, eggs hussard, pancakes, and some special Swiss breakfast dishes, such as eggs scrambled with toast cubes, potatoes, tomatoes, onions, and two cheeses. For the quality of the accommodations and service, the rates, between $150 and $175 a night, are reasonable. Merrywood is open all year. No smoking; no pets; no children. Call (866) 637–7993.

## Places to Stay in the Heartland

**Butternut Farm,**
1654 Main Street,
Glastonbury;
(860) 633–7197.
Inn offers four guest rooms.
Moderate to expensive.

## Places to Eat in the Heartland

**Brookside Bagels,**
563 Hopmeadow Street,
Simsbury;
(860) 651–1492.
Inexpensive.

**Carville's Ranch House**
(dogs and burgers),
27 Windsor Avenue,
Windsor;
(860) 522–2266.
Moderate.

**Cottage Restaurant and Café,**
427 Farmington Avenue,
Plainville;
(860) 793–8888.
Contemporary American.
Moderate.

**First & Last Tavern,**
26 West Main Street
(US 44),
Avon;
(860) 676–2000.
Casual Italian.
Inexpensive to moderate.

# The Litchfield Hills

West of Hartford is Litchfield County, an area largely synonymous with Connecticut's western uplands. As one moves north and west through Litchfield, one moves deeper into the Litchfield Hills, a forested spur of the Berkshires that typifies what comes to most people's minds when they think of New England. Steepled white churches, romantic old inns, quaint antiques shops, and small establishments run by Yankee craftspeople still abound. In recent years, though, the Litchfield Hills have become home to many of the rich and famous: Susan Saint James in Litchfield, Philip Roth and Dustin Hoffman in Roxbury, Henry Kissinger in Warren, and Meryl Streep in Salisbury, to name but a few. Their arrival has brought upscale shops and nouvelle restaurants that give the area a cosmopolitan flavor. The southern portion of this hill mass merges into the region's "Alpine Lake" country, an area reminiscent of Switzerland, with cool forest-shrouded lakes and tranquil meadows. This region is home to some of the state's best inns. Cutting between the Litchfield Hills and New York's Taconic Mountains, from the extreme northwestern corner of Connecticut to Stratford on the coast, is the Housatonic River. In its northern reaches, the Housatonic is a wild freshet that is surely one of the prettiest rivers in New England. Litchfield County is bordered by Massachusetts on the

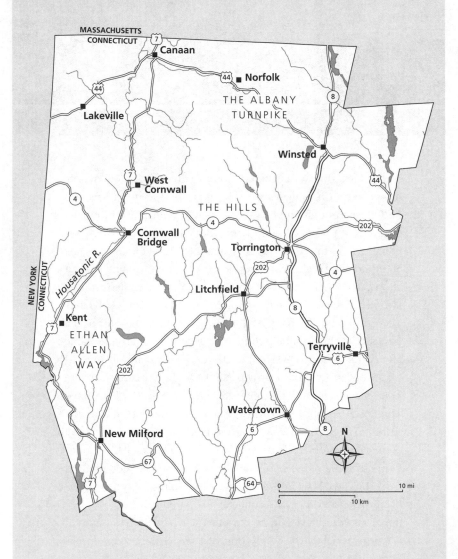

north and New York on the west. To the south of the lake country are the populous counties of Fairfield and New Haven.

# The Albany Turnpike

In the days before railroads and superhighways, Hartford and Albany, New York, were linked by a rutted roadway called the Albany Turnpike. This highway of sorts was the main route through the rugged northwestern uplands, and its location determined the patterns of settlement in this part of the state. Today the successor to the old turnpike is a gleaming asphalt ribbon dubbed US 44, and any traveler through this part of Connecticut must pass over it.

The easternmost township along the Litchfield portion of US 44 is New Hartford. New Hartford is divided into four sections, of which **Satan's Kingdom** and Pine Meadow are the best known. Satan's Kingdom is named for the bandits who used to hide out in the rugged, wooded countryside flanking the turnpike to ambush and rob the Hartford–Albany stagecoach. Today a company called **Farmington River Tubing**, on US 44 inside Satan's Kingdom, will rent you an inflated rubber tube in which you can float down the Farmington River past the gorges where the robbers made their homes. Trips take two to three hours and cover 3 miles and three sets of rapids, ending up in Canton. The company picks you up and returns you to your starting point by bus. The service operates from Memorial Day through Labor Day. Call (860) 693–6465 for age restrictions and prices. We suggest that you wear shoes you don't mind submerging in water.

**Blue Sky Foods**, 431 Main Street (US 44) in New Hartford, likes to call itself a blend of Key West and Nantucket. Two words describe the ambience of this charming roadside eatery—Jimmy Buffett (whose music also dominates the sound system). The decor is simple but manages to communicate the laid-back sensibilities of the tropics with vibrant colors (vivid sky-blue dominates), shells scattered around the tables, and of course, plenty of pink flamingos. Service is friendly but somewhat minimal. You order at the counter, choosing from the

## AUTHORS' FAVORITES

| | |
|---|---|
| Action Wildlife Foundation | Carole Peck's Good News Cafe |
| Blue Sky Foods | The Last Post |

menu, the blackboard specials, or whatever looks good in the cold case, grab a chair, and pretty soon a member of the waitstaff zips your food to the table. You won't find lots of tricky, trendy food, but you will find what might be referred to as "the food real people eat." The fried whole-belly clams or fried oysters (which sell out at lightning speed) are almost as good as those at Johnny Ad's in Westbrook, and you'll like their New England take on a Cuban sandwich (grilled ham and cheese, pickles, mustard, and mayo). Blue Sky pays homage to Mr. Buffett with their Cheeseburger in Paradise, and it is a heavenly burger. The Couch Potatoes (fries topped with chili, cheese, and onions) make a light lunch or a hefty side. Desserts change with the seasons; you might find mango crisp in summer and gingerbread in winter. Not surprisingly, the key lime pie is the perfect blend of creamy, tart, sweet, and tangy, topped with a cloud of real whipped cream. Patio dining starts around Memorial Day and ends around Columbus Day. From May through mid-October, open Wednesday and Thursday 11:00 A.M. to 8:00 P.M.; Friday and Saturday from 11:00 A.M. to 8:30 P.M.; and Sunday from 11:00 A.M. to 6:00 P.M. Winter hours are curtailed, so call before going: (860) 379–0000. E-mail: blueskyfood@earthlink.net.

If you're in New Hartford at sugaring-off time (February and March), visit the **Kasulaitis Farm and Sugarhouse,** 69 Goose Green Road, to watch the process and buy some tasty maple products. If you miss sugaring-off, stop by anyway and watch the lambs frisk and frolic in the spring pasture. Such things are good for the soul. Call ahead: (860) 379–8787.

North of New Hartford, US 44 loops through Barkhamsted. This township's combination of sparse population, winding roads, heavy forest, and large lakes makes it one of the most dramatic parts of Connecticut for leaf peeping.

One of the best fall foliage jaunts through Barkhamsted starts north of the town at the junction of Routes 20 and 181 in Hartland. If you approach this intersection from the east on Route 20, you'll pass through West Hartland on the way. Don't let this confuse you; with typical Yankee contrariness, *West* Hartland is actually *east* of Hartland, so keep driving for another mile. At the intersection in Hartland, take Route 181 south. This road runs between the Barkhamsted Reservoir and the Farmington River, for much of the way under the limbs of the lovely Peoples State Forest. At the tip of the reservoir, Route 181 meets Route 318. Take 318 east to the Saville Dam, separating Barkhamsted and Compensating Reservoirs. There's parking nearby and even on the dam itself; this is a great spot to stop for pictures or for an informal picnic. From the dam, continue east to Route 219. From there you can either drive south to pick up Route 44, return west for more leaf peeping, or loop back up to Route 20 in Granby.

If you loop south you'll pass the **Compensating Reservoir** on your right. Also known as Lake McDonough, this body of water is a major state recreational area, with facilities for boating, swimming, picnicking, hiking, and fishing. Boating is allowed from mid-April through September; rowboats can be rented. Fishing is allowed mid-April through Labor Day. Open weekdays, 10:00 A.M. to 8:00 P.M., weekends and holidays, 8:00 A.M. to 8:00 P.M. No admission; parking fee. Call (860) 278–7850.

If, after reaching Saville Dam, you're still in the mood for more fall color, head back west on Route 318 for ½ mile beyond the intersection of Route 181. Turn right on East River Road. This will take you directly through **Peoples State Forest** along the banks of the West Branch of the Farmington. It is one of two roads that run along the riverbank. The other, West River Road, runs through the forest on the west bank, intersecting with Route 318 a few yards west of, and across the bridge from, East River Road. The two roads don't quite intersect several miles north of the bridge in the village of Riverton, former home of the Hitchcock chair, first produced in 1825.

While other Connecticut entrepreneurs were experimenting with the use of interchangeable parts in the manufacture of rifles and clocks, Lambert Hitchcock set out in 1818 to mass produce furniture in a little factory at the junction of the Farmington and Still Rivers. A decade later, Hitchcock was turning out 15,000 chairs each year, and his factory employed a hundred people in the rapidly growing village of Hitchcocksville. The mass-produced Hitchcock chairs, selling for between 45 cents and $1.75, were an instant success. They were also extremely sturdy. Quality control consisted of dropping each assembled chair from a second-floor workshop into a waiting wagon; only those items that survived the drop unscathed were considered sufficiently sturdy to wear the Hitchcock label. Once the chairs were assembled, workers finished them by hand, often using multiple stencils that produced a colorful and distinctive look.

In the middle of the nineteenth century, Hitchcock's business foundered; in 1852 its owner died penniless. About the same time, the village that bore his name disappeared from the map. Tired of constantly being confused with nearby Hotchkissville, the residents of Hitchcocksville, in typically pragmatic Yankee fashion, changed the town's name to Riverton. Present-day Riverton (population a mere 200) is a sleepy, picturesque, quarter-mile-long village—little more than a quaint neighborhood tucked inside the larger town of Barkhamsted—where all three streets run alongside the Farmington River. Local stature and "image" were almost completely dependent on the venerable Hitchcock Furniture Factory and Factory Store (for bargain-priced chairs and other Riverton-made furnishings), both of which ceased operations in April 2006. But even without the Hitchcock-related attractions, the village is worth a leisurely visit.

Village attractions are easily reachable. It's only a five-minute walk along Route 20 from the local Grange Hall on the banks of Sandy Brook at the west end of town to the bridge spanning the Farmington River at the east end. But that stretch of road abounds with enticing stores and snack shops. You might, for example, wrap up your visit with a bite at the *Catnip Mouse Tea Room* or grab a deli sandwich and Moxie at the *Riverton General Store* and picnic along the river. Or you could just stroll along with one of the *Village Sweet Shoppe*'s quality ice-cream cones; if you like strange mix-ins, try the coconut ice cream with dark chocolate. Peek inside *Beautiful Things* for Italian hand-lacquered music boxes, gourmet gift baskets, Hummel figurines, and Steiff Teddy bears.

Riverton has always been a delightful village to visit, but getting a really good meal has been problematic at best. *Sweet Pa's,* 6 Riverton Road (Route 20), billeted in an antiques-filled, yellow Victorian house, offers a new dimension to dining in Riverton. Pa's serves new American cuisine featuring many fish dishes and fresh, in-season ingredients. There is also a children's menu, complimentary wine tasting, and outdoor dining. Open 11:30 A.M. to 2:30 P.M. and 5:00 to 9:00 P.M. Tuesday through Saturday and 10:30 A.M. to 8:00 P.M. Sunday. Call (860) 379–7020 for reservations.

If you fish, mark your calendar for the first day of trout season (the third Saturday in April). That's when Riverton holds its annual *Fishing Derby* on the Farmington River. The Farmington is a National Wild and Scenic River, and probably offers the best fly fishing in Connecticut. Rainbow and brown trout don't exactly beg to be caught, but it's pretty easy to catch one. The contest runs from 6:00 to 10:00 A.M., rain, sun, or snow. There's no entry fee; all you need is a Connecticut fishing license. Non-anglers are welcome to observe, and presumably applaud when a particularly promising catch is landed. Kids under twelve can fish in a specially stocked area. For more information, call the Riverton General Store at (860) 379–0811, where you can also buy that all-important Connecticut fishing license.

If you intend to overnight in this part of Connecticut, we recommend the *Old Riverton Inn* on Route 20. Opened as the Ives Tavern, a stagecoach stop on the old Boston-to-Albany Turnpike (US 44), this twelve-room inn bills itself as offering "hospitality for the hungry, thirsty, and sleepy since 1796." And it retains its colonial charm to this day. Small, quaint, and friendly, the Old Riverton Inn is famous for the hospitality of its staff. The twelve guest rooms have private bathrooms and include a full breakfast. The inn is nonsmoking.

The floor of the enclosed Grindstone Terrace is made of grindstones quarried in Nova Scotia, sent by sailing ship to Long Island Sound, then dispatched upriver to Hartford and hauled by oxcart from Hartford to Collinsville, where they were used to grind axe heads and machetes in the Collinsville Axe Factory (now an antiques store). The inn's dining room is decorated with Riverton's famous Hitchcock chairs. The fare here is pretty good, although some dishes are regrettably institutional, and includes tasty homemade soups.

Located on the west bank of the Farmington River, just across from the Hitchcock factory, the Old Riverton Inn is open year-round except the first three weeks in January. The restaurant serves lunch from noon to 2:30 P.M. on Saturday. Dinner runs from 5:00 to 8:30 P.M. Wednesday through Saturday, and noon to 5:00 P.M. Sunday. The inn is closed on Monday, Tuesday, and Christmas Day. Call (860) 379–8678.

Southwest of Riverton is another beautiful forest: the **American Legion State Forest** in Pleasant Valley. Even on

### thomastontrivia

Many Americans grew up with a Seth Thomas clock on the mantel. And, yes, Virginia, there really was a Seth Thomas and he really was a clockmaker. The town of Thomaston is named after him.

the hottest day, the tall trees and pines keep the forest shady and glade cool, and at night, it's mouse quiet and real country dark. You can fish or tube on the Farmington River, and there's good hiking all around. Moderate fee for campsites. Most state parks and state forests are open from 8:00 A.M. to sunset. For detailed information, including maps, on Connecticut's state parks and forests, contact the Bureau of Outdoor Recreation, State Parks Division, Connecticut Department of Environmental Protection, 79 Elm Street, Hartford 06106-5127; (860) 424–3200; http://dep.state.ct.us.

You probably won't meet up with the *New York Times* food critic in the **Winsted Diner** at 496 Main Street (US 44). If so, he or she would like it, and chances are that you will, too. Part restaurant, part local gathering place, the Winsted Diner has been a town institution since 1941. It's tiny and easy to miss because it's angled off from Main Street. But persevere. The atmosphere is friendly, and the pancakes and French toast are good. Or you might try the Ra-Doc-a-Doodle, a breakfast sandwich that is what an Egg McMuffin only wishes it were. Call (860) 379–4429.

On your way down the hill into Norfolk, make sure you stop to look at the route marker on the green (across from the library). It's a lovely piece of primitive folk art, decorated with deer, bunnies, and other woodsy creatures. Definitely worth a photograph.

Located at the junction of US 44 and Routes 272 and 182 and with **Campbell Falls** and **Haystack Mountain State Park** just north of the town center, Norfolk is a crossroads of tourism in northwest Connecticut. While outdoor recreation is popular, the activity for which the town is famous is the **Norfolk**

## Three Civic-Spirited Families

The philanthropic, much-intermarried Eldridges, Battells, and Stoeckels have left their mark on Norfolk. Its shingle-sided, barrel-vaulted library (1889) was donated by Isabella Eldridge. High-society architect Stanford White designed that same year's village-green fountain, commissioned by Mary Eldridge and named in honor of her uncle, Joseph Battell. Mary Alice Bradford Eldridge paid for 1892's Town Hall. The Battell Memorial Chapel (1928) features priceless Tiffany stained-glass windows depicting the four seasons, and Ellen Battell Stoeckel's estate now is home to Norfolk's summertime music festivals.

*Chamber Music Festival.* Think of this annual summer event as a Tanglewood without the crowds. The Norfolk Chamber Music Festival and the *Yale Summer School of Music* perform summer concerts in the brown-shingled Music Shed on the grounds of the Stoeckel estate on US 44, west of the Norfolk Green. The concert schedule varies from year to year, but the New York Woodwind Quintet, the New York Brass Quartet, and the Tokyo String Quartet have all appeared in the past. There are Friday and Saturday evening performances throughout June, July, and August. Call (860) 542–3000.

Norfolk has what many people consider the prettiest village green in the state. What better way to see the sights of charming and historic Norfolk than in a horse-drawn carriage? The *Horse and Carriage Livery Service* (Loon Meadow Drive, off US 44) offers a horse-drawn tour of the town or horse-drawn hayrides with bonfires afterward. In winter (snow permitting) you can arrange for a private sleigh ride for two or for a larger sled that can handle groups on a romantic sleigh ride through snow-hushed woods. Warm up afterwards with a cup of mulled cider in the wood stove–heated barn. Open 9:00 A.M. to 10:00 P.M. daily. Reservations required; call (860) 542–6085; www.loon meadowfarm.com.

Located just off the Norfolk Green in a castlelike brownstone adorned with stained-glass windows and turrets is *The Pub.* The decor is laid back and includes posters, memorabilia, and one very cool chair made from antlers. The beverage list is notable not only for its 150 beers, mostly microbrews, but also for its microbrewed *root beers.* The food stretches beyond pub grub, with the veggie burgers (little patties of shredded veggies with a dipping sauce and a dollop of onion marmalade); good, filling soups like the baked potato soup; very good burgers; and salads like chicken, apple, and walnuts over baby greens. Desserts tend to the chocolate side. Without a doubt, this place offers one of the best deals on meals in the Litchfield Hills. Open 11:30 A.M. to 9:00

P.M. Tuesday through Thursday, 11:30 A.M. to 10:00 P.M. Friday and Saturday, and 11:00 A.M. to 9:00 P.M. Sunday. Throughout the year, The Pub cooks up various special dinners, for example, an Octoberfest German dinner. When things get quiet in the winter, pub hours change, so call ahead. Call (860) 542–5716 for information. Parties of five or more need to make reservations.

Just outside of town, at 105 Greenwoods Road East, is an unassuming bed-and-breakfast called **Greenwoods Gate.** *Yankee* magazine has called it the "most romantic [B&B] in New England," and our readers seem to agree. A couple from New Jersey wrote us that their twenty-fifth anniversary at Greenwoods Gate was their most romantic ever. The pineapple, the colonial symbol of hospitality, greets you as you enter the white clapboard structure, a 1797 restored colonial with three opulent suites. Each suite has its own entrance, assuring guests maximum privacy. The three-level Levi Thompson suite has its own living room and a bathroom with a large whirlpool that would be the envy of many spas. Splendid gourmet breakfasts are served on weekends and less elaborate country continental breakfasts are served on weekdays, but only for guests. Call (860) 542–5439; www.greenwoodsgate.net.

Way up in the farthest northwest corner of Connecticut is the **Mount Riga** area, a system of peaks that marches north and west from Salisbury to the New York and Massachusetts borders. The Appalachian Trail crosses the region, running over **Bear Mountain,** at 2,316 feet the highest peak in the state. The highest *point* in the state is a shoulder of **Mount Frissel** that rises to 2,380 feet in the northwesternmost corner of Connecticut. According to tourist brochures, you can stand on that mountain and (assuming that you are reasonably limber) place one foot in Connecticut and one foot in Massachusetts and bend over and put both hands in New York. Very near this summit is Crying Child Rock, which, they say, makes a soft crying sound just like an infant whenever the wind is right. For detailed information on this area, call the state parks division of the Department of Environmental Protection at (860) 424–3200 or log on to http://dep.state.ct.us.

*Chaiwalla* means tea-maker in Hindi. So what else could a place named **Chaiwalla** be but a teahouse? Located at 1 Main Street in Salisbury, this establishment somehow fits the town (you should pardon the expression) to a T. Salisbury has always been a simple, pastoral village, with a small measure of sophistication and a lot of country charm. In recent years these qualities have made it a popular destination for weekending New Yorkers. The combination of a rustic setting and a sophisticated audience made this a perfect place for tea lover and importer Mary O'Brien to set up shop.

Chaiwalla serves light lunches and teas. The lunches are quite good, but high tea is what is done best. This is not your simple tea and a bun, but rather

## OTHER ATTRACTIONS WORTH SEEING IN THE LITCHFIELD HILLS

**Cricket Hill Garden,**
670 Walnut Hill Road,
Thomaston;
(860) 283–1042.
www.treepeony.com

**Elephant's Trunk Flea Market,**
Route 7,
New Milford;
(860) 355–1448.
New England's largest outdoor
flea market.

**The Golden Age of Trucking Museum,**
1101 Southford Road,
Middlebury;
(203) 577–2181.

**Hillside Gardens,**
515 Litchfield Road,
Norfolk;
(860) 542–5345.

**H.O.R.S.E. of Connecticut,**
43 Wilbur Road,
Washington;
(860) 868–1960.
Nonprofit rescue organization gives
tours to view and feed horses.

**Morris Historical Society Museum,**
Route 61,
Morris;
(860) 567–1776.

**Quassy Amusement Park,**
Route 64,
Middlebury;
(203) 758–2913.

**The Silo/Hunt Hill Farm Trust,**
44 Upland Road (off Route 202),
New Milford;
(860) 355–0300, (800) 353–SILO.
Everything you need for cooking, dining,
or collecting.

a bounty of scones and lemon curd and a selection of desserts. The kitchen really shines when it comes to desserts. Fruit tarts glistening with fresh fruit on crisp, ultralight pastry are always a good choice, as are the butter cakes and a rich whiskey cake bursting with coconut and raisins. Chaiwalla serves twenty-three different teas, all of which are blended at the restaurant. The tea is proper tea, of course, not bag tea. Freshly brewed, it's available in half or full pots. In addition to conventional blends, tea enthusiasts can choose from such rare and exotic brews as *banarshi,* brewed with vanilla and cardamom, and Moroccan mint tea, made with—what else?—crushed mint leaves. Open 10:00 A.M. to 6:00 P.M. Wednesday through Sunday. Call (860) 435–9758.

It must be something in the water because Salisbury is also home to *Harney & Sons Tea,* 11 Brook Road. Should Connecticut ever appoint ambassadors, John Harney would be a natural envoy for tea. He could turn Pacific Northwest coffee drinkers into tea fanatics without breaking a sweat. Naturally, you can buy any of Harney's teas at the shop, but even better, you can sample the teas in a tasting room. Sip the decaf teas and the fruit teas for iced tea. The shop sells other accoutrements dear to the hearts of tea fans such as cozies, pots, spoons, spreaders, biscuits, and jams. Tea tastings are open to the public, 10:00 A.M. to 5:00 P.M. Monday through Saturday; and 11:00 A.M. to 4:00 P.M. Sunday. Call (800) TEATIME (800–453–5051) for information or to request a mail-order catalog. You can also find them on the Web at www.harney.com.

West of Salisbury on US 44, you'll come across Lakeville, where you'll find the *Holley-Williams House Museum.* By now your eyes are probably glazing over when you see the words "restored house," but hang in there. The Holley House is worth a look for several reasons. First, it's just about the purest example of classic revival architecture we've seen. More important the house tour is something special. Instead of the usual dry mix of trivial facts and obscure decorating information, this place offers living, breathing history. Using diaries, letters, and the household accounts of the Holley family, the tour presents a spirited portrayal of what life was like in the eighteenth and nineteenth centuries. Tours are given by a costumed guide playing the role of Maria Holley Williams. Maria led a remarkable life for a woman in the nineteenth century; among other things, she negotiated a prenuptial agreement, which saved her from penury when she divorced her husband. After the tour be sure to spend some time in the 1844 Heritage Garden, which includes specimens of antique flowers and plants. Open Memorial Day through September, Saturday and Sunday from noon to 5:00 P.M. or by appointment. Call (860) 435–2878 for tour information and special events.

## The Hills

No one driving past 192 Main Street in Torrington can possibly ignore the awe-inspiring symphony in Roman brick and rosy-red slate that occupies the property. At first, all you see is the big, round, three-story corner tower. Then the eye begins to jump from dormer to porch to porte cochere, taking in the Victorian carvings, the intricate sashes, the many small details that speak of another age, when decoration for its own sake was a common element of American home-building.

The magnificent sixteen-room *Hotchkiss-Fyler House* is now the headquarters of the Torrington Historical Society. It still displays the original mahogany paneling, hand stenciling, and parquet floors that made it such an opulent example of Victorian excess when it was built by Orsamus Roman Fyler back in 1900. The original furnishings, on display here, are almost as extravagant as the house itself. Several of the rooms feature wonderful little collections of art objects, including gold Fabergé spoons, Sevres porcelain, Victorian art glass, and Meissen porcelain figurines.

The Hotchkiss-Fyler House and an adjacent museum devoted to local history are open Tuesday through Friday from 10:00 A.M. to 4:00 P.M. and Saturday and Sunday from noon to 4:00 P.M. Both are closed during November and January through March. Call (860) 482–8260.

One of the nicest places to take a leisurely fall hike is located in **Burr Pond State Park,** Route 8 in Torrington. The circuit around the 88-acre pond in the park is a pleasant walk. There's history in the park, too; it was the site of Borden's first American condensed milk factory. The 436-acre park offers swimming, hiking, fishing, camping, and picnicking. Admission (lower on weekdays than weekends). Call (860) 482–1817 for more information.

## torringtontrivia

Torrington was once known by the rather odd moniker of "Mast Swamp."

In 1856 Gail Borden of Torrington created a way to preserve milk. His creation, condensed milk, was called the "milk that won the Civil War."

They say that at one time, travelers passing through the Bridgeport area during the spring were shocked to see elephants plowing nearby fields; they were rented to local farmers by circus impresario P. T. Barnum. These days if you see an elephant strolling through a field along Route 4, it won't be plowing it—it and the other circus animals on the property are on vacation. That field located just across Route 4 from the Village Marketplace belongs to **R. W. Commerford & Sons Circus Animals** and serves as a Club Med of sorts for animals on break from the circus. You can't tour Commerford's, but, at any given time, a fair number of the residents will be exercising and thus visible from the road.

**Nodine's Smokehouse,** 65 Fowler Avenue (Route 63), just north of the Goshen rotary and on your left as you leave town, is one of the two or three best smokehouses in New England. It's also something of a Connecticut institution. Nodine's (it's pronounced *no-DINES*) carries more than eighty specialty items, ranging from smoked hams, turkeys, and chickens to more exotic smoked pheasants, shrimp, and venison sausage. If you hunt or hike and have had your fill of trail mix, try the beef jerky; it keeps forever and makes a satisfying meal that you can eat on your feet. The bacon and many other meats can be purchased with or without nitrites, and the non-nitrited variety will change your whole concept of how bacon should taste. If you like the flavor of game animals but you don't want them smoked, the freezer case includes such items as buffalo, quail, pheasant, and venison (including packages of stewing meat that are perfect for venison chili).

Nodine's more common meats can be had in made-to-order sandwiches. The bread is an import from Canada that comes frozen in huge loaves; it is grainy and chewy, a perfect match for the tender tasty meats. You can also get some very good sausage and bacon-and-spinach rolls and similar items for a cold-weather picnic; they'll be heated up for you on the spot. Open 9:00 A.M. to 5:00 P.M. Monday through Saturday and 10:00 A.M. to 4:00 P.M. Sunday. If you see something you like, but don't want to drag it along for the rest of your trip, never fear; they have a mail-order operation. Call (860) 493–3213 or visit www.nodinesmokehouse.com.

The ***Litchfield Green,*** which was laid out in the 1770s, is probably the best known location in this part of Connecticut. The stark white Congregational church with the towering spire on the green's north side is almost certainly the most photographed church in New England. Opposite the church, on West Street, there's a row of upscale shops and restaurants, behind which you'll find Cobble Court, an easily overlooked nineteenth-century cobblestone courtyard, around which several merchants have set up shop in rustic settings.

For moderately fancy fare, Litchfield's chic ***West Street Grill*** (43 West Street, on the green) is the place. In just a few years, the West Street Grill has become such a part of the Litchfield landscape that its changes in management and chefs make front-page news in the local newspaper. The frequent upheavals in the kitchen haven't hurt the food, which seems to get better with each passing chef. The cuisine is New American, meaning lots of fish and steak, with a slight Asian and Irish influence. You can't go wrong by taking the easy way out with one of the daily specials or any of the pastas from the set menu. And take a minute to check out the wine list. You'll find some unusual wines at moderate prices. Reservations are a must for dinner, and you may need to call far in advance to get a table on a peak fall weekend. Call (860) 567–3885 for reservations and operating hours.

The heart of historic Litchfield consists of a block or two of North Street and the few blocks of South Street (Route 63) immediately off the green. There you'll find the

Congregational church on Litchfield Green

## A Highland Fling in Goshen

In the Highlands, they'd call it a Gathering. The time, usually after harvest, when Scots would get together to buy and sell their wares, swap some yarns, and play a few tunes on the bagpipes. These days, in Connecticut, such things are called folk festivals. Even if you're not a Scot—nobody's perfect, after all—you'll probably find something to amuse you at the Scottish Festival held at the Goshen Fairgrounds on Route 63 on the first Saturday in October. Naturally, there's Celtic music and folk dancing, including periodic performances by half a dozen local pipe bands. Also Scottish games, most of which seem to involve big sweaty guys tossing around rocks and logs. If you're looking for a souvenir, there are dozens of booths flogging everything from custom-made kilts to clan badges. Other booths sell Scottish food, everything from shortbread to forfar bridies (meat pies). Sorry, no haggis. The booths in one section of the fairgrounds are given over to the clan associations. On the agenda, too: border collie trials and demonstrations. If you've never actually seen the way an eagle-eyed, spirited sheltie or border collie operates, the sheep-herding demonstration is an eye-opener, and kids seem to be especially delighted by the duck-herding demonstration.

Call the **Goshen Agricultural Society** for more information at (860) 491–3628 or (860) 491–2308. Note that there's a similar folk festival in the town of Scotland, over in Connecticut's northeastern corner.

New England autumn weather is a "bonus extra." The rolling, flame-clad October hills just seem to be a perfect background for this event. Even when it rains, early October is a fine time for being outdoors. If you go, try to be there for the stirring opening ceremony, with its massed pipes and evocative Calling of the Clans. And if you visit the clan tents, you can learn more about the different clans and maybe discover that you're a Scot, too. Admission. For more information, write to St. Andrew's Society of Connecticut, P.O. Box 1195, Litchfield 06759, or call (860) 485–2692.

1760 home of Benjamin Tallmadge, once an aide to George Washington, and the house where Harriet Beecher Stowe was born. There's also the 1760 Sheldon Tavern, where George Washington really did sleep (he visited town five times), and the 1792 Pierce Academy, the first academy for girls in America.

Much of Litchfield's historic heritage is summarized in an exhibit in the **Litchfield History Museum,** at the corner of South and East Streets. Here you can trace the history of Litchfield from the first contact between Europeans and Indians back in the seventeenth century to the end of the town's "golden age" in the middle of the nineteenth century. The museum also features a display of antique furniture and a gallery of eighteenth-century portraits, plus several galleries of changing exhibits. There's also a research library and gift shop. The museum is open between mid-April and the end of November, 11:00 A.M. to

5:00 P.M. Tuesday through Saturday and 1:00 to 5:00 P.M. Sunday. The museum shop is open year-round, weekdays from 10:00 A.M. to 5:00 P.M. Admission. Call (860) 567–4501.

A block south of the museum is the ***Tapping Reeve House & Law School.*** Founded in 1773, this was America's first law school. Here's a chance to tour the school that trained political conspirator and former vice president Aaron Burr. Of course, it also schooled the likes of John C. Calhoun and some 130 other congressmen and senators, not to mention three Supreme Court justices, six cabinet members, and a dozen governors. Today the Reeve House exhibits tell the story of students who attended the school. Open April through November, 11:00 A.M. to 5:00 P.M. Tuesday through Saturday and 1:00 to 5:00 P.M. Sunday. Admission. Call (860) 567–4501.

Farther out Route 202 is the ***White Memorial Foundation and Conservation Center,*** whose 4,000 acres constitute Connecticut's largest nature center and wildlife sanctuary. This privately owned facility is administered by a nonprofit corporation, the White Memorial Foundation. It contains numerous picnic areas, nine camps, two family campgrounds, a number of bird-watching platforms, 35 miles of riding and hiking trails (including a hiking trail for the blind with Braille signs), more than seventy acres of open water, and more than half of the Bantam Lake shoreline. The property is open year-round for fishing, canoeing, cross-country skiing, and similar activities.

## The Wild Life in Goshen

Just before you get to the rotary in Goshen, you'll see several large, intriguing stone cairns, surrounded by stout stone fences. You've reached the home of the 115-acre *Action Wildlife Foundation,* 337 Torrington Road (Route 4 west). This former dairy-farm-turned-game-park is home to about 170 exotic creatures, including zebra, yak, miniature donkeys, and American bush llama. The aoudad (wild sheep) live in one of the cairns called "Aoudad Mountain" and share quarters with fainting goats. Yep, when under stress, the goats go stiff and fall over in a faint just like a proper Victorian maiden. Visitors can tour the various animal areas on foot via walking paths throughout the thirty-five acres of the park that are open to the public or on tractor-drawn wagons. If you are visiting with very small children, take the wagon tour as the paths can get a little steep and the footing difficult. In addition to the exotic animals, the foundation has a picnic area and a petting zoo in the farm's former dairy. Plans are also in the works for a museum that will house mounted animals shot by the owner and other hunters in South Africa, Siberia, Tanzania, and New Zealand as well as other places around the globe. Admission. Open 10:00 A.M. to 5:00 P.M. daily, June through October, and Wednesday through Sunday in April, May, November, and December. Hayrides on fall weekends only. For information call (860) 482–4465.

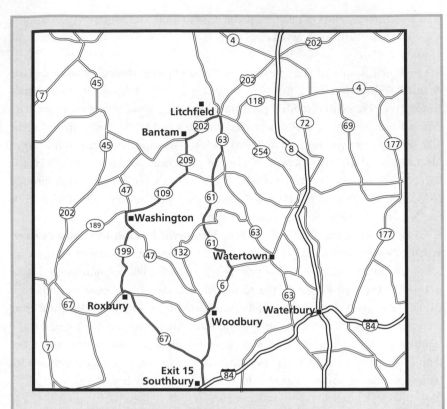

## Litchfield Driving Tour

One of the best fall driving tours through Litchfield County gives you spectacular views of foliage and the chance for some antiquing as well. Start in Southbury on U.S. Highway 6 (exit 15 from Interstate 84) and head north on Route 67 to Roxbury and north on Routes 199 and 47 to Washington. Along the way, you'll come across the Institute for American Indian Studies and the Gunn Memorial Library (read about both later in this chapter).

Follow Route 47 to Route 109 north to Bantam, then take Route 209 north to U.S. Highway 202 into Litchfield. Out of Litchfield follow Route 63 south to Route 61 and then south on US 6 to Woodbury.

The newly renovated Conservation Center building is the focus for the White Memorial Foundation's work. The first floor features fluorescent rocks, a working beehive, and a variety of exhibits, including some stunning nature dioramas and a collection of more than 3,000 species of butterflies. The center is open 9:00 A.M. to 5:00 P.M. Monday through Saturday during the winter and

8:30 A.M. to 4:30 P.M. the rest of the year; also open noon to 5:00 P.M. Sunday year-round. Admission. Call (860) 567–0857.

A little more than 3 miles south of Litchfield center on Route 63 is *White Flower Farm,* an establishment comprising more than ten acres of cultivated plants and thirty acres of wildflowers, plus assorted greenhouses. There are flowers blooming here all summer: From mid-May to mid-June the Exbury azaleas and tree peonies are in flower; throughout June, you can see tall bearded iris and herbaceous peonies; and around the middle of the month, the Japanese irises take over—they last until the middle of July. The stars of the farm, though, are its tuberous begonias that bloom throughout July and August. These have to be seen to be believed; the pictures in the farm's catalogs (written under the pen name of "Amos Pettingill") just don't do them justice. White Flower Farm also has a great gardening store. Open 9:00 A.M. to 5:30 P.M. daily April through October. Call (860) 567–8789.

As you travel east from Litchfield on Route 118, just past the East Cemetery is the *Lourdes in Litchfield Shrine.* For thirty-two years, Montfort Missionaries have operated this thirty-five-acre shrine, which features a replica of the famous grotto at Lourdes, France. An outdoor Stations of the Cross path winds its way to a spectacular crucifixion scene at the top of the hill. The grounds are open year-round and include a picnic area and gift shop. In addition, outdoor services are conducted throughout the pilgrimage season (May 1 to mid-October), and the Blessing of the Motorcycles occurs the third Sunday in May. At the blessing, each person, biker or not, and his or her vehicle is blessed. In recent years, more than 500 bikers from as far as Maine and New York have attended the celebrations. Even if you aren't a biker, it's worth a visit to see some really fine bikes. Call (860) 567–1041 for schedule and details.

Located on Chestnut Hill Road, off Route 118, about a mile east of Litchfield, the *Haight Vineyard & Winery* may not be quite *haut médoc,* but it is really quite a nice place for a Saturday afternoon vineyard walk, winery tour, and wine tasting. With vines that were first planted in 1975, this is Connecticut's oldest continuously operating winery and the first in the state to make sparkling wine using the French *méthode champagne.*

Tours are free. You can view the wine-making operation and vineyards from an outdoor balcony and picnic on the grounds. There's also a gift shop. The staff is friendly, knowledgeable, and eager to answer questions. Open 10:30 A.M. to 5:00 P.M. Monday through Saturday, noon to 5:00 P.M. Sunday. The winery is also the site and sponsor of the annual Taste of Litchfield Hills festival each June and the site of a harvest festival in the fall. For more details call (860) 567–4045.

# Eagle Watching

Not so long ago, your chances of seeing eagles hunting and soaring in the wild were somewhere between slim and none, and Slim was out to lunch. Today, thanks to the Endangered Species Act, the American eagle population is itself soaring. In winter Connecticut bald eagles find the Southbury area much to their taste. In fact it's such a popular place that their eagle buddies from as far away as Canada and Maine flock there, too. NE Energy has developed an eagle observation area for visitors. The observation area is staffed by knowledgeable guides to coach you in observing these beautiful birds—some of whom have a wing-span of 7 feet—while they fish, hunt, and soar. To use a worn-out phrase, they take your breath away. Eagle observations are held Wednesday, Saturday, and Sunday from late December through March. Reservations, far in advance, are a must. To protect the eagles and maintain their habitat, details about the site are not released until you make your reservation. After making the reservation, you'll receive a reservation number, directions to the site, and an eagle fact sheet that describes what will happen during your visit. NE Energy usually starts taking reservations in mid-December. Call (800) 368–8954 to reserve your spot. Visit the eagles on the Web at www.neenergyinc.com/eagles/default.asp.

By the way, bald eagles aren't really bald. In truth, they have a glorious head of white feathers. The bald part comes from the word *piebald*, which means white.

*Wisdom House Retreat Center,* formerly a convent for the Sisters of Wisdom, 229 East Litchfield Road, is the scene of Connecticut's only outdoor labyrinth. Don't arrive thinking you'll find a high, boxwood maze like those in England or in Colonial Williamsburg. The low circular path is a symbol older than time and one that transcends religions. Walking the spiral path helps you meditate and heighten your awareness. You'll find a helpful pamphlet at Wisdom House suggesting different meditative approaches to walking the labyrinth. We like entering the labyrinth in silence and keeping our eyes focused on the path until we reach the center, then retracing our steps in silence. Whichever approach you take, it's a peaceful way to get in touch with yourself, to find some peace in the silence, and to shed the cares of twenty-first-century life. Many visitors use the labyrinth for silent meditation, so it probably isn't a place to visit if you are accompanied by rowdy children. Call (860) 567–3163 for hours and more information about programs offered by Wisdom House. Or visit the Web site at www.wisdomhouse.org.

East of Haight Vineyard on Buell Road (off East Litchfield Road) is *Topsmead,* an estate-turned-park that looks like it belongs in the British midlands. When Waterbury heiress Edith Chase came home from a European tour enchanted with English manor houses, she was determined to build herself an authentic Cotswold cottage, complete with leaded-glass casement windows, hand-hewn beams, and buttery stucco exteriors. She found the right location in Litchfield. The Cotswold cottage of her dreams was designed by architect Richard Dana, who shared Miss Edith's love for English cottage architecture.

Topsmead, however, was more than a building. It was also a vast garden and a working farm. Miss Edith was as fond of English country gardens as of English architecture, and she surrounded her home with formal manicured gardens and with cutting gardens full of the flowers most beloved by English gardeners: roses, sweet William, and phlox. Even in her late seventies, she reputedly walked a daily mile around these gardens, inspecting, issuing orders, and sipping from an ever-present glass of skim milk.

When Miss Edith died, she left her 511-acre estate to the state of Connecticut so that everyone could enjoy a touch of England in Litchfield. The Topsmead gardens and grounds are now Topsmead State Forest and are open all year for picnicking, sledding, cross-country skiing, and hiking. You can tour the house on the second and fourth weekends of each month from June to October. Call (860) 567–5694.

If it's not springtime when you pass the junction of Routes 118 and 254 just east of Litchfield, make a mental note to come back to visit **Morosani Farms** on Wigwam Road. Something of a local legend, the ten-acre farm grows twenty varieties of daffodils, and in late April it's like looking at fields of gold. Visitors from all over New England, starved for a bit of springtime, stop by for a visit as do local artists and photographers. Take Route 118 east from Litchfield and then Route 254 south. The farm is near the village of Northfield. Just look for a patch of spring, you can't miss it.

On Route 209, southwest of Litchfield, you'll find the **Bantam Cinema,** just south of Route 202. The Bantam Cinema is an old-fashioned movie theater that screens those offbeat, independent, or imported films that never seem to get much play at suburban theaters. Even though the screening rooms and sound systems are modern, it's a wonderfully intimate and kind of old-fashioned way to see a film. Besides the well-chosen films and the really great snacks, what makes the Bantam Cinema so much fun is the synergy of the audience. Just standing around in the lobby and eavesdropping on conversations is a lot like taking a Film 101 class. From time to time, the cinema holds special programs with celebrities, such as Bridgewater's Mia Farrow, talking about their work and film. Call (860) 567–0006 for show times and film information, or log on to www.bantamcinema.com.

It would be a mistake to bypass the **Bantam Bread Company.** This is the type of hearth-baked bread that people line up for in New York and Los Angeles. Pick the Holiday Loaf, a whole-wheat sourdough loaf packed with toasted walnuts, plump and tender golden raisins, and tart dried cherries. The shop also turns out a variety of other breads—sourdough semolina, rosemary-scented kalamata olive, sourdough raisin—plus biscotti, cookies, and memorable tarts, including a lemon-strawberry number that is to die for. Open 8:00 A.M. to 5:30 P.M. Tuesday through Saturday and 8:00 A.M. to 4:00 P.M. Sunday; closed Monday. Call (860) 567–2737.

You'll find a great spot for a pre- or post-movie lunch or dinner right next door to the Bantam Cinema. **Wood's Pit BBQ & Mexican Cafe,** 123 Bantam Lake Road (Route 209), may be somewhat incongruous amid the Litchfield Hills' studied country casual, but it's a good place for a casual meal of smoked stuff, and kids and families are treated well here. Most of them like the shredded beef brisket, smoky, tender, and simmered with a jaunty BBQ sauce, but the pulled pork and ribs are good, too. On each table rest squeeze bottles of BBQ sauce: a traditional, hot, ketchup-based variety and a mustard-vinegar Carolina-style sauce, so you can doctor your 'cue to fit your taste. Don't expect much of the side dishes—coleslaw, baked beans, potato salad, or green salad —but the desserts, especially the silky-textured pecan pie, are good. Open 11:30 A.M. to 9:00 P.M. Monday through Thursday, 11:30 A.M. to 10:00 P.M. Friday and Saturday, and 11:30 A.M. to 9:00 P.M. Sunday. Call (860) 567–9869.

As one would expect from the name, the **Lock Museum of America** at 230 Main Street (US 6) in Terryville is all about locks. In fact, its two floors house a unique collection of 22,000 locks, keys, and related paraphernalia, tracing the development of the American lock industry back to its local beginnings; there were once forty lock companies in Terryville (which was known as the Lock Town of America), and the Eagle Lock Company formerly occupied the site of the shopping mall across the street.

This is the largest collection of locks and keys in the United States, and there are all manner of locks and lock-related items on display. The oldest is a 4,000-year-old Egyptian pin tumble lock, but there are also a number of colonial locks and many nineteenth-century items. There are big locks and little locks, plain locks and fancy locks, safe locks and padlocks. There are also mail locks, which were invented by former Eagle Lock Company employee Burton Andrus when he was superintendent of the U.S. Mail Service Department in Washington, D.C. Many of the locks are part of doorknob assemblies, and some of these are quite beautiful. The oddest item is a modern dog-collar lock. Open May through October, 1:30 to 4:30 P.M. Tuesday through Sunday. Admission. Call (860) 589–6359 for special tours.

If you want to truly get away from it all and do something really different at the same time, try floating over the Litchfield Hills in a hot-air balloon. In mid-October, when the fall-color change is at its peak and the clear blue skies are just starting to bluster their way toward November, a balloon ride can make you a little giddy from sun and wind. Take a friend who's not too chatty; the best thing about the experience is that except for the sound of the wind, it's absolutely quiet up there.

Ballooning, both private and public, is quite popular in Connecticut, and there must be a score of operations in the state that offer passenger rides. Many of these, however, are seasonal or operate over the less scenic parts of the state. **Watershed Balloons** at 179 Gilbert Road in Watertown offers year-round flights lasting about an hour each, and the normal flight takes you directly over Litchfield into the heart of the hills.

Generally passenger operations charge a couple hundred dollars per person per ride; Watershed Balloons is priced a little below average. Like most such operations, this one can normally accommodate two to four guests. If you have a larger party, pilot Tom Murphy can arrange for an extra balloon and pilot to handle the overflow. All balloon pilots are licensed by the FAA. Reservations are required. Call (860) 274–2010.

Situated south of Watertown on US 6, Woodbury was one of the first towns established in inland Connecticut. During the early eighteenth century, it was home to Moll Cramer, the best known of Connecticut's witches. Known as the Witch of Woodbury, Cramer resided in a hut she built on Good Hill and supported herself by begging. Good Hill got its name from the fact that while Moll lived there storms and high winds never seemed to cross Woodbury. After she disappeared from Good Hill without a trace, Woodbury was hit by a series of destructive storms. Even today, old-timers speak of needing a "Moll Cramer storm" after a summer dry spell. If you enter Woodbury from Roxbury on Route 317 (Good Hill Road), you'll pass over the crest of the hill near the township line.

Today, US 6 runs through the center of Woodbury past rows of eighteenth- and nineteenth-century houses, many of which have been converted into antiques and gift shops. In fact, in this neck of the woods, Woodbury's Main Street is nicknamed **Antique Avenue.** Some travel guides create the impression that unless you roll up in a chauffeured Rolls, you won't get very good treatment at many of the antiques shops in Woodbury. Not so! Even if you show up in faded jeans and scuffed-up sneakers, you can look forward to being treated with great kindness and helpfulness.

**Mill House Antiques,** 1068 Main Street North (US 6); (203) 263–3446. It's a pleasure just to walk through this restored mill house with its imaginative displays of top-quality English and French furniture. The Welsh dressers, armoires, and harvest tables are noteworthy. Open 10:00 A.M. to 5:00 P.M. daily, except Tuesday.

## Good News in Woodbury

Roadfoodistas Jane and Michael Stern adore *Carole Peck's Good News Cafe,* 694 Main Street in Woodbury, as do other restaurant critics and celebrity diners-out. This gem of an eatery has been compared to Berkeley's Chez Panisse. For many epicures, it's like going home, except the food is better and you don't have to clean your plate to get dessert. Carole Peck buys most of her produce and other foods from local suppliers, so everything you get is fresh and high quality, and the food is healthful without being grim or preachy. It's also some of the tastiest and most innovative food we've ever encountered. Special favorites: warm smashed potato salad with blue cheese and corn on a bed of greens, corned beef hash with frizzled leeks, rotisserie chicken with buttermilk mashed potatoes and wok-fried veggies. The desserts are as splendid as the entrees, with the standout being a delightful white chocolate banana cream pie. The truth is, no matter what you order, the food is great, and the service remarkable, the art wonderfully watchable, and the atmosphere comfortable. Open daily for lunch and dinner; closed Tuesday. Call (203) 266–4663.

*The Woodbury Guild,* 4 Main Street South; (203) 263–4828; www.woodbury guild.com. Owner Michael Bird calls himself a "twelfth generation Yankee and just as eccentric as anything." He may be eccentric, but his store is beautiful. You'll find lots of Americana primitives, beautiful bronzes, and some really lovely reproduction pottery. Open 10:00 A.M. to 5:00 P.M. Wednesday through Saturday and noon to 5:00 P.M. Sunday.

For a complete directory of Woodbury antiques dealers, write to the Woodbury Antiques Dealers Association, P.O. Box 496, Woodbury 06798 or call (203) 263–3233.

For a taste of the Woodbury that antiquers rarely see, visit the *Canfield Corner Pharmacy* on North Main Street. It has an old-fashioned soda fountain and is crammed from floor to rafters with every nostrum and homemaker's convenience on the market. Call (203) 263–2595. Also on Main Street (US 6), *Philips Country Kitchen* serves such old-fashioned comfort food as chicken pot pies and cinnamon doughnuts. Sharp-eyed celebrity-watchers swear that Dustin Hoffman regularly bikes in from nearby Roxbury for breakfast. Call (203) 263–2516.

Although they are not antique pewter, the pewter plates, mugs, lamps, and other accessories at the *Woodbury Pewter Outlet,* 860 Main Street South, look as authentic as any antique you buy in Woodbury. Featured in *Victoria* magazine, Woodbury Pewter has been around since 1952 when it was a tiny shop tucked into a blacksmith's shop. Today it's a modern retail operation that features not only its own products but also the pewter work and jewelry of pewterers from across America. Be sure to look for the birthday flower pins, earrings, and lockets; they're great gifts at exceptional prices. Speaking of prices, those at the outlet are very good, with significant discounts over what you'll find in well-known department stores. Seconds, on a hit-or-miss, what's-available basis, are also for sale. The staff is friendly and professional and more than willing to help you pick out just the right purchase, whether it's an expensive lamp or a simple key chain; it's not uncommon for a sales associate to spend a good half hour helping a little girl pick out just the right $5.00 pin for her grandmother's birthday. Open daily, from 9:00 A.M. to 5:00 P.M. Woodbury Pewter holds several very good sales throughout the year. Call (800) 648–2014 or visit www.wood burypewter.com for more information or to request a catalog.

A *glebe* is the parcel of land granted to a clergyman during his tenure of office. The gambrel-roofed 1740 **Glebe House** on Hollow Road, off US 6 in the center of town, has always had ecclesiastical connections. Mere weeks after the start of the American Revolution, a group of clergy secretly assembled in the house to elect the first American bishop of the Episcopal Church, the Reverend Dr. Samuel Seabury. His election broke the American connection with the Church of England and laid the foundation for the separation of church and state in America. Today the old farmhouse is used as a museum and kept much as it was. The original paneling remains, and the rooms are stuffed with period furnishings collected locally. The most interesting item, however, is outside, where you will find the only garden in America designed by renowned British horticulturist Gertrude Jekyll. The garden blooms with candytuft, iris, lavender, lamb's ear, and other flowers beloved by Jekyll. Open 1:00 to 4:00 P.M.

Glebe House

Wednesday through Sunday, May through October, and weekends only in November (other times by appointment). Donation requested. Call (203) 263–2855 or visit www.theglebehouse.org.

During most of the year, Bethlehem (on Route 61 north of Woodbury) is just another quiet, pretty New England country town. During the Christmas holiday season, however, all that changes, and for a few brief weeks, Bethlehem bustles with activity.

The reason, of course, is the name. The local post office doubles its staff each December to accommodate the thousands of folks who want a Bethlehem postmark on their Christmas cards. If you're going to be passing through during early December, bring yours along and they'll be glad to add them to the bin. There's also a *Bethlehem Christmas Town Festival* in mid-December that draws a lot of people to listen to the music, ride hay wagons, and look at holiday arts and crafts and a small festival of lights; a far cry, you will agree, from the days when the Puritans who wrote the colony's stringent blue laws prescribed a five-shilling fine for "Christmas Keeping." For details call the town clerk's office during the morning: (203) 266–5557.

With so much holiday traffic passing through town, businesses have sprung up to capitalize on the captive audience. One of the newer ones is *Town Gifts,* which sells gifts and home decorations for all holidays but which specializes in Christmas merchandise. The shop sells Department 56 holiday homes and Krinkles as well as Willow Tree angels and nativities. It also carries a wide variety of Christmas tree ornaments. Town Gifts is located at 5 Sunny Ridge Road in Bethlehem. It's open 11:00 A.M. to 4:00 P.M. Tuesday through Saturday and noon to 4:00 P.M. on Sunday. Call (203) 266–7801 for expanded holiday hours.

South of Bethlehem, about 1½ miles down Flanders Road (off Route 61) is the *Abbey of Regina Laudis,* which operates a Little Art Shop offering items hand-crafted on the premises by Benedictine nuns. Among crafts represented are printing, potting, and blacksmithing. You can also buy beauty products, honey, herbs, and postcards showing the abbey grounds. The Sisters of the Abbey also produced a CD, called *Women in Chant,* which is available at the gift store. The abbey's holiday decorations include a nativity scene composed of eighteenth-century Neapolitan figures. Open by appointment. Call ahead for hours and information on special events: (203) 266–7727.

*Lake Waramaug,* with its surrounding forests and hills, is often likened to Switzerland's Lake Lucerne, and the inns that ring its waters reflect the same alpine charm. Even though the lake is named for Chief Waramaug, the atmosphere and food at the inns are Swiss. One of the best ways to see the area, especially during leaf-peeping season, is to take the 0.9-mile drive around the lake. The burning autumn colors of the surrounding hardwoods, reflected by the cool, crystal-clear lake, make this a picture-postcard setting. Two outstanding inns grace this beautiful setting: Hopkins Inn and the Boulders Inn.

The food at the ***Hopkins Inn*** on Hopkins Road in New Preston is so stellar that people tend to recommend the inn solely for its cuisine and forget that it is a warm and comfortable hostelry in its own right, with eleven guest rooms and two private apartments at reasonable rates. The outdoor patio, open for dining spring through fall, provides a spectacular view of the lake. The cuisine is contemporary Austrian, complete with rich desserts. The inn is open year-round; the restaurant is open from late March to January 1. It can be difficult to find, so call ahead for directions: (860) 868–7295 or visit the Web site at www.thehopkinsinn.com.

Except for the name, there's no connection between the inn and the ***Hopkins Vineyard*** located at 25 Hopkins Road. But the dairy farm turned winery and the inn do share a spectacular view of Lake Waramaug and the surrounding countryside. The Hopkins family has farmed the land around the lake since the late 1700s but didn't plant its first grape vine until 1979. The vineyard pro-

## The Legend of Chief Waramaug and His Great Lodge

About the time settlers first arrived in northwestern Connecticut, the Native Americans who lived along the banks of the Housatonic River were led by a great leader, Chief Waramaug. Waramaug lived in a lodge high above the west banks of the Housatonic, not far from the beautiful alpine lake that bears his name. The lodge was so majestic that it was called Waramaug's Palace and, in its time, was without a doubt the most elegant dwelling in Connecticut. According to legend, Waramaug's longhouse was 20 feet wide by 100 feet long. Native American artists from all over New England worked ceaselessly for months to create Waramaug's Palace. Using bark gathered from all over New England, they intricately painted the bark with sumptuous colors distilled from herbs and flowers. Although much of the decoration came from Waramaug's own people and from the Iroquois from nearby New York, the Hurons, Delawares, and even the fearsome Mohawks all sent their greatest artisans to decorate Waramaug's great lodge.

The interior of the lodge was as magnificent as the outside. Waramaug's council chamber was decorated with portraits of the great chief, his family, and the elders and wise men of the tribe. Other rooms were alive with pictures of the animals who shared the forests with Waramaug and his people. According to legend, Chief Waramaug died peacefully in his great lodge and was buried nearby. For years after his death, passing warriors would add a stone to his gravesite as a gesture of respect for the great leader. The great chief's lodge is no more, but the elegant inns that ring Lake Waramaug carry on the tradition of graceful living by the beautiful lake.

duces a variety of wines, including a pretty good sparkling wine made in the traditional champagne method. Try their off-dry cider as an ingredient for autumn recipes or as a celebratory drink before Thanksgiving. You'll find tastings, sales, and a gift shop in the winery's bright red barn. Open every day for sales and tastings. Open 10:00 A.M. to 5:00 P.M. Monday through Saturday and 11:00 A.M. to 5:00 P.M. Sunday. Closed Monday through Thursday in January and February, and Monday and Tuesday in March and April. Be sure to visit the hayloft wine bar on weekends. Self-guided tours are always available; guided tours for twenty or more must be arranged in advance. Call (860) 868–7954 or log on to www.hopkinsvineyard.com.

The **Boulders Inn** on East Shore Road (Route 45) in New Preston takes its name from the large fieldstone boulders from which it was constructed. Some people say it is the best inn in the Alpine Lake region. They could be right. Renovated in 2003, the Boulders Inn is nestled below Pinnacle Mountain. The main inn building has five comfortable bedrooms, and the carriage house has seven rooms. Typical of the inn's comforts is the samovar in the living room that dispenses tea to guests in the late afternoon. The dining room serves a spare but enticing menu of French-American fusion cuisine with herbs and produce from its own gardens. The outdoor patio is open Memorial Day to Labor Day. There is also a private beach for swimming, paddle boats, kayaks, canoes, bicycles, and an exercise facility. If you like hiking, you can reach the top of Pinnacle Mountain from the inn's backyard; the reward, aside from all that healthful exercise, is a breathtaking view of three states.

The Boulders Inn is open year-round. The restaurant is open for dinner Wednesday through Sunday. Breakfast for houseguests is served seven days a week. Call (860) 868–0541 or visit www.bouldersinn.com for prices and hours.

The crossroads village of New Preston at the southeast tip of Lake Waramaug contains several delightful little shops that are well worth a short stop, especially if you like antiques. **Black Swan Antiques** (710 Bantam Road, 860–567–4429) is always fun. Its specialty is seventeenth- and eighteenth-century English country furniture, but the store has also been known to carry Elizabethan, Queen Anne, and William and Mary pieces. **J. Seitz & Co.** (Route 45, 860–868–0119) handles both Southwestern antiques and reproductions, and the **Village Barn and Gallery** (Main Street, 860–868–0501) carries an eclectic selection of antiques and collectibles in a country-store atmosphere.

Southeast of New Preston, on Curtis Road off Route 199 near the village of Washington, is the **Institute for American Indian Studies.** Splendid Indian craft exhibits and authentic re-creations of Indian dwellings are among the features of this museum. The institute attempts, fairly successfully, to cover 10,000 years of Native American life; displays include a seventeenth-century Algonquian village and garden, a furnished longhouse, a simulated archaeological site, a prehistoric rock shelter, and a variety of nature trails. There's also a museum shop. The institute holds several special events throughout the year. The museum is open 10:00 A.M. to 5:00 P.M. Monday through Saturday and noon to 5:00 P.M. Sunday. Be sure to keep a sharp eye out for signs directing you to the museum because they are easy to miss. Call (860) 868–0518.

The *Gunn Memorial Library and Museum,* 5 Wykeham Road in Washington, was named after Mr. and Mrs. Frederick Gunn, who founded the Gunnery school in Washington. The library was designed by architect and Washington resident E. K. Rossiter and features oak paneling and a beautiful stained-glass window. The ceiling mural, called the Mowbray mural, is exceptional. Donated by painter and muralist H. Siddons Mowbray in memory of his wife, it depicts Persephone's abduction to the underworld by Pluto and the world's ensuing four seasons. The Gunn Museum next to the library is stocked with heirlooms from the estates of townspeople. Call (860) 868–7756 for more information.

# Ethan Allen Way

Someone once estimated that the tiny village of Kent had one gallery for every 300 residents. One of the more interesting of these establishments resides in a red freight car beside the railroad tracks at Kent Station Square. This modest housing is home to Jacques Kaplan's *Paris–New York–Kent Gallery,* which exhibits an eclectic and ever-changing mix of local stuff and major pieces by world-famous artists whose work is seldom seen outside of major metropolitan centers. Kaplan is the man who almost single-handedly started the gallery boom in Kent. Usually open Wednesday through Sunday, but call ahead: (860) 927–3357.

Viewing all that art can work up quite an appetite, so it just makes sense to stop off at *Belgique Patisserie and Chocolatier* at the intersection of US 7 and Route 341 in Kent for a little treat to raise your blood sugar, purely for medicinal reasons. The tiny chocolate shop, owned by Belgium-born chocolatier Pierre Gilissen and his wife, Susan, offers intricately shaped filled chocolates and amazing truffles. There's no seating in the chocolate shop, but the owners have thoughtfully placed some benches outside so you can rest your weary feet, enjoy a little chocolate, and sip hot or cold coffee and chocolate drinks. The separate patisserie is a jewel box of a place with pastries that sparkle like something from Tiffany's window. The variety is impressive with choices ranging from glazed fruit-topped cakes to fruit mousses to madeleines.

## Tall Tales of Ethan Allen

Being of a question-authority bent ourselves, Ethan Allen is our favorite Connecticut hero. Here are a couple of our favorite Ethan Allen stories.

Ethan Allen was a big guy (6 feet 6 inches) with a big thirst. According to one "tall" tale, on a hot August afternoon, Allen and his cousin, Remember Baker, having overindulged, repaired to a nearby shady woods to sleep it off. A besotted Remember was awakened by a strange noise, and he watched in horror as a rattlesnake bit his drink-befuddled cousin over and over. Before Remember could find a weapon to subdue the serpent, it moved away from Allen, gazed at Remember with a certain drunken stare, then wobbled its way into the bushes where it collapsed in a stupor. Allen awoke refreshed from his nap, except for complaints about "these eternal, damnable, bloodsucking mosquitoes," which had disturbed his rest.

It stands to reason that Ethan Allen would marry a woman as formidable as himself. His wife, Fanny, was, by all accounts, his equal in temper and independence. The story is told that Allen's friends became concerned about his drinking and decided to frighten him into leading a more temperate life. They wrapped themselves in sheets and hid beneath the bridge Allen passed on his way home from his favorite tavern. Making the requisite booing, moaning, and keening sounds, they jumped out at their friend, only to scare his horse into rearing. Despite his snozzled state, Allen managed to control his mount and greeted the "apparitions" by proclaiming, "If you are angels of light, I'm glad to meet you. And if you are devils, then come along home with me. I married your sister."

Best-in-show could well be the delightfully dark and rich chocolate ganache cake, which rivals Hartford's own David Glass Chocolate Mousse for top chocolate cake honors. The Gilissens have opened a tearoom that serves pastries. Open 9:00 A.M. to 6:00 P.M. Thursday through Saturday and 10:00 A.M. to 6:00 P.M. Sunday; winter hours may be shortened, so call ahead before visiting. Call (860) 927–3681 for more information.

If you're looking for other attractions, Main Street (US 7) is lined for several blocks with restaurants, antiques stores, craft shops, and the like. You'll also find interesting establishments on Maple Street and Railroad Street. Businesses come and go fairly frequently, so if you want to know what's there currently, you'll just have to visit.

A mile and a half north of North Kent on US 7 (Ethan Allen Way) is **Kent Falls State Park.** The broad meadow and shaded picnic areas visible from the road are inviting enough, but you might be inclined to pass it by if you weren't specifically looking for a place to spread a picnic lunch. Don't. The best part of the park is a 250-foot waterfall that is easy to miss, especially when the foliage of high summer obscures it from view. If you like tramping through the woods, you can hike to the top of the falls; or, if you prefer less demanding pleasures, you can simply sit out on the rocks in the middle of the falls and dangle your toes in the torrent. Even though the water may be a tad cool for toe-dangling come autumn, we highly recommend visiting the park after the leaves have turned and the summer crowds have thinned. Call (860) 927–3238.

About a mile north of Kent, you'll find a big maroon L-shaped barn set back a short distance from the west side of US 7. The ground on which it sits used to be the Kent town dump, but all that changed back in the 1970s. At that time, New Britain's Stanley Tool Company was looking for a site for a museum to house a collection of American tools and implements collected by noted artist and author Eric Sloane. Stanley wanted the state of Connecticut to run the place, but the state would accept ownership only if the museum's site was somehow historically significant. As it turned out, down at the foot of the hill behind the town dump in Kent were the ruins of an old blast furnace that produced pig iron during most of the nineteenth century. The presence of this jumble of stone made the dump suitably historical, so Stanley acquired the

## Falling Waters

*Kent Falls* is probably Connecticut's most spectacular waterfall. At 250 feet, it's certainly the largest, but other nearby parks offer equally beautiful, if somewhat more hard to find, waterfalls.

At *Campbell Falls* on Route 272 in Norfolk, you can see the Whiting River boil over rocks in a narrow gorge. You'll need to take a short hike to reach the falls; just follow the sounds of rushing water. The water drops in two levels, with a small pool in between and one at the bottom. The first level is a good place for a picnic among the weathered rocks. Campbell Falls is off Norfolk Road, just south of Southfield, Massachusetts, just before Spaulding Road. If you are traveling from the other direction, it's about 5 miles north of Haystack Mountain, on Route 272 in Norfolk.

You'll want to bring your camera with you to *Southford Falls* in Southbury, where you'll find a lovely cascade of Eight Mile Brook as it rushes to meet the Housatonic River. The park also includes the remains of the Diamond Match factory, which was destroyed by fire in 1923. The ruins include an old steam engine foundation, a grinding stone, and some of the sluice pipe. The little covered bridge, built by carpenter Ed Palmer with the help of author/artist Eric Sloane, is based on an eighteenth-century arch design. There are picnic tables by the bridge, just the place for a romantic spring picnic, or perch on a rock by the falls and spend some time just listening to the water or reading. The park also includes a lookout tower, great for viewing fall foliage. Southford Falls State Park is located just south of Southbury on Route 188, south of Interstate 84.

property and had Sloane design a building for his collection. Thus was born the **Sloane-Stanley Museum.**

The one thing to understand about this place is that it is not so much a museum of artifacts as it is a gallery of art objects. The tools collected here, some of which date from the seventeenth century, probably do have some historical interest as a link with everyday life in America's past; but Sloane vehemently rejected the image of himself as what he called "a nurturer of nostalgia." The contents of this museum are oddly beautiful. Sloane personally arranged and lighted the displays, and the resulting jumble of wooden bowls and woven baskets, yokes and mallets and pitchforks, axes and scythes, and weathered sawhorses has an internal order that is both pleasing and restful. It's as if each arrangement were a small work of art in itself.

## ethanallentrivia

Litchfield-born Ethan Allen is one of the most colorful personalities in American history. The guy was a crusty old coot. You probably learned in fifth grade history that Allen ordered the British commander of Fort Ticonderoga to surrender by declaiming, "Surrender in the name of the great God Jehovah and the Continental Congress." What he really said was something like: "Come out of there, you goddamn old billy goat." Spin doctors, even then.

In addition to the fine tool collection, the museum also contains a recreation of Sloane's studio with some of his works on display. And don't forget that historic blast furnace; it's the tumbled pile of rocks surrounded by the split-rail fence down at the bottom of the hill behind the barn. Open May 15 to October 31, 10:00 A.M. to 4:00 P.M. Wednesday through Sunday. Adult admission. Call (860) 927–3849 or (860) 566–3005.

Located just off US 7 about 4 miles south of Kent, **Bull's Bridge** is one of three remaining covered bridges in Connecticut and one of two that are still open to traffic (the other is in West Cornwall, also off US 7 a few miles north). Bull's Bridge spans the Housatonic River between New York State and the small Connecticut town of Bull's Bridge on the river's eastern bank. George Washington didn't sleep here, but he did pass over the bridge, and he (or a member of his party) did manage to lose a horse in the Housatonic while so doing. If looking at the bridge gives you a sense of déjà vu, it's because it's probably been the source of more quaint New England covered-bridge photographs on postcards and calendar covers than any other bridge in this part of the world.

## kenttrivia

Macedonia Brook State Park in Kent is the largest state park in Connecticut.

Bull's Bridge

After you cross the bridge, about 3 miles up the road on the ***Schaghicoke Indian Reservation,*** you'll find an old cemetery with many timeworn head-stones, including one commemorating the last resting place of a "Christian Indian Princess." We've never been able to find out the story behind this intriguing inscription. As with any visit to a cemetery, remember to show proper respect and not to take rubbings without permission.

The ***National Audubon Society's Northeast Center*** on Route 4 in Sharon consists of 2,000 acres of woodlands, flower and herb gardens, and rural coun-tryside. There are also a pond, a swamp, and a marsh, and the entire area is crisscrossed by trails and nature walks. Both guided and self-guided nature walks are available. A large house on the property contains exhibits, offices, a library, and a gift shop. The center offers programs for both children and adults.

The building is open 9:00 A.M. to 5:00 P.M. Tuesday through Saturday and 1:00 to 5:00 P.M. Sunday; closed major holidays. Trails open dawn to dusk. Admission. Call (860) 364–0520.

Up US 7 from the Audubon Society's Northeast Center and only 1 mile south of the covered bridge at West Cornwall is another type of outdoor experience. ***Clarke's Outdoors*** is one of several outfitters along the Housatonic that offer kayaks, canoes, and rafts for those who want to try the river's white water. Look at the expressive anthropomorphic critters adorning Clarke's signs and vans. These are original Sandy Boynton paintings. A safety talk is given before each trip, and members of Clarke's staff are happy to answer any questions you have. Clarke's is open 10:00 A.M. to 5:00 P.M. daily from March through November and 9:00 A.M. to 6:00 P.M. on weekends. Call (860) 672–6365.

# White Water

Outdoor activities belong on any state's roundup of tourism attractions. To the dismay of couch potatoes, Litchfielders talk about a hardy fellow who thinks nothing of kayaking the Tariffville Gorge on the Connecticut River for two hours before heading off to work. Here are some of his favorite places:

**The Small Boat Shop,** 144 Water Street, Norwalk, offers guided tours of the Norwalk Islands. You must make reservations in advance; the tours carry a fairly hefty per person price tag. Call (203) 854–5223 for more information.

**Clarke's Outdoors** offers guided tours on the Housatonic River, including a lovely trip under the covered bridge or a somewhat wilder white-water rafting trip down Bull's Bridge Gorge. The Bull's Bridge trip is usually offered only in spring. Reservations for the guided rafting trips are a must. Tip: Prices are lower during the week. Shuttle service available. Call (860) 672–6365 for more information.

**Mountain Workshop Inc.,** Ridgefield, offers a trip past Gillette Castle on the Connecticut River and a family canoe trip on the Croton River that winds through Croton Swamp. (Children must be at least six years old.) For prices and more information, call (203) 438–3640.

On the west side of US 7, a couple hundred yards south of Cornwall Bridge, is something right out of an H. P. Lovecraft horror novel. There, jutting out from under a canopy of overhanging trees right along the side of the road, is a big rock painted to resemble a most lifelike giant frog whose leering mouth seems to be reaching for the occupants of the passenger side of the car. We don't know the story behind it, but every so often it gets refurbished with a coat of paint. Really, we're quite sure that there are no Marshes or Whateleys in the area; try Rhode Island.

About 6 miles north of Cornwall Bridge on US 7, the largest and handsomest covered bridge in Connecticut spans the Housatonic at West Cornwall. Originally designed by Ithiel Town, the bridge has been in continuous service since 1841. Route 128 runs from US 7 across the one-lane bridge to become the main street of West Cornwall.

Be sure to hit the **Cornwall Bridge Pottery Store.** Ever since Todd Piker started his pottery and store in 1972, this place has been selling world-class stoneware, much of it featuring a celadon glaze made from slag recovered from a local riverbed, where it was deposited by the ironworks that used to dominate the area's economy. None of the glazes, however, contain lead. Most items are decorated with simple blue or brown brushwork designs with an oriental flavor.

The firing is done in a 40-foot, wood-fired kiln at Piker's pottery in Cornwall Bridge, and the flames give the finished pieces distinctive two-tone markings.

In addition to Piker's pottery, the Cornwall Bridge Pottery Store features an assortment of museum-quality crafts and a showroom of furniture by Shaker Workshops, makers of fine Shaker accessories and furnishings. Open noon to 5:00 P.M. Friday and Monday; 10:30 A.M. to 5:30 P.M. weekends. Call (860) 672–6545 or visit them on the Web at www.cbpots.com.

Housed in a rambling, high-ceilinged, former Masonic hall at the top of the hill is ***Barbara Farnsworth, Bookseller.*** This establishment can be a near-religious experience for bibliophiles and collectors of old prints and maps. The bottom floor of the shop contains nonfiction, cookbooks, reference books, and a variety of antique prints and ephemera. The top floor contains the bulk of the store's 50,000 volumes. Parking in West Cornwall can be tricky, especially during fall foliage season. Try the lot across the street from Farnsworth's, between the deli and the post office. Open 9:00 A.M. to 4:00 P.M. Saturday, seasonally, and by chance or appointment. Much of Barbara Farnsworth's business is now conducted online, so check out her Web site at www.farnsworthbooks.com or call (860) 672–6571.

Up at the end of Dibble Road in West Cornwall there's a little piece of heaven. Set on a wooded hilltop and surrounded by stunningly landscaped grounds, Everett Van Dorn's ***Hilltop Haven*** affords a view of the northwest hills that is hard to match. Each guest room in this inn's elegant country house has its own bath and a small sitting area overlooking the woods and the gardens (perfect for tea and a snack). The public rooms include a parlor with its own baby grand piano and a library whose fireside rockers beckon the browsing bibliophile to find a good story and sit a spell. Breakfast is served in the library or in the conservatory, which has a wonderful view of the Housatonic Valley. The grounds are open for strolling and the woods for hiking. These are fairly untamed woods, where you're likely to spot deer and many species of birds, including wild turkeys. No smoking; no pets; no gratuities; breakfast included; children over fourteen only. Call (860) 672–6871 or visit www.hilltopbb.com.

Go a little north from West Cornwall on US 7 and west on Route 112 and you'll find ***Lime Rock Park,*** probably Connecticut's most famous sports-car race track. From time to time, you can see celebrities behind the wheel. Paul Newman is something of a regular at the track, and racing buffs Walter Cronkite, Tom Brokaw, and Tom Cruise have also made appearances. For us un-famous people, it's a fun place to spend Memorial Day. The Dodge Dealers Grand Prix, held on Memorial Day, is one of the largest sports-car races in the country. Racing fans can get free race information and sign up for the free newsletter (800–RACE–LRP). Wanna-be drivers can learn the ropes at Skip Barber Racing and Driving School at Lime Rock. Call (860) 435–5000.

East of West Cornwall is **Mohawk Mountain State Park.** The big draw here is skiing, but if that's not your thing, avoid the crowds and take a scenic warm-weather 2½-mile stroll to the top of the 1,683-foot-high Mohawk Mountain instead. The view from the wooden observation tower is absolutely breathtaking. One of our favorite picnics is sandwiches from Nodine's Smokehouse in Goshen eaten at one of the handful of picnic tables atop Mohawk Mountain.

## trivia

In 1948 Mohawk Ski Area in Cornwall became the first ski resort in the country to make artificial snow. The first (unsuccessful) attempt involved trucking in 700 tons of ice from Torrington.

Although the festival in nearby Norfolk tends to be better known, the tiny community of Falls Village in Canaan also boasts an excellent summer musical program. From mid-June to mid-September the town is home to the **Music Mountain Chamber Music Festival,** the oldest continuous chamber music festival in the United States. During the season a variety of string quartets play chamber music. Located off US 7. On Saturday evenings there are folk, jazz, and baroque music performances. Call (860) 824–7126 for details.

Wanna take home a real slice of Connecticut? Well, south of West Cornwall is a small, family-run bakery called **Matthews 1812 House,** 250 Kent Road (US 7) in Cornwall Bridge, housed in, what else, a vintage 1812 house. Stop by and sample the Lemon Rum Sunshine Cake, called "moist and deliciously spirited" by the *New York Times.* Lush with imported rum and zippy with lots of lemon, this old-fashioned poundcake is rich but still light enough to eat with a clear conscience. A small loaf-size cake sells for around $7.75. The bakery also cooks up several other types of loaf cake for sale or mail-order shipment. Open 9:00 A.M. to 5:00 P.M. Monday through Friday. Call (800) 662–1812 for information or to request their mail-order catalog.

Originally built in 1872, Canaan's **Union Station** (located at the junction of US 7 and 44) is supposedly the oldest train station still in use in the United States, and it celebrates the fact with an annual Railroad Days festival. It is also the main facility of the **Housatonic Railroad Company,** a tiny firm that operates a seasonal shortline across 17 miles of track between Canaan and Cornwall Bridge. Vice President Peter Lynch claims that his company's line is "one of the most scenic railroads east of the Mississippi," and we are inclined to agree. The 34-mile round-trip excursions that run down the Housatonic Valley and back pass through the most beautiful and unspoiled part of Connecticut.

# Cats in Retirement

*Falls Village,* in Canaan, is also the site of one of the state's truly unique establishments, though not, perhaps, one that you would normally think of as a tourist attraction. Located on thirty-five rural acres off Route 126, *The Last Post* is a private animal sanctuary and no-kill shelter. It's also a retirement home for cats.

New York radio personality Pegeen Fitzgerald founded The Last Post in 1982 as a home for felines whose human companions had passed away. Since then, hundreds of cats have been willed to the place, along with bequests for their care. Depending on the provisions of the will, some live out their lives there, while others stay only until they are adopted. Over the years, these "retirees" have been joined by a legion of strays and drop-offs. Today, over 375 of the fattest, sassiest, friendliest cats we've ever seen live uncaged in two huge airy halls connected by a 100-foot-long sundeck, which they can get to through cat doors and floor-level windows. There are cats of all shapes and sizes, ages, and appearances. They sprawl on couches, recline in stuffed chairs, and laze in tangled masses of fur on beds set next to the windows. Overhead, cats with swishing tails and mock feral eyes crouch on the exposed beams, while their somnolent cousins lounge under the skylights catching some rays. Others line the railing around the deck or prowl the five acres of fenced-in fields and trees set aside for their use. It's all very much like something out of Alfred Hitchcock's *The Birds*—only with cats.

The cat rooms are open to the public from 11:00 A.M. to 3:30 P.M. daily, including holidays, and The Last Post encourages visitors. So do the cats. In fact, if you sit down and hold still for even a moment, you'll find yourself bedecked with purring felines, all vying for your attention. Beware, though. It takes a hard heart to spend even a little time with these guys and not want to take one home. So many Connecticut residents' kitties come from right here. Call (860) 824–5469. Visit The Last Post on the Web at www.thing.net/~flux/lastpost.

It's an area that is especially popular among fall-color fanciers, and business has been so brisk on peak color days that would-be riders have sometimes had to be turned away. The Housatonic Railroad Company's steam-powered trains operate daily from Memorial Day through the end of October. Call (860) 824–0850 for daily schedule and rates.

## Places to Stay in the Litchfield Hills

**Curtis House,**
506 Main Street,
Woodbury;
(203) 263–2101.
Connecticut's oldest inn; also
serves lunch and dinner.
Moderate.

**Manor House,**
Maple Avenue,
Norfolk;
(860) 542–5690.
Lovely Victorian home.
Moderate.

**The Rose & Thistle,**
24 Woodland Acres,
Barkhamsted;
(860) 379–4744.
Located on ten hidden acres.
Moderate.

**Tir'na nO'g Farm B&B,**
261 Newton Road,
Northfield;
(860) 283–9612.
Charming and comfortable
B&B.
Moderate.

## Places to Eat in the Litchfield Hills

**The Birches Inn,**
233 West Shore Road,
New Preston;
(860) 868–1735,
(800) 525–3466.
Contemporary American.
Expensive for dinner.

**Mayflower Inn,**
118 Woodbury Road
(Route 47),
Washington;
(860) 868–9466.
Eat in the main dining room
or the Tap Room.
Moderate to expensive.

**The Sheik Sandwich Shop,**
235 East Elm,
Torrington;
(860) 489–5576.
Inexpensive.

**South Side Café,**
361 South Main Street,
Torrington;
(860) 489–5888.
Inexpensive.

# Gateway to New England

For most of America, Connecticut's southwestern shore is truly the Gateway to New England, the place where mid-Atlantic names, customs, and speech patterns begin to drop away and we Yankees start to quietly assert our personality. Most visitors to New England form their first impressions of our region from what they see in the busy towns and cities of Fairfield and New Haven Counties.

Geographically, the Gateway country is really just one long, lightly wooded coastal plain, with elevations ranging from sea level along the shore to 800 feet inland. The coastline of this low-lying plain is broken by many small bays and inlets and by the mouths of five rivers: the Mianus, Saugatuck, Mill, Housatonic, and Quinnipiac. A few miles inland, numerous lakes and ponds dot the countryside. The neighboring Long Island Sound helps temper the climate, making for pleasant summers and relatively mild winters, with plenty of rain but only moderate snowfall.

The southernmost of Fairfield County's towns (Greenwich) is only 28 miles from Times Square, and many of its residents commute daily to jobs in the banks, brokerage houses, and corporate headquarters of Manhattan. So do thousands of others in the southwestern towns. The wealth they bring back to

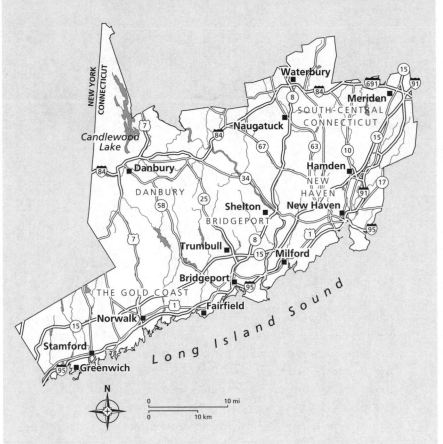

the state combined with that generated by the dozens of corporations that have their headquarters here has helped earn this area the nickname of the Gold Coast. As you move north and east, the tony quality of the Gold Coast gives way to the working-class atmosphere of cities such as Bridgeport and Norwalk. This transition is complete by the time you cross the line into New Haven County, the bridge between the commuter towns of the southwest and the outlying communities of Metro Hartford. New Haven, the easternmost city in the Gateway area, is a

## greenwichtrivia

In 1640 European settlers gave Native Americans twenty-five coats in exchange for the land now occupied by the prosperous town of Greenwich.

mixture of town and gown, famed as the site of Yale University, but also revered by the cognoscenti as the home of Louis' Lunch, birthplace of the American hamburger. Across the Quinnipiac River from New Haven, population density begins to fall away quickly as one moves east, and the eastern townships of New Haven County are really more typical of the shore than of the populous southwestern part of the state.

## The Gold Coast

As its mission statement proclaims, Greenwich's ***Bruce Museum of Arts & Science*** (One Museum Drive) "bridges the arts and sciences for people of all ages and cultures to foster learning and to preserve the past for the future." Sounds uplifting, to be sure. Fortunately it's also fun. For big people, the collection includes works by some of Connecticut's famed impressionists, including Childe Hassam, plus a wealth of art honoring diverse cultures. For the youngsters, there are scads of well-thought-out interactive exhibits. Open 10:00 A.M. to 5:00 P.M. Tuesday through Saturday; 1:00 to 5:00 P.M. Sunday. A donation is suggested; free on Tuesday. Call (203) 869–0376 for information on special events and the museum's calendar of exhibits.

## AUTHORS' FAVORITES

Bruce Museum of Arts & Science

Discovery Museum

Goulash Place

Military Museum of Southern New England

United House Wrecking Inc.

When the Merritt Parkway was opened in 1938, it was praised for its beauty and efficiency. Today it is acclaimed as a scenic alternative to the newer, grittier, and truck-laden Interstate 95. The Merritt, which is on the National Register of Historic Places, runs 37 miles, from Greenwich on the state line to Milford's border at the Housatonic River. At that point it becomes the Wilbur Cross Parkway, and the scenery and architecture become less distinguished.

Credit for the Merritt's unique charms goes especially to its landscape architect, Weld Thayer Chase, and to George Dunkelberger, designer of the sixty-eight distinctive bridges. Watch closely and you will see the Connecticut state seal, an owl, a blue-and-white Yale textbook, and a pair of Nike wings on the many art deco spans that cross the parkway. (If you're driving with restless children, point out the bridge ornamentation, urging them to see what will come next and choosing their favorites.) The grassy median that separates the Merritt's north and southbound lanes is also a delight with its varied landscape of trees and shrubs. Two bonuses: The Merritt is toll-free, and trucks are not allowed. Although there have been periodic attempts to widen it in an effort to lessen the traffic congestion, preservationists have always risen up to defeat such misguided ideas. During your Connecticut travels, if you have a choice between taking I–95 or the Merritt to reach your destination, choose the latter, even if it takes you a bit out of your way.

When you visit the **Stamford Cone** on Tresser Boulevard in downtown Stamford, you'll feel like you're standing inside a giant kaleidoscope. This 45-foot-tall structure is made up of 204 panels of glorious stained glass. There's something magical about standing inside and watching the play of light and color. The Stamford Cone is open to the public from 9:00 A.M. to 4:00 P.M. After dark, the cone is lit inside until dawn. For more information, call (203) 719–3000.

You can't miss **United House Wrecking Inc.** (535 Hope Street, Stamford). Just look for a rambling collection of buildings surrounded by a chain-link fence and guarded by a bunch of stone yard animals and lots of other junk.

Inside, there are more than two-and-a-half acres of every type of antique something or other you can (or can't) imagine. The main display area contains antique furniture, some salvaged from Gold Coast mansions, some from manor houses in England and France; others are quality reproductions. There's so much of it that they organize it in sections; tables here, cabinets there, chairs over in that section. Everywhere, you'll find artifacts and structural elements removed from stately homes; for example, an entire room with nothing but mantels, some clearly intended for ox roasts. Several side rooms contain stained-glass windows, authentic Victorian gingerbread trim, antique lighting, doors, plumbing fixtures, clocks, collectibles, curiosities; and so it goes.

The establishment's discovery by both Oprah Winfrey and Martha Stewart has caused the size of weekend crowds to balloon. If you really want to browse, go during off-peak hours. Open 9:30 A.M. to 5:30 P.M. Monday through Saturday; noon to 5:00 P.M. Sunday. Call (203) 348–5371 or visit www.united housewrecking.com.

*The Stamford Museum and Nature Center,* 39 Schofieldtown Road, is something of a hybrid with plenty to appeal to a variety of tastes. For many visitors, the animals on the small working farm are the main attraction. Gentle, wheelchair-accessible paths wind around pastures and barns with cows, oxen, sheep, goats, pigs, llamas, alpacas, horses, donkeys, and barnyard fowl. One of the neatest features is the live pond life exhibit, which includes a microscope/television system for viewing the mysteries of pond life. SMNC's 118-acre woodland site also includes galleries for interactive exhibits, a planetarium, picnic tables on a meadow overlooking the pond, a state-of-the-art observatory with research telescope, two stores, and a vast hardwood forest with miles of hiking trails. For more information call (203) 322–1646 or log on to www.stamford museum.org.

What kid doesn't like a swing? And what could be better than a single swing? A whole playground full of swings and playscapes. The *Timbertown Swing Set Company* of Stamford, 633 Hope Street, sets aside part of its facility as a giant indoor playscape open to the public. Kids can swing and play to their hearts' content, and it's not a bad way for a big kid to work off a little workweek stress. You'll find playhouses—actually more like play châteaux—pirate ships, complete with portholes and planks for walking, and a supercharged tree house. Timbertown is a dandy spot for a kid's birthday party. There's an admission charge, and reservations are encouraged. Call (203) 352–1222 for information and reservations. (There are two other Timbertown playscapes: one in Milford at 65 Woodmont Road, (203) 876–5004, and the other in Newington, on 94 Pane Road, (860) 594–8888.)

Fairfield isn't the most pastoral of Connecticut's counties, but smack dab in the middle are a couple of towns—Wilton and Weston—that have managed to preserve their bucolic atmosphere. Weston is especially pretty, thanks to tough zoning regulations and restrictions on development. According to folklore, old Mr. Scratch himself left

## fairfieldtrivia

The Wiffle ball was invented by David N. Mullaney of Fairfield in 1954. By the way, *wiffle* comes from the sandlot baseball term *wiff* (strike), which is what you usually do when you try to hit that crazy ball (the plastic ball with holes).

some hoofprints on the rocks thereabouts. Lucifer's purported stomping grounds are now the site of the ***Lucius Pond Ordway Devil's Den Preserve*** on Pent Road (take Godfrey Road, which is off either Route 53 or 57, to Pent Road). Owned by the Nature Conservancy, Devil's Den consists of more than 1,756 acres with 20 miles of hiking trails. This is a great place to scout out examples of rare or unusual plant species, including hog peanut and Indian cucumber root. Or you can just have a pleasant hike. If you plan to do so, be sure for your own safety that you pick up a map at the Pent Road entrance and sign in. Special programs and guided walks are held on some weekends, with attendance by reservation only. The park is open from dawn to dusk daily. There are no restrooms, and dogs and bicycles are not allowed. Call (203) 226–4991.

Technically, ***Norwalk's City Hall,*** 125 East Avenue, is neither museum nor gallery, but it does contain one of the largest collections of Depression-era murals in the United States. During the 1930s, unemployed artists were commissioned under the Works Progress Administration (WPA) to paint murals, many portraying the art of everyday life in America, in public buildings. Most of the structures that once housed these underappreciated masterpieces have fallen victim to the wrecker's ball, but some of Connecticut's Depression-era buildings, especially post offices, still display these modern wonders. Norwalk's WPA murals were originally painted on the walls of the old high school. When that building was torn down, the art was carefully preserved, restored, and rehung in the city hall. Free. Open 9:00 A.M. to 5:00 P.M. Monday through Friday. Call (203) 866–0202.

## norwalktrivia

At one time Norwalk was the oyster capital of Connecticut. Severe pollution changed all that for a while. Today, thanks to tough environmental legislation that is cleaning up Long Island Sound, Connecticut is once again one of the country's top oyster producers. And the new home base for Connecticut's oystering industry is, once again, Norwalk.

***SoNo,*** shorthand for South Norwalk, was once an all-too-common decaying inner-city neighborhood, but the area around Washington and South Main Streets has pulled itself up by its bootstraps to become a home to artists and artisans, much like Manhattan's trendy SoHo. This restored waterfront, included in the National Register of Historic Places, is now home to dozens of galleries, specialty shops, and restaurants.

The centerpiece of the SoNo revival is the ***Maritime Aquarium at Norwalk*** at 10 North Water Street. Part museum, part aquarium, and part theater, what ties the center together is life on (and by) the sea. The building also contains restaurants and a nice gift shop. Open daily 10:00 A.M. to 5:00 P.M. Closed Thanksgiving and Christmas. Admission. Call (203) 852–0700.

The *SoNo Switch Tower Museum,* 77 Washington Street, is an interesting part of the district's thriving cultural scene. Run by the Western Connecticut chapter of the National Railroad Historical Society, the museum was originally the switch tower in the timing building. Now it is a participatory museum. There is some memorabilia on display, but the main attraction is standing above the tracks and watching the trains roar by beneath you. Visitors can also pull the levers that move the switches and signals on the main line. The museum is open May through October, noon to 5:00 P.M. Saturday and Sunday. Call (203) 246–6958 or visit www.westctnrhs.org.

SoNo is known for its fine restaurants. One of the best is *Pasta Nostra,* located at 116 Washington Street. The style and the prices are high, but the food is worth it. All pasta is made fresh on-site; there's also a takeaway pasta store. The lunch and dinner menu changes daily, featuring high-quality food such as linguine with puttanesca, a zesty, quickly prepared red sauce invented by Rome's working girls. Open for dinner 5:00 to 9:30 P.M. Wednesday through Saturday. Call (203) 854–9700 for reservations.

At *Calf Pasture Park* on Calf Pasture Road, families loll on the beach, picnic, or wander the shore looking for seashells. Open daily from 8:30 A.M. to 11:00 P.M. A food concession, restrooms, changing areas, and eating areas are available. If you're an out-of-towner, there's a fairly stiff parking fee.

Just a short ferry ride off Norwalk, the historic *Sheffield Island Lighthouse* is a pretty cool place to spend a hot summer day. Sheffield is the outermost of the thirteen Norwalk islands and offers scenic views of both Long Island Sound and the Norwalk River. *G.W. Tyler,* a forty-nine-passenger ferry, leaves for the island from

## yankeedoodle

During the French and Indian War, Col. Thomas Fitch was preparing to lead his troops from Norwalk. When his sister, Elizabeth, came to say good-bye, she was troubled by the shabbiness of the soldiers' uniforms. Gathering feathers from a nearby chicken coop, she placed one in each man's cap. When they arrived at Fort Crailo near Albany, British army surgeon Richard Shuckburgh declared, "Now stab my vitals, they're macaronis," slang for dandies. He wrote a jeering rhyme that was later set to music: "*Yankee Doodle* (slang for a simpleton) *went to town a ridin' on a pony/He stuck a feather in his cap and called it macaroni.*" But the Americans grew so fond of the ditty that it became the battle theme during the Revolutionary War. It was the celebratory tune played as the beaten British troops were marched out of Yorktown to end the war, and today it is the Connecticut state song.

Hope Dock (corner of Water and Washington Streets in South Norwalk) twice a day on weekdays and three times on weekends. Weekend and holiday service starts Memorial Day weekend; daily service runs from late June through Labor Day. On the round-trip cruise, the ferry's crew offers lively commentary on Norwalk's oystering past and the island's sometimes racy history and folklore. Island clambakes are held Thursday evening throughout the summer. Visitors

## Dogs Off the Beaten Path in Fairfield County

Should Fairfield County be christened Connecticut's "Hot Dog" capital? Who knows? Who cares? For those who do, several of the state's top hot dog shops can be found in Fairfield County.

For years chef Gary Zemola and his colorful Super Duper Weenie Truck were a familiar sight around Fairfield Country. Now the SDWT is off the road (except for special occasions), and Gary cooks up his superlative dogs in a permanent home at his tiny eatery, **Super Duper Weenie** (the "Fortress of Weeni-tude"), 306 Black Rock Turnpike, Fairfield. For the uninitiated, the SDWT is a restored Chevy van featured in a painting by diner artist John Baeder in his book *Diners*. Chef Gary, who trained at the Culinary Institute of America, creates fast food with panache. All ingredients are high quality, but what really makes the sandwich are his homemade relishes. The fresh-cut fries also get raves. You can eat inside at the counter, but why? Head for the picnic tables outside. The quality of the food is as high as the prices are low (lunch for under a fin). Open 11:00 A.M. to 8:00 P.M. Monday through Wednesday; 11:00 A.M. to 4:00 P.M. Thursday, Friday, and Saturday; and 11:00 A.M. to 6:00 P.M. Sunday. Call (203) 334-3647. Visit the SDW on the Web at www.superduperweenie.com.

Not far from the Birdcraft Museum and Sanctuary is **Rawley's Drive-in,** 1886 Post Road, a place where the doyenne of domesticity, Martha Stewart, chows down, as do the likes of Paul Newman and David Letterman. Obviously, along with most of the people in Fairfield, Martha, Paul, and David know a good thing. This small, shingled eatery offers no-frills, fundamental drive-in eating at its best. The chili dogs and plain hot dogs in butter-toasted French rolls topped with the works (sauerkraut, mustard, relish, and bacon) are excellent, and the prices are rock bottom. Open 11:00 A.M. to 6:45 P.M. Monday to Saturday, closed Sunday. Call (203) 259–9023.

Is it too Fairfield County or what that Ridgefield would have a hot dog cart named **Chez Lenard Sidewalk Cafe and Catering?** And, naturally, Chez Lenard's offerings are called "le hot dogs." Snobbery aside, Lenny does cook up some swell dogs. We like "le hot dog façon Mexicaine" (chili dog) and "le hot dog Logano Suisse," an all-beef frank drenched with a cheese fondue–like mixture. You'll find Chez Lenard open year-round on Main Street. He opens for business around 11:00 A.M. Call (203) 431–6324.

can tour the lighthouse, picnic, or walk to the trail of the McKinney Wildlife Refuge. Fee for ferry ride and clambake. The light, which is now on the National Register of Historic Places, was constructed in 1868 and was an active working light until 1902. For a copy of the Sheffield Island Lighthouse schedule and more information, call the Norwalk Seaport Association at (203) 838–9444 or visit http://lighthouse.cc/sheffield.

Norwalk's picturesque **Silvermine Tavern,** 194 Perry Avenue, was built in 1785 in the crossroads town of Silvermine. Since then, several nearby towns have swallowed up the village, but the tavern still occupies the crossroads (now Silvermine and Perry Avenues). Today, as in the past, Silvermine Tavern could very well be the ideal of a picturesque New England tavern inn. The 200-year-old establishment overlooks a waterfall and a charming mill pond populated by fat ducks and swans who seem to feed quite well on the bounty cast their way by strolling guests. The ten rooms are amply furnished with antiques, including, in some cases, canopy beds.

Most people, however, come here to eat and drink. There is a cozy cocktail lounge and six dining rooms, including a main dining room decorated with more than 1,000 antiques. The food is traditional New England cooking. Thursday night the inn serves up a locally famous buffet, and a plentiful brunch is offered on Sunday. Lunch is served from noon to 3:00 P.M.; dinner, 6:00 to 9:00 P.M. (10:00 P.M. on weekends). The inn is open all year; the restaurant closes on Tuesday from September to May. Call (203) 847–4558.

Downtown Westport, with its collection of small quaint shops, has its own charm, although the streets and boutiques can get crowded on peak shopping days. The shops come and go, so just park and go where your fancy takes you.

One of the best reasons for visiting Westport even on the busiest days is a place called **Coffee An'.** This establishment at 343 Main Street is a world-class doughnut shop. The doughnuts are made from scratch, and they keep coming fresh out of the oven all day. There are no special ingredients or secret recipes involved, but the results bear the same resemblance to franchise fare as Dom Perignon does to Ripple. Just about anything that comes out of the oven— including the plain variety—is superb, but we're particularly partial to the coconut crullers and the cinnamon twirls. Westport resident Paul Newman has been known to slip into Coffee An' for his Sunday-morning doughnuts, but we don't know *his* preferences. Open daily 7:00 A.M. to 3:30 P.M., to 3:00 P.M. Saturday, and 8:00 A.M. to 1:00 P.M. Sunday. Call (203) 227–3808.

One of the oldest nature centers in Connecticut is a good place to walk off doughnuts from Coffee An'. **Earthplace Nature Discovery Center,** 10 Woodside Lane in Westport, has good trails (open dawn to dusk) and an excellent

# Chili-Dog Sauce

Collecting recipes for this book hasn't always been an easy task. Sure, some chefs willingly share their "kitchen secrets" because they appreciate winding up with free publicity. Others, though, guard their recipes like Scrooge McDuck guards his gold—and it seems no recipe is as highly cherished as chili sauce for chili dogs. Nevertheless, what follows has been around so long it's become widely known. Some restaurants take credit for it, but New Britain's original Metropole seems to be the most likely source.

1 small onion, chopped

1 clove garlic, crushed

1 tablespoon vegetable oil

1 pound hamburger

2 cups water

1 tablespoon best-quality chili powder

½ teaspoon cinnamon

1 teaspoon paprika

½ teaspoon nutmeg

½ teaspoon allspice

salt and pepper to taste

Brown onions and garlic in oil. Add meat and brown. Stir with a fork to break up meat. Add water and remaining ingredients. Simmer over medium-low heat for twenty to thirty minutes until mixture is thick and water evaporates. If you prefer your chili-dog sauce with a finer texture, let it cool and then buzz it a little in a food processor. Reheat as needed. *NOTE:* You can freeze leftover sauce, but spice balance will change.

display of native plants in a courtyard. On weekends the hands-on marine aquarium exposes kids to marine life, and the Discovery Room has many hands-on natural history activities, puzzles, artifacts, and scientific equipment to use. Since 2005 the exhibit hall has featured activities for kids. There is also an animal rehabilitation center where injured and abandoned animals are cared for. The center also has a wheelchair-accessible trail. The center is open 9:00 A.M. to 5:00 P.M. Monday through Saturday and 1:00 to 4:00 P.M. Sunday. There's a very modest admission fee, and family memberships are available. Call (203) 227–7253 for information on special programs.

*The Connecticut Audubon Birdcraft Museum,* 314 Unquowa Road in Fairfield, is housed in the first privately owned songbird sanctuary in America. It was established in 1914 by Mable Osgood Wright, a pioneer in the American conservation movement and founder of the Connecticut Audubon Society. Recognized as a National Historic Landmark in 1993, the Birdcraft Museum includes a natural history exhibit. It also features dioramas of Connecticut's wildlife as it existed at the turn of the twentieth century. The Four Seasons Room explores bird diversity throughout the years. There is also a honeybee hive, the Frederick T. Bedford Collection of African Animals, changing exhibits, and hands-on children's activities. There is a bird-banding station, which has mist-netted and documented more than 18,000 birds before releasing them unharmed. The station operates weekdays in the spring and fall. Demonstrations are available to any group by appointment. The museum is open 10:00 A.M. to 5:00 P.M. Tuesday through Friday and noon to 4:00 P.M. Saturday and Sunday. Admission. Call (203) 259–0416.

# Bridgeport

Phineas Taylor (P. T.) Barnum is probably the country's most famous entertainment entrepreneur. Born in 1810, in an era when entertainment was pretty much divided along class lines between the cultural and the popular, Barnum revolutionized show biz by presenting entertainments designed to appeal to people of all classes. Over time his name came to be linked with three things: showmanship, the circus, and a legendary quote, which he never said: "There's a sucker born every minute."

Today Barnum is remembered in Bridgeport's refurbished and expanded **Barnum Museum** (820 Main Street), three stories of circus exhibits and P. T. Barnum memorabilia, housed in what has been described as a "Byzantine-Romanesque-Gothic-Barnumesque" building with a red sandstone facade and lots of domes and terra-cotta friezes. The third floor, "Showman to the World," is the tour's grand finale. Here is Barnum's famous 2,500-year-old Egyptian mummy (Pa-Ib), one of the favorite exhibits. There's also an exhibit of Barnum oddities, including the *Feejee Mermaid,* a two-headed calf, and a fragment from Noah's Ark; a wonderful gallery on "clowning"; and displays of memorabilia related to Jenny Lind—the so-called Swedish Nightingale—and General Tom Thumb (two of many proteges Barnum collected during an active life as a promoter). Finally there's the museum's most famous holding: William Brinley's 1,000-square-foot scale model circus, based on one the artist saw in 1915, when he was nine years old. The model took sixty years to complete and contains more than 3,000 hand-carved miniature figures. It alone is well worth the trip.

The Barnum Museum is open 10:00 A.M. to 4:30 P.M. Tuesday through Saturday and noon to 4:30 P.M. Sunday (mornings by appointment). Gift shop. Admission. Call (203) 331–1104.

Any town would be lucky to have a museum as good as the Barnum. Bridgeport has two. Someone once described the ***Discovery Museum*** (4450 Park Avenue) as "more fun than a basket of puppies." It is indeed a splendid place for kids of all ages.

The Discovery was born in 1987, when the stuffy old 1950s-era Museum of Science and Industry decided on a change. Its new focus is the relationship between the arts and physical science. This required a makeover of the museum's interior and the installation of more than fifty hands-on exhibits. The result is a place where you can make a variety of delightful things happen by simply pulling a lever, turning a crank, or pushing a button. When your hands have had enough pulling, turning, and pushing, you can jump aboard a bicycle and pedal enough electricity to run a radio or test your reflexes by driving a bumper car or interact with the museum in what seems like a zillion and one other ways. Some museums are "don't touch" places; the Discovery is a "please touch" place.

The exhibits are only part of the fun here. You can also visit the ***Henry B. DuPont Planetarium*** and the ***Wonder Workshops,*** where kids can make their own souvenirs. As part of a special program, school groups can even suit up and go to Mars as crew members aboard a spaceship. For a small additional charge, kids ten and up can participate in one of the Challenger mini-missions that are held most weekends. You might like checking your weight on a "Martian" scale;

## bridgeporttrivia

Famous last words: On his deathbed, P. T. Barnum is reported to have said, "How were the receipts today at Madison Square Garden?"

you'll weigh about one-third less. Be sure to check out the gift shop; it's thoughtfully stocked with lots of low-priced goodies. Open 10:00 A.M. to 5:00 P.M. Tuesday through Saturday and noon to 5:00 P.M. Sunday.

The planetarium shows start at 1:00 P.M. for children seven and under, 3:30 P.M. for eight and older. There are more shows on weekends, so call for the full schedule. Admission. Call (203) 372–3521 or visit www.discoverymuseum.org.

Bridgeport's ***Beardsley Zoo,*** in Beardsley Park on Noble Avenue, is Connecticut's biggest zoo, featuring large North American mammals in addition to various exotics. There is also a children's zoo set up like a New England farm within the main zoo, a thirty-six-acre rain forest, and an indoor carousel museum. The facility includes a picnic area, snack bar, and gift shop. It is open weekdays from 9:00 A.M. to 4:00 P.M. There is a modest admission charge and a fairly stiff parking fee. Call (203) 394–6565.

# Star Power in Connecticut

Because it offers suburban living in close proximity to New York, a host of celebs from the world of entertainment have made their homes in Connecticut, mostly in Fairfield and Litchfield Counties. But Connecticut is also the birthplace of many well-known actors.

Bridgeport: Robert Mitchum, Peter Falk, Brian Dennehy, and John Ratzenberger (*Cheers*)

Fairfield: Meg Ryan

Hamden: Ernest Borgnine

Hartford: Sophie Tucker, Linda Evans, Katharine Hepburn, and Louis Nye

Redding Ridge: Hope Lange

Stamford: Christopher Lloyd

Waterbury: Rosalind Russell

Westport: Glenn Close

*Bloodroot* (85 Ferris Street) in Bridgeport is one of those places that make you wonder whether you've accidentally stepped through a time warp. It's not so much the rigidly vegetarian fare. Sure they don't serve meat or fish, but lots of places are that way today. Maybe it's the fact that this restaurant thinks of itself as feminist to the point of redefining what the restaurant business is all about. It's not a cafeteria, but no one waits on anyone else, either. You order your food and pay for it. Then you sit down and relax. When the food is ready, you pick it up, course by course, and carry it to your table. When you're ready to leave, you clear the dishes yourself.

Bloodroot is committed to animal rights, so the only animal products on the menu are eggs and milk products. You won't miss red meat, though. Soups, thick hearty ones such as curry-scented lentil, sided with a few slices of Bloodroot's homemade bread, thick with husks and shards of different grains, make a lovely meal. The pasta and salad dishes are also tasty and filling. Desserts are excellent, especially the Indian pudding.

Bloodroot is open for lunch 11:30 A.M. to 2:30 P.M. Tuesday, Thursday, Friday, Saturday; dinner 6:00 to 9:00 P.M. Tuesday, Thursday and 6:00 to 10:00 P.M. Friday and Saturday; Sunday brunch, 11:30 A.M. to 2:30 P.M. No credit cards. Wheelchair accessible through a side entrance, but restrooms are a tight squeeze. Call (203) 576–9168 or visit www.bloodroot.com.

# Danbury

Time was, a good hat was an essential item of apparel, and you weren't really dressed without a good topper. In those days, Connecticut was hat maker to America, and Danbury was the center of the hat-making business. Today the glory days of hat making are remembered along with other Danbury history in the ***Danbury Museum and Historical Society*** at 43 Main Street. There are actually several buildings at this address, and exhibits are scattered among them. The exhibit on Danbury's hatting industry is in the 1790 John Dodd Shop. Other exhibits deal with early American life, the Revolutionary War, and the history of Danbury. A highlight is the recording studio of singer Marion Anderson, who was a Danbury native. The studio houses many artifacts from her career and life. Gift shop. Call (203) 743–5200 for hours.

The ***Military Museum of Southern New England,*** 125 Park Avenue (just off Interstate 84, exit 3) is the product of a volunteer army of helpers who don't want the sacrifices of those who served in World War II forgotten. Unlike so many volunteer-run museums that seem to suffer from lack of a professional staff, this one thrives. It's one of the best military museums we've seen anywhere.

You'll know you've arrived when you see what looks like a tank park. This is actually an outdoor display of fighting vehicles and small guns in front of the museum. Most of the material is American, but there are items from other countries, too. The condition of the armored fighting vehicles varies. Some have been fully restored, while others look like what they are: vehicles that have been moldering away for half a century. Whatever their condition, standing directly under the guns of these steel monsters is awe-inspiring. To get a real feel for what the soldiers of that era meant by "tank fright," stand behind the 37mm antitank gun by the museum's front entrance and peer along its barrel at the tanks out in the yard. Some variant of this was the main weapon that the grunts of most armies used to stop enemy tanks during the first half of World War II. Really.

Inside the museum you'll find enough dioramas, maps, models, pictures, and paraphernalia of war to occupy your attention for several hours. The most impressive items are fully restored weapons and vehicles exhibited against realistic backgrounds, complete with mannequins dressed in authentic period uniforms. The experience is enhanced by World War II–era background music. The museum also holds monthly open turret days when visitors can enter the tanks. There's a gift shop. Admission. Open 10:00 A.M. to 5:00 P.M. Tuesday through Saturday and noon to 5:00 P.M. Sunday. Closed Monday and nonpatriotic holidays. Reduced hours during the winter. Call (203) 790–9277 for information about special events and exhibits. Find it on the Web at www.usmilitarymuseum.org.

Adults commuting into Manhattan may think of trains as something to be endured, but most kids will always see trains as romantic and vaguely magical. At the **Danbury Railway Museum,** housed in a restored 1903 train station and adjoining a six-acre railyard at 120 White Street at Union Station, a group of dedicated volunteers is doing its bit to keep that magic alive. They've transformed the old station into a museum of train paraphernalia and restored trains. Call ahead and ask about special events.

The museum holds some neat ones, such as shopping trips to Manhattan, Christmas and Halloween trips, and "rare mileage" trips (their term for trips along tracks not in regular use). Near the front of the museum is a small but interesting gift shop. If Union Station looks familiar, it should. Alfred Hitchcock used it in *Strangers on a Train* as the setting for his own cameo appearance. Open April through December, 10:00 A.M. to 5:00 P.M. Tuesday through Saturday and noon to 5:00 P.M. Sunday. Closed Monday. Shorter hours January through March. Call (203) 778–8337 or log on to www.danbury.org/drm.

danburytrivia

Zadoc Benedict founded the nation's first hat factory in Danbury in 1780. It produced a dizzying three hats a day! By the mid-1800s, the Hat City led the world in hat production, and by 1949, more than 66 percent of the nation's hats carried a "made in Connecticut" label. From 1949 to 1977, Connecticut honored the hat industry with Hat Day, and both houses of Connecticut's legislature would be filled with examples of the hat-makers art, from tough-guy fedoras to Miss Porter's–perfect pillboxes.

The Danbury Fair Mall is one of the largest shopping malls in the Northeast, but that doesn't mean you should skip downtown Danbury, where you'll find plenty of neat shops such as the **Cow's Outside,** 286 Main Street (exit 5 off I–84). Perhaps the name comes from the fact that this is a leather store (the cow's outside) or because there really is a *cow outside* (in this case a life-size, mooing, boot-shod cow). The Cow's Outside is a leather outlet, with an emphasis on boots with prices "cheaper than in Texas." Even at outlet prices (discounts ranging from 15 to 50 percent), the boots here are on the high side, but then so's the quality. As for the selection, it's just about impossible to beat. You'll find thousands of pairs of boots, made from ostrich, alligator, lizard, and leather, in a wide range of sizes. In the summer, look for nice discounts on sandals. You'll also find leather jackets for men and women at 30 to 50 percent discounts. Open 10:00 A.M. to 6:00 P.M. Tuesday through Saturday and noon to 5:00 P.M. Sunday. Call (203) 797–1924.

Danbury has its share of fast-food strips and chain restaurants, not to mention the usual urban mix of "family" and "gourmet" establishments. We figure you can find the name eateries on your own. Here are some places you might miss but shouldn't. If you're bored with overpriced eateries where the chef thinks that "gourmet" and "eccentric" are synonyms, head for the **Goulash Place,** in a secluded residential neighborhood at 42 Highland Avenue. The food is first-rate, and the prices, as they say in Fargo, are indeed "reasonable."

The specialty is goulash, and there are five different varieties to sample. If you've never eaten Transylvanian goulash, take a chance. This tender stew of pork, sauerkraut, paprika, onions, and dill comes topped with a dollop of sour cream and is completely different from any other goulash you've ever tasted. The goulash arrives piping hot, with *nockerl* (pumped-up noodles) and fresh veggies. In the unlikely event that you save room for dessert, go for the apricot or cheese *palacsinitas* (dessert crepes). Open 11:00 A.M. to 10:00 P.M. Tuesday through Saturday and 1:00 to 8:00 P.M. Sunday. Closed Monday. Call (203) 744–1971. Parking is in the rear and is presided over by the owners' dog, Gypsy.

If you like motorcycles, you'll want to hit **Marcus Dairy Bar** at 5 Sugar Hollow Road (intersection of US 7 and I–84, near Danbury Fair Mall). On any given Sunday, you'll find the bikes lined up and down Sugar Hollow Road as bikers and bike-watchers bop in for morning coffee and to check out each other's rides. On a Super Sunday, it looks like every bike in New England is parked there. Super Sunday events include vendors, motorcycle crafts, shows, competitions, and club displays. By the way, the food, especially breakfast, is pretty good, plentiful, and cheap. Open daily 6:00 A.M. to 9:00 P.M. for three meals. Call (203) 748–9427.

Danbury was a center of Portuguese settlement in New England, and great Portuguese cuisine is one of the city's cultural assets. If you're in the area during June, you might want to try one of several outdoor Portuguese festivals on Liberty Street: the **Feast of Saint Anthony** is the first weekend in June, **Portuguese Day** is June 10, and the **Feast of Saint John** is the third or fourth weekend in June.

East of Danbury is Newtown, where the **Second Company of the Governor's Horse Guards,** Fairfield Hills Complex No. 4, Wildlife Drive (I–84, exit 11), practice, usually in full uniform. A horse guards practice is something no horse- or animal-loving kid can resist. Chartered in 1808, the Second Company of the Governor's Horse Guards was mainly used to escort the governor and distinguished visitors on ceremonial occasions. Today, the troop is a cavalry militia designated by the governor to serve the people of southwestern Connecticut. The troop's horses, which were donated, are a variety of breeds. Tours of the barns are often available. Summer practices are held in Newtown April through October on Thursday at 7:30 P.M. For more information call (203) 426–9046. (The First Company of the Governor's Horse Guards, headquartered in Avon, also holds public drills and special events. See The Farmington Valley in The Heartland chapter.)

When J. Alden Weir saw his first impressionist painting in a Paris gallery, it gave him a headache, but by 1881, the American artist was honing his own distinctively impressionistic style. Today, his home, **Weir Farm,** 735 Nod Hill Road in Wilton, is a National Historic Site. Weir designed his farm as he would a painting, mixing and matching visual elements until everything was perfect. The farm, which he called the Land of Nod, provided inspiration for his own paintings of late nineteenth-century family life and for the works of fellow artists Childe Hassam, John Twachtman, and John Singer Sargent. The self-guided Painting Sites Trail is a living landscape. It's well marked to highlight a series of views from Weir's paintings, including Weir Pond, which he built with the prize money from his 1895 painting *The Truants.* Admission is free, but you'll want to spring for the excellent inexpensive brochure that illustrates the tour. Open April through November, 8:30 A.M. to 5:00 P.M. daily. Call (203) 834–1896 for hours and information.

The **Brookfield Craft Center** north of Danbury on Route 25 houses a school of contemporary arts and crafts within six colonial buildings (including a 1780 gristmill) set on the banks of Still River. The associated arts-and-crafts gallery and retail shop is open 10:00 A.M. to 5:00 P.M. Monday through Saturday and noon to 5:00 P.M. Sunday; closed major holidays. Call (203) 775–4526 or log on to www.brookfieldcraftcenter.org.

If your kids normally gag at being dragged off to a craft center, try bribing them with a visit to **Mother Earth Gallery & Mining Company,** 806 Federal Road in Brookfield. It's a great way to occupy kids during school vacations. You and the kids can suit up with natty lighted miners' helmets and buckets and go digging for amethyst, quartz, mica, pyrite, tourmaline, peridot, and galena. The best part: You get to keep whatever you find. The florescent mine, glowing with green, red, orange, and blue rocks, is spooky but neat. The complex includes a gift shop that is well stocked with products from conservation organizations such as Greenpeace. Mother Earth is one cool place for a kid's birthday party. Admission; open to kids five and older. Open 10:00 A.M. to 6:00 P.M. Monday and Wednesday through Saturday, and noon to 5:00 P.M. Sunday. Call (203) 775–6272 for information about special events.

You don't have to travel to Napa for an authentic wine tour. Brookfield's **DiGrazia Vineyards & Winery** (131 Tower Road) is one of New England's smaller wineries, but it's also one of the most interesting. The grapes come from vineyards in New York as well as Sharon and Southbury, but it all comes together at the Brookfield site, which is a family-run boutique winery. While other area vintners make fruit wines or grow the French hybrids traditional to

New England, Dr. Paul DiGrazia and family focus on specialties. You might find Beaujolais, port, mead (honey wine), or wines made from pears, sugar pumpkins, raspberries, or apples. If you're sensitive to sulfides, ask about the wines made with honey. This winery has been around since 1984, and the original line has expanded greatly. Open daily, 11:00 A.M. to 5:00 P.M., with reduced winter hours. Free tours and tastings are run by Barbara DiGrazia on weekends and are conducted in a small, but pleasant, tasting room and retail area. Call (203) 775–1616.

## southbury trivia

Kettledown State Park in Southbury gets its name from the story that settlers paid the Native Americans who originally lived on the spot one brass kettle for the land.

When Washington's Northern Army went into winter quarters at the end of November 1778, it was dispersed in an arc from New Jersey to Connecticut to ring the British garrison in New York. Three of the army's brigades had their winter encampment at Redding, where they were strategically positioned to defend the region from British raiders. Their commander was Maj. Gen. Israel ("Old Put") Putnam, a larger-than-life hero, who is often called Connecticut's Paul Bunyan.

That winter was relatively mild, but the harvest had been poor, and supplies were scarce. The men, many of whom had been through the hell of Valley Forge the previous year, began to mutter about a similar privation winter in Connecticut. Then in December the state experienced one of the worst winter storms in New England history. Two days after it ended, the men of one brigade mutinied and prepared to march on the colonial assembly in Hartford to demand overdue supplies and wages. Putnam was able to break up the protest only with the greatest of difficulty. Thus began the winter encampment at Redding that came to be known as Connecticut's Valley Forge.

The original encampment is now the site of **Putnam Memorial State Park** at the junction of Routes 58 and 107 in West Redding. These days, the twelve-man huts are just piles of stone where their chimneys stood, and the old magazine is only a stone-lined pit. The officers' barracks have been rebuilt, though, and there is a museum containing exhibits dealing with the Redding encampment. There's also a great statue by the front gate showing Old Put riding his horse down a flight of stairs to escape capture during a British raid in February 1779. Open daily, 8:00 A.M. to sunset. Call (203) 938–2285.

South of Danbury, nearby Ridgefield was the site of a minor 1777 skirmish known as (what else?) the **Battle of Ridgefield,** in which Benedict Arnold led the colonists against Gen. William Tryon's British. The historic 1733-vintage Keeler Tavern at 132 Main Street still carries a legacy of the battle in the form

## OTHER ATTRACTIONS WORTH SEEING IN GATEWAY TO NEW ENGLAND

**Bishop Farms,**
500 South Meriden Road,
Cheshire;
(203) 272–8243.

**Bovano,**
430 South Main Street,
Cheshire;
(203) 272–3200.
Gift shop includes Bovano Enamelware.

**Images,**
32 North Colony Street (Route 5),
Wallingford;
(203) 265–7065.
Heirloom linens.

**Knights of Columbus Museum,**
1 State Street,
New Haven;
(203) 865–0400.
Art, artifacts, and archival material
relating to the history, formation, and
activities of the Knights of Columbus.

**Lockwood-Mathews
Mansion Museum,**
295 West Avenue,
Mathews Park,
Norwalk;
(203) 838–1434.

**Meeker's Hardware,**
86-90 White Street,
Danbury;
(203) 748–8017.

**Railroad Museum of New England,**
176 Chase River Road,
Waterbury;
(860) 283–RAIL (860–283–7245);
www.rmne.org.

**St. James Church,**
25 West Street,
Danbury

**St. Peter Church,**
built in 1870,
at Main and Center Streets,
Danbury

**Stepping Stones Museum
for Children,**
303 West Avenue,
Mathews Park,
Norwalk;
(203) 899–0606.
Focusing on the arts, science and
technology, culture and heritage.
Rain forest exhibit.

**Tarrywile Mansion and Park,**
70 Southern Boulevard,
Danbury;
(203) 744–3130.

**United Crafts,**
127 West Putnam Avenue,
Greenwich;
(203) 869–4898;
www.ucrafts.com.
A gallery of beautiful Arts and Crafts
stoneware, bronzes, and textiles.

of a British cannonball embedded in the wall. Now the ***Keeler Tavern Museum,*** the inn has been restored and furnished with authentic eighteenth-century furniture, appointments, and artifacts. Guides in colonial dress conduct half-hour tours in season. Open 1:00 to 4:00 P.M. Wednesday, Saturday, and Sunday (last tour is at 3:30 P.M.). Gift shop. Admission. Call (203) 438–5485.

A short distance down Main Street, at number 258, is a large 1783-vintage clapboard house. It doesn't really look much different from most of the other historic houses on this street, whose exteriors are frozen in time. This building's interior, however, is another matter. This was the *Aldrich Museum of Contemporary Art.* Now it houses the museum's administrative offices. The museum is in a new 19,000-square-foot-building behind the house. The new facility has twelve flexible galleries, performance space, a sound studio, and a screening room. The museum mounts twelve exhibits a year, plus a full calendar of arts & educational programs. It is one of America's better small art museums. This private facility is definitely contemporary, and this close to New York, it tends to get works from the best of America's young artists. Often the artists represented are relative unknowns whose first important exposure comes at the Aldrich.

Behind the museum is the most exciting part of the Aldrich. Sloping away from the building is a broad green lawn dotted with several dozen pieces of modern sculpture. Most are massive, towering over the strollers in their midst. All are imbued with a special strangeness that comes partly from their staid colonial surroundings. Scattered about this sculpture garden are wrought-iron tables and chairs where visitors can sit and relax.

The Aldrich is open noon to 5:00 P.M. Tuesday through Sunday. The garden is always open, even when the museum is closed. Admission. Call (203) 438–4519.

To fortify yourself before tackling art and culture at the Aldrich, you can't go wrong with breakfast at *Gail's Station House* at 378 Main Street (between Bailey Avenue and Governor Street) in Ridgefield. This is a cozy place with sort of a town clubhouse feel to it. Gail's breakfast specialty is the "skillet breakfast," cooked and served in a black cast-iron skillet. Each skillet meal includes scrambled eggs, hash browns, and some special touch, such as chunks of lox and green onion. The pancakes here are also splendiferous, especially the apple variety. For a lighter meal, try the muffins; muffins are New England's favorite quick bread, and nobody does them much better than this place. Open for breakfast daily, 8:00 A.M. to 3:00 P.M.; lunch daily 11:30 A.M. to 3:00 P.M. Mid-day menu, 3:00 to 5:30 P.M. Friday and Saturday. Dinner runs from 5:30 to 9:30 P.M. Friday and Saturday. Live music on Friday. Call (203) 438–9775.

Every now and then, you deserve a big splurge. One of the best getaways and fine dining experiences to be had in Connecticut is at the *Elms Restaurant & Tavern,* 500 Main Street in Ridgefield. The menu shines with updated versions of American classics such as curried butternut squash and apple soup, succotash, sweet potato spoon bread, creamed collards, and Rhode Island johnnycakes. On the dessert menu, go for anything chocolate. Thanksgiving dinner (reservations required far in advance) at the Elms is the essence of a colonial holiday. Prices are moderate to high. The main dining room (reservations a must) is open 5:00 to around 9:00 P.M. Wednesday through Sunday. The more casual, less expensive tavern is open 11:00 A.M. to 3:00 P.M. for lunch and 5:30 P.M. to closing for dinner. No wheelchair access; no children's menu. Call (203) 438–9206.

The pleasant inn rooms, furnished in a colonial style with antiques and high-quality reproductions, are spacious and comfortable. The breakfast included in the room rate (moderate to high range) makes the inn a good value. Call (203) 438–2541 for more information.

If inns were film stars, Ridgefield's **Stonehenge Inn,** 35 Stonehenge Road, would be Cary Grant: nothing ostentatious, just impeccable, gracious, and charming, with a tiny touch of reserve—the perfect mix for an extended stay or an exquisite dinner. Located on US 7 in Ridgefield, the inn features sixteen rooms of understated opulence designed for grace and comfort. The ten acres of landscaped grounds, including a duck pond and gardens, are almost as inviting as the elegant interior.

The food, with a French flair, follows the same path. Fresh and well prepared, the tastefully presented cuisine is matched by professional service. If you eat dessert, the Grand Marnier soufflé is the only way to go. Prices are in the high range. Dinner reservations are a must. Open for dinner 6:00 P.M. to 9:00 P.M. Monday through Saturday. Call (203) 438–6511 for reservations and details.

The **Bethel Cinema,** 269 Greenwood Avenue in neighboring Bristol, screens art and independent films, attracting a large audience who want more than the latest blockbuster sequel. The two-screen theater is known for showing films long before the rest of the world hops on the bandwagon. Generally two films are shown during a run. The matinees are kind to tight budgets. Local restaurants offer discount deals. The theater publishes a newsletter with information about upcoming features and film-related lectures. To get on the mailing list, call (203) 778–3100; for film information call (203) 778–2100.

After a show, head over to Bethel's **Dr. Mike's** at 158 Greenwood Avenue. If, as some say, (Eric) Clapton is God, then Dr. Mike must be his archangel. One favorite Dr. Mike creation, Chocolate Lace ice cream, starts with rich, unflavored ice cream and then is packed to bursting with Chocolate Lace candy, a filigree of spun sugar dipped in bittersweet chocolate. The contrast between the crunchy candy and the puff of bland ice cream is almost indescribable, especially for a G-rated book. Dr. Mike rotates an impressive array of flavors throughout the year, but only a handful (maybe six) are on the menu at any one time because the Doc makes his product in small (five-gallon) batches. Open daily noon to 10:00 P.M. (Shorter hours in winter; call ahead.) Call (203) 792–4388. Note that this is a very tiny establishment, so don't plan on eating inside. (There's another Dr. Mike's at 44 Main Street at the junction of Routes 25 and 59 in Monroe; 203–452–0499.)

Readers of a certain age might have spent their teen years hanging out at drive-in restaurants where the uniformed carhops roller-skated out to your car and delivered the food on steel trays that clipped to the window! In Connecticut, we know of only one place that still has carhops. The **Sycamore,** 282 Greenwood Avenue, is an old-fashioned drive-in restaurant that has been a Bethel favorite since the 1940s. Carhop service is available spring, summer, and fall. Just pull in and flash your lights. It's not all atmosphere, either. The burgers are juicy and tasty. The brewed-there root beer (the recipe for which is a deep dark secret) can taste sweet and full or sparkly and dry, depending on its age. The malts are made with real malt powder. The egg creams are the best we've found in Connecticut, too. Prices are rock bottom. The Sycamore sponsors Cruise Nights throughout the summer, but you might see a vintage car pull in at any time (with Sunday often having a regular traffic in these vehicles). Open 6:30 A.M. to 6:30 P.M. Sunday through Wednesday and to 9:30 P.M. Thursday through Saturday. Call (203) 748–2716 for information.

# New Haven

New Haven's **Yale University** is one of those American treasures that can be measured only in terms of firsts, bests, and similar benchmarks. In 1861 it granted the first doctor of philosophy degree ever awarded in the United States. In 1869 its School of Fine Arts, the first in the country, opened its doors. Yale numbers among its graduates men of the caliber of Eli Whitney and Noah Webster, and since 1789 almost 10 percent of major U.S. diplomatic appointees have been Yale grads.

Yale boasts some of the best Gothic architecture in the country. Start at Phelps Gate on College Street. Beyond the gate is the Old Campus, ringed with Gothic buildings. Dwight Hall introduced Yale to Gothic architecture in 1842. Built as the college library for the then mind-boggling sum of $33,253, it was a strange marriage of spare New England Puritanism with Gothic overindulgence. It boasts thirty-two carved heads of man and beast mounted on turrets on its 90-foot tower. Over the next seventy years, other architects designed additional Gothic buildings for the Old Campus. Bingham and Vanderbilt Halls on Chapel Street and the bridge over High Street each has its own menagerie of mythological beasties.

Yale graduate James Gamble Rogers's 221-foot 1921-vintage Harkness Tower on High Street honors people and events associated with Yale history, including university founder Eli Yale and graduates Samuel F. B. Morse, Eli Whitney, John C. Calhoun, James Fenimore Cooper, Noah Webster, Nathan Hale, and eighteenth-century fire-and-brimstone preacher Jonathan Edwards. Higher on the tower are figures from ancient history, such as Phidias, Homer, Aristotle, and Euclid. Rogers also designed the Sterling Memorial Library, the Sterling Law complex, and the Hall of Graduate Studies. The library's decorative sculpture has a surprisingly whimsical theme, with its bookworm perched above the Wall Street entrance. The Law School is a veritable jungle of legal symbols, including Minerva and her owl. A feisty bulldog serves as the school mascot. Free student-guided tours of Yale are available through the Yale Visitor Information Office, 149 Elm Street. Call (203) 432–2302. Tours run Monday through Friday at 10:00 A.M. and 3:00 P.M. and on weekends at 1:30 P.M.

Yale University's ***Beinecke Rare Book and Manuscript Library,*** 121 Wall Street, is like no other building you've ever seen. To protect the fragile documents inside from sun damage, it was built without windows. Instead, the

Harkness Tower

exterior walls are made of wafer-thin marble slabs. When the sun shines, the building's interior has a cloudy amber glow. The library, which is open to the public, has five major collections. The permanent exhibit on the mezzanine features the Gutenberg Bible. Printed in about 1455 in Mainz, Germany, it is regarded as the first book printed from movable type in the Western world. Audubon's *Birds of America* is also on display. Open 8:30 A.M. to 8:00 P.M. Monday through Thursday, to 5:00 P.M. Friday, and 10:00 A.M. to 5:00 P.M. Saturday. Call (203) 432–2977.

## yaletrivia

The Yale Bowl, completed in 1914, was the first enclosed football stadium in the United States. And a nameless bunch of Elis gets the credit (and happy thanks from dogs everywhere) for inventing Frisbee by tossing empty pie tins from Mrs. Frisbie's bakery back and forth. Oh yes, and while it wasn't quite the Final Four, the first intercollegiate basketball game was played in New Haven in 1896.

They call it The Tomb and the name fits. If you walk down High Street between Chapel and Elm Streets in downtown New Haven, you will come across a spooky stone edifice with no windows and a padlocked front door. This is the headquarters of *Skull and Bones,* the infamous secret society at Yale University. Its alumni include George Herbert Walker Bush and his son George W. Bush plus a host of CIA agents and big-shot dignitaries. Skull and Bones had an unwanted national spotlight shined upon its Greco-Egyptian facade during the 2004 presidential campaign, which featured the eerie coincidence of two "Bonesmen" (Bush the younger and U.S. Sen. John Kerry) running against one another. Neither of them would discuss their membership in an elite group that supposedly practices secret rituals involving coffins. According to folklore, Geronimo's skull is inside the building. If you're contemplating trying to get inside, forget about it. Just walk on and wonder.

Yale is also home to several of America's finest museums. A showcase for British art and life, the *Yale Center for British Art,* at 1080 Chapel Street in New Haven, was built around the extensive collection of Paul Mellon, who spent forty years amassing works by a host of British artists. Mellon's holdings have been expanded since the center opened in 1977, and the building now houses the largest collection of British art outside of Great Britain. It also houses a 13,000-volume research library. Open 10:00 A.M. to 5:00 P.M. Tuesday through Saturday and noon to 5:00 P.M. Sunday. Call (203) 432–2800 or (203) 432–2850 or visit www.yale.edu/ycba.

On the opposite corner of Chapel and York Streets from the Yale Center for British Art, at 1111 Chapel Street, is the *Yale University Art Gallery.* Founded in 1832, this is the oldest university art gallery in the Western Hemisphere, and its collection spans eras, cultures, and art styles. Four floors cover everything from ancient to early modern art. There's also a sculpture garden, with works by Moore, Nevelson, and others, that makes an awfully nice setting in which to dream away a spring afternoon. Open 10:00 A.M. to 5:00 P.M. Tuesday through Saturday (until 8:00 P.M. on Thursday from September 15 to May 15) and 1:00 to 6:00 P.M. Sunday. Call (203) 432–0600 or log on to http://artgallery.yale.edu.

The **Yale Peabody Museum of Natural History** (170 Whitney Avenue, at the intersection of Whitney Avenue and Sachem Street) is the largest natural history museum in New England. Big deal, you say. Ah, but all children and those adults who are truly tuned in to kid kool know that "natural history" is just an adult euphemism for what it's really all about: dinos. The big guys. The all-time king bad butts of the natural kingdom. T-Rex, Raptor red, and their buddies.

The Peabody has the largest collection of mounted dinosaurs in the world, including a 67-foot brontosaurus. It also boasts the original *Age of Reptiles* mural by Pulitzer Prize–winner Rudolph Zallinger. Sure, it has been reproduced countless times in dino books from coast to coast. But it's the biggest mural of its kind in the world, and nothing beats the overwhelming experience of standing in front of the real thing.

The Yale Peabody is open 10:00 A.M. to 5:00 P.M. Monday through Saturday and noon to 5:00 P.M. Sunday and holidays. Admission. Call (203) 432–5050.

But there's much more to New Haven than Yale University. For starters, there's the crypt under **Center Church on the Green.** For tourists who are truly committed to getting off the beaten path, this attraction is hard to beat. It's not so much creepy as it is historic. These graves are believed to be unique to America. Nowhere else, historians

Dinosaurs at the Yale Peabody Museum of Natural History

say, was a church built over a colonial graveyard, a decision that helped protect the graves from the elements. The original graveyard dates back to the 1600s. Here lie the remains of up to 1,700 early New Haveners, including Benedict Arnold's first wife and the family of President Rutherford B. Hayes. Headstones and tomb "tables" abound in the cold subterranean expanse. The crypt's visiting hours are from April to November. For a tour appointment call (203) 787–0121. The tours are free, but donations are accepted to help preserve the crypt and its remarkable contents.

Famed as the birthplace of the hamburger, **Louis' Lunch** at 261–263 Crown Street in New Haven is open 11:00 A.M. to 4:00 P.M. Tuesday and Wednesday and noon to 2:00 A.M. Thursday through Saturday. It is closed Sunday and Monday and the month of August—to count spoons. The way locals tell it, proprietor Louis Lassen invented this now ubiquitous American dish in 1895. Having some scraps of steak that he wanted to use up, the frugal Lassen chopped them up fine and made patties, which he then broiled and served on toast. Among the first customers to whom he served his concoction, the story goes, were sailors from the port of Hamburg in Germany. When they asked for the name of the unknown item, Louis decided then and there to call it a "Hamburg."

This Old English pub–style cafe seats about twenty people. It serves burgers in much the same style as Louis' original: finely chopped meat patties on white toast, not buns. Ask for a cheeseburger, they'll glop on some Cheese Whiz. Onions? Absolutely. Ketchup? No way. Like the sign in the window says: THIS IS NOT BURGER KING. YOU GET IT MY WAY OR YOU DON'T GET THE DAMN THING AT ALL. Call (203) 562–5507.

Connecticut pizza lovers claim that **Pepe's Pizzeria Napoletana** (157 Wooster Street) in New Haven makes the best clam pizza in the Western world. There is some reason to accept that claim. Everything at Pepe's is prepared by hand on the premises. And Pepe's has never heard of a microwave. The splendiferous pies are baked in a coal-fired oven to emerge as flat crisp circles of dough with a firm chewy crust.

newhaventrivia

Famous New Haven inventions include the meat grinder, the corkscrew, and Isaac Strouse's misogynistic little torture device: the corset.

Pepe's special white clam pizza is topped with fresh littlenecks, olive oil, garlic, oregano, and Romano cheese. For other types of pies, if you want cheese, you have to ask for it; otherwise, you get a marvelous pie crust topped with tomato sauce. (If you can't handle the lines at Pepe's, try Sally's, at 237 Wooster Street. It rivals Pepe's in the quality of the pizza it serves.)

Pepe's is open 4:00 to 10:00 P.M. Monday, Wednesday, and Thursday, 11:30 A.M. to 11:00 P.M. Friday and Saturday, and 2:30 to 10:00 P.M. Sunday. Closed Tuesday. It doesn't matter when you're there; it's always crowded, and there's always a wait. No checks, credit cards, or reservations. Pepe's is closed during August. Call (203) 865–5762.

The ***Five-Mile Point Light,*** 1 Lighthouse Road in New Haven, was built in 1847. The 65-foot-high stone lighthouse was a functional light until it was taken out of service in 1877. Now it dominates Lighthouse Point Park. The park includes lots of nature trails and a bird sanctuary, but the main reason to visit is the 1916-vintage carousel. It's one of the biggest in America (52 feet in diameter) and holds seventy-two figures: sixty-nine horses, one camel, and two dragons (in our opinion, the only place to ride). The park is free; there's a small admission for the carousel. Carousel rides are available 11:00 A.M. to 6:00 P.M. Tuesday through Sunday from Memorial Day through Labor Day. Call (203) 946–8005.

## Arts in New Haven

New Haven likes to call itself the cultural capital of Connecticut, and it's a sobriquet that is well deserved. Besides the well-known museums mentioned elsewhere, the Elm City has nearly a dozen smaller museums and galleries, many nestled off the beaten path in residential neighborhoods and old factories. Below is a partial list. We recommend you check their Web sites for a sense of the kind of work each exhibits. Also, call ahead for hours of operation.

**Creative Arts Workshop**
80 Audubon Street;
(203) 562–4927.
www.creativeartsworkshop.org

**ArtSpace**
50 Orange Street;
(203) 772–2709.
www.artspacenh.org

**Small Space Gallery**
Arts Council of Greater New Haven
70 Audubon Street, Second floor;
(203) 772–2788.
www.artscouncil-newhaven.org

**Gallery 81**
81 Chestnut Street;
(203) 785–9130.
www.gallery81.com

**All Gallery**
319 Peck Street;
(203) 671–5175.
www.allgallery.org

**City Gallery**
994 State Street;
(203) 782–CITY (203–782–2489).
www.city-gallery.org

**John Slade Ely House**
51 Trumbull Street;
(203) 624–8055.
www.elyhouse.org

**White Space Gallery**
1020 Chapel Street;
(203) 495–1200.

New Haven is justifiably proud of its role in liberating the captives aboard the ship *Amistad*. In 1839 a group of Africans who had been kidnapped from their homes in Sierra Leone by slave traders mutinied and took over the ship. But they were seized by naval authorities and taken to New Haven for trial. After being imprisoned in a jail on the New Haven Green, where abolitionists took up their cause, the prisoners were acquitted, first in Connecticut courts and then by the U.S. Supreme Court. This amazing and courageous saga received wide attention when Steven Spielberg's movie *Amistad* was released in 1997. Three years later a reproduction of the *Amistad* was completed in Mystic and arrived at its home port of New Haven in July 2000. The storied ship is available for tours when it is docked at Long Wharf, alongside New Haven Harbor. But during many times of the year, it's on tour at other ports or in winter storage. Call Amistad America at (203) 495–1839 to find out if the *Amistad* is in port. You can always see the 11-foot bronze statue of the man who led the mutiny, Sengbe Pieh, outside New Haven's City Hall, opposite the green.

The **Shore Line Trolley Museum** at 17 River Street in East Haven can show off more than a hundred classic trolleys, including the world's oldest rapid transit car, the world's first electric freight locomotive, and a rare parlor car. There are also some interpretive displays, including hands-on exhibits and audio-video displays. We suspect, though, that most people will be drawn by the trolley rides. The museum offers 3-mile round-trip rides in vintage trolley cars on the nation's oldest operating suburban transportation line. Hard-core trolley freaks are also welcome to hang around the carbarn watching the restoration process. You can picnic on the grounds, and there's also a gift shop.

This attraction charges a fairly hefty admission, but group rates for parties of fifteen or more are available; parking is free. Trolleys run every thirty minutes, and the round-trip takes an hour. For most of the year, the museum opens at 10:30 A.M.; the last trolley leaves at 4:30 P.M. Charters are available in winter. Open Memorial Day through Labor Day daily. The rest of the year the schedule is more sporadic, so call ahead: (203) 467–6927.

**Fair Haven Woodworks** at 72 Blatchley Avenue in New Haven advertises itself as "where SoHo meets Vermont." Put another way, this woodworking shop and gallery offers sophisticated furniture and accessories characterized by fine workmanship. While most of the pieces, especially the settees, side chairs, and Morris chairs, obviously owe their inspiration to the Arts and Crafts movement, these are not slavish reproductions of old Gustav Stickley designs, but lighter, modern designs that are rooted in a shared tradition. Commissions are welcome, and you choose the type of wood, finishes, and fabrics.

In addition to its own furniture, the two-story gallery showcases the work of other furniture designers. The gallery also has a variety of Arts and Crafts–

style decorative items, including copperwork, kilim rugs and pillows, mica lamps, and stained glass. Open 10:00 A.M. to 6:00 P.M. Monday, Thursday, Friday, and noon to 4:00 P.M. Saturday and Sunday. Call (203) 776–3099 or (800) 404–4754 or log on to www.fairhavenwoodworks.com for more information.

When in the New Haven area, be sure to make a side trip north of the city to suburban Hamden. The town's *Eli Whitney Museum* (Whitney Avenue at Armory Street) includes displays tracing two centuries of industrial growth on the site plus various technology-oriented interactive hands-on exhibits. The museum is mainly devoted, however, to the achievements of Eli Whitney, one of the towering figures of the industrial revolution. Whitney was a local firearms manufacturer who pioneered the use of interchangeable parts. He also changed the course of American history by inventing the cotton gin, a device that became the foundation of the Southern plantation economy, spurred the spread of slavery, and contributed mightily to the political crisis that ended in America's Civil War. You'll find a waterfall, covered bridge, and walking trails behind the museum. Open noon to 5:00 P.M. Wednesday, Thursday, Friday, and Sunday and 10:00 A.M. to 3:00 P.M. Saturday, with shortened hours during the summer. Call (203) 777–1833 or (203) 777–0299 or visit www.eliwhitney.org.

Hamden also contains some great picnic spots, most of them located within the confines of *Sleeping Giant State Park* on Route 10. According to a legend that predates European settlement, the basalt mountain where the park is sited is actually an evil giant by the name of Hobbomock, who was put to sleep to prevent him from doing harm to local residents. When you approach it from the north, the chain of high, wooded hills that make up the park really does resemble a sleeping giant. Many of Sleeping Giant's eleven color-coded trails lead to gentle or moderate hikes, so even if you're out of shape you can still get in a good walk. All told, the park's 13,000-plus acres include more than 28 miles of trails, some with spectacular views.

For information write the Sleeping Giant Park Association, P.O. Box 14, Quinnipiac College, Hamden 06518. As with any hike, it's a good idea to check in with the ranger station. The telephone number of the ranger station on the mountain is (203) 789–7498.

Our vote for best ice-cream parlor in Connecticut goes to *Wentworth's* (3697 Whitney Avenue, Route 10) in Hamden. Located just down the road from Sleeping Giant State Park, Wentworth's occupies a clapboard house on your right as you're leaving Hamden. Wentworth's makes

## onlyinconnecticut

You probably know that Connecticut inventors invented the submarine and anesthesia, but did you know that the Nutmeg State was also where somebody invented the lollipop?

all of its own ice cream on-site. Incredibly dense and not too sweet, Wentworth's products seem to capture the essence of each of the dozens of flavors in its ever-changing repertoire. Almond Amaretto (one of many "adult" flavors that use real liquor) will win you over even if you don't care for sweet liqueurs. The best flavor of all, though, is the peach, a gift of ambrosia lovingly crafted from fresh tree-ripened fruit. For kids, there are silly flavors such as Cookie Monster, neon-blue vanilla with cookie bits.

Wentworth's is open daily, noon to 9:00 P.M. (until 10:00 P.M. in the summer). It usually closes for a few months during the winter. Call (203) 281–7429 for current hours and to find out when peach ice-cream season starts, which is usually in July.

Its extensive collection of rare books, maps, and prints aside, what we *really* like about **Whitlock Farm Booksellers** in Bethany (northwest of Hamden on Route 63) is that it's so quiet, isolated, and hard to find, but worth the search. The address is 20 Sperry Road, and it's a straight shot down that back road from Route 69 (the old Litchfield Turnpike), but, even knowing all that, it's easy to miss this place. If you're traveling south on Sperry, look to your left for two big red barns. If you find yourself on Dillon Road or back on the Litchfield Turnpike, you've gone too far. Don't worry about it. Just turn around and try the road from the other direction; once you've seen the lovely, pastoral countryside around Bethany, you won't mind seeing it some more.

Most of Whitlock's inventory of 50,000-plus books is packed into two rustic barns. The turkey barn serves as the main office and showroom for the more expensive items and is a bonanza for collectors of military history, philosophy, and Connecticut history. Less expensive books and more recent books

## Connecticut Haunts

West of the Shelton-Derby area is Monroe, which is home to what might be Connecticut's most famous ghost, the White Lady, who is said to haunt the Stepney Cemetery near Monroe and nearby Pepper Street. Visitors to the cemetery report that the apparition wears a white nightgown with a bonnet. Others say they've seen not only the **White Lady** but also shadowy specters who try to grab her. Ed Warren of Monroe, Connecticut's top ghostbuster, believes she is a Mrs. Knot, whose husband was murdered near Easton in the 1940s. It is believed Mrs. Knot met the same fate as her husband shortly after his unfortunate demise. The White Lady—or perhaps another lady in white—is also said to haunt the **Union Cemetery,** near the Easton Baptist Church on Route 59 in Easton. As with any cemetery, visit with respect and only during the cemetery's operating hours.

(including popular fiction, science fiction, magazines, and paperbacks) are housed in the sheep barn. Old maps and prints are available on the upper floor of the sheep barn. Open 9:00 A.M. to 5:00 P.M. Tuesday through Sunday. Call (203) 393–1240.

If you've never seen cider being made, stop in at **McConney's Farm,** 795 Roosevelt Drive in Derby (near Shelton), any time from mid-August to Christmas or during late March. After watching the pressing, you can sample the result. The farm also sells local apples, candy apples, and fresh home-baked apple crisp and apple pies; and the greenhouse is open during spring and summer. Open 9:00 A.M. to 6:00 P.M. daily. Call (203) 735–1133.

There's something about a sunflower that just makes us happy. If you agree, then don't miss taking a summer or fall drive to Ernie and Sabrina Santoro's **Sunflower Farms,** 767 Derby-Milford Road (off Route 34 or Route 121 or exit 56 from the Merritt Parkway) in Orange. The Santoros are the largest growers of ornamental sunflowers in Connecticut. Throughout the late summer and into the fall, their two-acre farm blazes with brilliant sunflowers in a surprising range of colors from the traditional golden yellow to cream and wine. It's not unusual to find painters and photographers mingling with garden lovers as everyone tries to take in the essence of summer in a flower. You can buy flowers potted or in bouquets. In May and early June, they'll sell you seedlings for your own sunflower garden. In the fall Sabrina paints pumpkins with great flair and creativity in traditional harvest and Halloween motifs and in some not-so-traditional motifs such as customers' pets and kids, crows, and Elvis and other famous personalities. Open during summer and fall, noon to 6:00 P.M. Monday through Friday and 10:00 A.M. to 6:00 P.M. on weekends. Call (203) 795–6829.

When intrepid OBPers Pat and Erasmus "Ray" J. Struglia recommended we visit **Rich Farm Ice Cream Shop,** 691 Oxford Road (Route 67) in Oxford, we hopped to it. We admire Dave Rich's philosophy of farming his land rather than selling it off for condos, and he churns up some really good ice cream, made from milk from his own herd of Holsteins. In summer the place is packed, and you might wait on line a good fifteen to twenty minutes. You won't be bored because this is a real farm with real farm looks and real farm smells. At haying time during the summer, just a whiff of the new-mown hay distills summer in a sniff. As for the ice cream, you can choose from among twenty-five flavors with seasonal favorites such as pumpkin and kid flavors like Cookie Monster. Or keep things simple and stick with a good old-fashioned chocolate cone. The ice-cream shop also makes ice-cream cakes and seasonal treats such as ice-cream Yule logs. Open daily April through October, noon to 10:00 P.M. and October to mid-December, noon to 5:00 P.M. Call (203) 881–1040.

Ed and Lorraine Warren of Monroe have been Connecticut's, maybe the country's, premier investigators of otherworldly occurrences for a very long time now. Their *Warren Occult Museum,* 30 Knollwood Street, is one spooky place, definitely not for the easily suggestible. The Warrens have investigated ghosts, spirits, and apparitions for years at such places as the U.S. Military Academy at West Point and Amityville, New York. Your tour starts only after Mr. Warren has provided each member of the tour with an aura of protection. The stories behind many of the displays are both truly terrifying and truly sad. Visitors are cautioned not to touch any of the artifacts as they still hold incredible evil. One display of local interest includes photos of Monroe's famed White Lady ghost; other displays include evil dolls and cursed chairs. Tours of the museum are by appointment only for groups of ten or more. The Warrens also host a Supernatural Halloween Program, which includes a dinner, guest speakers, and a special screening of a horror film. Their Halloween dinner seminar starts in the late afternoon and continues on through, what else, the witching hour. Call (203) 268–8235 for information about tours and special programs. Or visit www.warrens.net.

## South-central Connecticut

Way before there were golden arches on every street corner, the central Connecticut towns of Meriden and Middletown had developed a local specialty called the "steamed cheeseburger." Steaming the burgers makes them incredibly juicy and reduces the sharp Wisconsin cheddar to just the right degree of molten wonderfulness. Locals know to order theirs in the form of a "trilby" (a regional term for anything served up with mustard and onions). You do the same. Your best bet is probably *Ted's Restaurant* (1046 Broad Street in Meriden). Open 11:30 A.M. to 10:00 P.M. or so Monday through Saturday. Call ahead to check hours. Call (203) 237–6660.

At 487 North Brooksvale Road (Route 42), you'll find a restored section of the canal at *Lock 12 Historical Park.* In addition to the canal, the grounds contain a museum, a lockkeeper's house, a helicoidal bridge, and a picnic area. The park is open daily from March through November from 10:00 A.M. to dusk. The museum is open by appointment only except for limited Sunday hours in the fall. Call (203) 272–2743.

The *Farmington Canal Greenway* is a Connecticut attraction that is quite literally off the beaten path. It's also a marvelous example of recycling on a grand scale. In the early 1800s New Haven was a thriving port city. But there was a problem: The goods that arrived by boat couldn't be transported easily to the north. So in 1828 a canal, engineered by Eli Whitney and others, was built. It ran a total of 83 miles, from the harbor through Hamden, Cheshire, Plainville, and Farmington and up to Northampton, Massachusetts. The Farmington Canal became the economic lifeline of central Connecticut. But just twenty years later it was replaced by a railroad, which ran adjacent to the canal. The railroad operated until 1982, when floods washed out a portion of the line.

For years the railroad beds lay abandoned and neglected. At best, they became overgrown with grass and weeds. At worst, sections became eyesores, piling up with fast-food packaging, soda cans, old tires, and discarded shopping carts. But as the national rails-to-trails movement gained momentum, a grassroots effort emerged in southern Connecticut to restore this historic rail-canal corridor for recreational use. The result is a linear park for walkers, joggers, cyclists, and cross-country skiers that starts in southern Hamden and runs into Cheshire. The trail now stops near Hamden High School, off Dixwell Avenue, but municipal officials are confident it will run unbroken to downtown New Haven within a few years. Meanwhile, you can enjoy the path on a long, unbroken stretch northward through the rest of Hamden and into Cheshire. You can see the restored Lock 12 and the lockkeeper's house from the trail. It is wheelchair accessible, with entrances in Hamden at Cornwall

## It's A-MAZE-ing

Corn and hay mazes are rapidly becoming a fall tradition in Connecticut. It's a fun activity for the whole family. Since the mazes are located at farms or nurseries, you can combine your family's pumpkin-gathering expedition with a trip through a maze.

*Steck's Nursery* at 100 Putnam Park Road, Bethel, (203) 748–1385, creates a wonderful hay maze every fall. The maze is made completely of hay bales, and kids can crawl through hay tunnels, climb on top of hay pyramids, and work their way through the intricate maze. Free. Call for hours.

*Jones Family Farm* at 266 Israel Hill Road and Route 110 in Shelton, (203) 929–8425, is a fun-filled family farm throughout the year, but for us, the highlight is October's corn maze. After you're through tunneling through the maze, you can take a hayride, gather pumpkins from the pumpkin patch, or take home some cornstalks to make your own corn maze. In the summer you can pick strawberries and blueberries (starts in mid-June); winter brings a chance to cut your own Christmas tree, wend your way through the Christmas tree maze, and visit with Santa. You'll find berry picking and Christmas tree cutting at Valley Farm; the corn maze, pumpkin patch, and Christmas tree maze are located at Pumpkin Seed Farm. Both locations are just off Route 110. Open 8:00 A.M. to 8:00 P.M. Monday through Saturday, and 8:00 A.M. to noon Sunday. Hours change in the winter, so call ahead for information and directions.

Avenue, North Brooksvale Road, and Mount Sanford Road. Ample parking is available at each trail's entry point.

At **Roaring Brook Falls,** just off Roaring Brook Road (west of the junction of Route 70 and I–84), you'll find a wonderful hiking trail and overlook—the perfect place for a spring or fall picnic—and the foundation of an old mill to explore. But the draw here is Connecticut's second highest waterfalls, Roaring Brook Falls, an 80-foot main waterfall with smaller cascades above and below. Open from dawn to dusk. Call (203) 272–2689 for information.

Your kids might think that animation starts with the Simpsons and ends with SpongeBob, but a visit to the **Barker Character, Comic, and Cartoon Museum,** 1188 Highland Avenue (Route 10) in Cheshire, will set 'em straight. Herb Barker, the museum's guiding light, is a longtime collector of 'toon memorabilia, and he's packed a lot of history into his jewel-box museum. You'll find a lot of cartoon cells on view, but our favorite parts of the collection are the lunch boxes and pull toys featuring cartoon characters from our youth and the collection of McDonald's Happy Meals toys, once giveaways, now pricey collectibles. Animators and illustrators such as George Wildman of Popeye fame often visit the museum for talks and special events. The museum is open 11:00 A.M. to 5:00 P.M. Wednesday through Saturday. The animation art gallery is open 9:30 A.M. to 5:30 P.M. Monday to Saturday. Call (203) 272–2357 for information about special events.

**Brix Restaurant,** 1721 Highland Avenue in Cheshire, isn't a cute spelling for bricks; *brix* is a measurement of the sugar content of grapes that indicates how ripe the grapes were when harvested. Got that? Cool, pop quiz later. Jokes aside, Brix is a very unlikely restaurant for Connecticut; it feels like places we've visited in California's Napa Valley, but we're very glad it's located just a short hop down Route 10 from us.

Menu offerings are rotated seasonally, so what we enjoyed from the fall menu may not be around when you visit. Here's just a sampling of dishes we remember. Goat cheese has become something of a yuppie cliché, but it defies stereotypes in Brix's warm goat cheese over baby greens with a sweet beet vinaigrette. The pizza Popeye is a fusion of New Haven thin crispy crust and a California-designer pizza, strewn with fresh spinach, caramelized onions, black olives, and ricotta. On the dinner menu the perennial fave, rack of lamb, appears roasted perfectly with a wonderful side sauce of garlic and rosemary. The dessert list features some tried and true goodies like chocolate mousse. Prices are moderate for the quality of food and service. Open for lunch 11:30 A.M. to 2:00 P.M. Monday through Friday, dinner 5:30 to 9:30 P.M. Monday through Friday and 5:30 to 10:00 P.M. Saturday. Brix is a Cheshire hot spot, so reservations, especially on weekends, are advised. Call (203) 272–3584 for information and reservations.

*Sweet Claude's* at 828 South Main Street in Cheshire dishes up some of the best ice cream in the state in a rainbow of more than forty-five flavors. People on restricted diets can still spend quality time with their favorite treats because Fred Clason (the Claude behind the name) stocks sugar-free or lactose-free ice cream, tofutti, sorbets, yogurts, and Italian ice. We like their more adult (and higher butterfat) concoctions like the sublime bananas foster, a creamy banana ice cream with a praline taste. Kids tend to glom onto the special flavors like smurf (vibrantly red raspberry ice cream filled with marshmallows and stripes of equally vibrant blue). Open daily noon to 10:00 P.M. Shorter hours in winter; closed January and February. Call (203) 272–4237 for more information.

Ten miles or so northwest of Cheshire is the city of Waterbury. The brass industry moved into the city in the mid-1800s, and the Brass Capital of the World, as it was then known, was largely built on wealth derived from brass manufacturing. In the years since, the industry has moved elsewhere, but its architectural legacy remains. During the heyday of brass, Waterbury residents erected hundreds of rambling Victorian mansions and imposing public buildings. Entire neighborhoods of these buildings are preserved almost intact, and as part of an ongoing renaissance program, other neighborhoods have been restored to their former glory. As a result much of modern-day Waterbury is a living museum of nineteenth- and early twentieth-century architecture.

## waterbury trivia

Preserving food in tin cans was a good invention, but getting the food out of tins and into the mouth was, perhaps, a better one. So when in 1858 Ezra J. Warner of Waterbury found a way to quickly open tins, tummies all across American thanked him. Unfortunately, his invention looked more like something from a slasher movie than the latest housewife's helper. You stuck a rather intimidatingly big, curved blade into the tin and rammed it around. Since the opener tended to open the user as well as the tin, about ten years later, someone else invented the less dangerous cutting-wheel can opener.

In 1790 the Grilley brothers of Waterbury made Connecticut's first buttons.

Timekeeping pretty much put the Waterbury area on the map. In the 1850s Waterbury Clock and Waterbury Watch made clocks and watches inexpensively, which made giving the gift of a timepiece (once prized and expensive) possible for everyone. Around 1900 watchmaker Robert Ingersoll partnered with Waterbury Watch to make the popular $1.00 Yankee watch. In just two short decades, almost 40 million Yankees were sold. You can see the history of timekeeping and watch the industrial progress of this part of the Nutmeg State at the *Timexpo Museum,* 175 Union Street, Brass Mill Commons (exit 22 off I–84). The museum traces the history of timekeeping with an emphasis on the Waterbury-based Timex Corporation. You'll see about 150 years' worth of clocks and watches as well as those famous John Cameron Swayze commercials of our youth ("takes a licking and keeps on ticking"). Interactive displays and games keep kids interested and occupied. Perhaps the strangest part of the museum is a 40-foot replica of an Easter Island statue and an interactive display that challenges visitors to guess where the inhabitants of Easter Island came from. We're not sure what it has to do with watchmaking, but it's way cool. Admission; reduced admission for kids and seniors. Open 10:00 A.M. to 5:00 P.M. Tuesday through Saturday and noon until 5:00 P.M. Sunday. Visit the museum on the Web at www.timexpo.com. For details call (203) 755–8463 or (800) 225–7742.

If you're interested in architecture, you'll want to visit the *Hillside Historic District,* once home to Waterbury's captains of industry. Now carried on the National Register of Historic Places, the district includes 310 structures dating from the nineteenth and early twentieth centuries. The center of Waterbury's restoration program, however, is the tree-lined city green, one of the most beautiful greens in any northeastern city. Within a few blocks of the green, you'll find scores of lovingly restored structures. Among the more interesting are a marvelously misplaced railroad station modeled on the Palazzo Pubblico in Siena, Italy. There are also five municipal buildings designed by prominent American architect Cass Gilbert.

The modernized and expanded Masonic Hall, at 144 West Main Street on the northwest corner of the green, houses Waterbury's *Mattatuck Museum.* This establishment is an oddly satisfying combination of industrial museum and art gallery. The gallery portion includes items spanning three centuries and is devoted to the works of American masters who have an association with Connecticut. The museum portion contains displays of household items and furnishings dating from 1713 to 1940 as well as exhibits dealing with local history, especially the history of the region's industrial development. Its holdings include collections of nineteenth-century furniture, novelty clocks and watches, early cameras, and art deco tableware. The most curious item is Charles Goodyear's rubber desk. The museum is open 10:00 A.M. to 5:00 P.M. Tuesday through Saturday. Except during July and August, it is also open noon to 5:00 P.M. Sunday. There is a gift shop and cafe on-site. Call (203) 753–0381.

Wandering the halls of the Mattatuck or pounding the pavement on an architectural tour can burn a lot of calories, and Waterbury has some great eateries where you can replenish them. A large Italian population means that some of the best of these serve Italian cuisine. Two area restaurants that are

## The Holy Land in Miniature

Folks who travel through this part of Connecticut are apt to ask about the cross they can see from Interstate 84 in Waterbury. Some locals don't have a clue. Others know that the cross is what remains of Waterbury's Holy Land, an early version of a religious theme park. As you travel west on the interstate (exit 22) toward Waterbury, the cross is the most visible part of Holy Land, a model in miniature of Jerusalem and Bethlehem. Once upon a time, Holy Land was such a flourishing attraction that busloads of the faithful trekked to Waterbury from all over the East Coast to see the biblical scenes rendered in miniature and other attractions. Holy Land's been closed for many years now, and time, the weather, and vandalism have pretty much reduced the park to rubble. There don't seem to be any objections to visitors, at their own risk, wandering through the once-flourishing attraction. If you're of a mind to learn more, the Waterbury Public Library keeps an extensive file on Holy Land.

particularly well thought of are *Bacco's* at 1230 Thomaston Avenue, (203) 755–1173, and *Faces* at 702 Highland Avenue, (203) 753–1181.

When you drive past the Waterbury Green, slow down long enough to take a gander at the massive statue of a lively prancing horse. Knight the horse was owned by Waterbury heiress Caroline Welton, who lived in Rose Hill, one of Waterbury's most lavish mansions. Welton was an animal rights activist before her 1885 death in a mountain climbing accident. When originally installed in 1888, the statue included a horse trough at its front and two troughs at its back for dogs and cats. It's such a popular landmark in Waterbury that residents frequently make dates to "meet at the horse."

Souvenir hunters should check out what used to be the Howland-Hughes Department Store (120 Bank Street), a downtown stalwart built in 1890 and renowned throughout the state as the oldest free standing department store in Connecticut. Recent redevelopment under new ownership has transformed this landmark into the *Connecticut Store,* well named because the management focuses on inventory that consists exclusively of made-in-Connecticut merchandise. So here's your chance to browse for Woodbury pewter, wristwatches and buttons produced right here in Waterbury, Bovano enamelware from Cheshire, Liberty candles from Bolton, Allyn neckwear from Stamford, and Lego building blocks from Enfield—plus made-in-Shelton Wiffle balls, made-in-Orange Pez candy dispensers, and made-in-Norwich Thermos bottles. Also in stock: clothing, housewares, games, puzzles, and wood carvings. This one-of-a-kind place has weathervanes, too, custom-crafted in Meriden. The store is open 9:30 A.M. to 5:00 P.M. Tuesday through Saturday. Call (800) 474–6728 for more information, or visit www.ctstore.com.

You'd expect to find great barbecue at a Texas ranch or a Louisiana church social, but in a northern industrial city? *Uncle Willie's,* 1101 Huntington Avenue, Waterbury, serves up huge slabs of pork, smoky, meltingly tender, and savory with a variety of barbecue sauces, including Wichita Falls hot and Memphis classic sweet. If you aren't in the mood for ribs, try any of the other stellar barbecue offerings: pulled pork and beef brisket. Besides barbecue, you'll find other down-home cooking—fried okra (probably an acquired taste for most Yankees) and collards. Side dishes include good, creamy coleslaw; cornbread; and smashed potatoes, both plain and sparked up with a dash of jalapeño peppers. For dessert go traditional—try the sweet potato pie or the peach cobbler. Open 11:00 A.M. to 8:00 P.M. Monday through Saturday and noon to 7:00 P.M. Sunday. Call (203) 596–7677 for more information.

## Places to Stay in Gateway to New England

**The Homestead Inn,**
420 Field Point Road,
Greenwich;
(203) 869–7500.
Try dinner or a getaway weekend.
Very expensive.

**House on the Hill B&B,**
92 Woodlawn Terrace,
Waterbury;
(203) 757–9901.
Victorian atmosphere and period ornamentation.
Moderate to high.

**Three Chimneys Inn,**
1201 Chapel Street,
New Haven;
(203) 789–1201.
Stately 1870 Victorian landmark.
Expensive.

## Places to Eat in Gateway to New England

**Blackrock Castle,**
2895 Fairfield Avenue,
Bridgeport;
(203) 336–3990.
Cooking with an Irish flair.
Moderate.

**Claire's Corner Copia,**
1000 Chapel Street,
New Haven;
(203) 562–3888.
Vegetarian restaurant.
Moderate.

**King's,**
Route 25
(271 South Main Street),
Newtown;
(203) 426–6881.
For breakfast or brunch.
Inexpensive.

**Long Ridge Tavern,**
2653 Long Ridge Road,
Stamford;
(203) 329–7818.
New American cuisine.
Moderate to expensive.

**Marjolaine,**
961 State Street,
New Haven;
(203) 789–8589.
A bakery and coffeehouse.
Inexpensive.

**Whistle Stop Muffin Co.,**
20 Portland Avenue,
Ridgefield;
(203) 544–8139.
Inexpensive.

# Coast and Country

Connecticut has 253 miles of shoreline, all of it bordering Long Island Sound. This coastline was settled shortly after the first towns were built in the Connecticut River Valley. Today the southwestern portion of the state's coastal plain has been largely urbanized, while much of the eastern portion has been given over to tourism. It is the less densely populated portion of this coastline (between New Haven and Rhode Island) that most people envision as the Connecticut shore. Home to fried-clam shacks and posh inns, popular sandy beaches and lonely old lighthouses, modern submarines and ancient whalers, river-boats and coastal mail packets, the Connecticut shore reflects the romance of the sea like few other places on earth.

Even if you're not a big fan of the sea, this part of Connecticut has much to offer. The inland portion of the coastal plain and the lower reaches of the Thames and Connecticut Rivers, in fact all of New London and Middlesex Counties and the easternmost part of New Haven County, are all part of what we call the Shore. Here you'll find attractions as disparate as Stonington's Old Lighthouse Museum and a classic diner in Middletown, the glorious wedding-cake architecture of the Goodspeed Opera House and the Gothic extravagance of

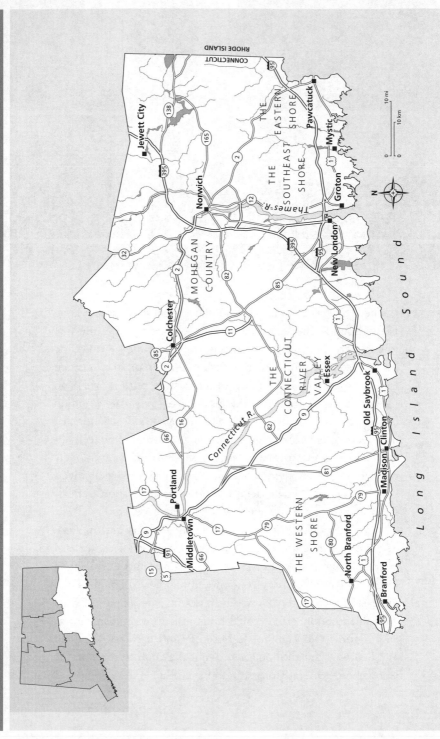

Gillette Castle, or the famous hunt breakfasts at the Griswold Inn and the renowned chili dogs and shakes at Higgies in Higganum.

# The Western Shore

According to legend, Captain William Kidd was a black-hearted pirate and bloody-handed murderer who savagely preyed upon America's eastern coast. Well, not exactly. As a matter of public record, the real Captain Kidd was a Scottish-born merchant transplanted to America, who was commissioned in 1695 to hunt down the pirate Thomas Tew (of Newport) in the Indian Ocean. While pursuing Tew, Kidd stretched the limits of his commission, which embarrassed his prominent British backers (including the Crown). When he returned home, Kidd was seized and, after a rigged trial in which evidence of his innocence was suppressed, convicted of murder and piracy and hanged in 1701.

Whether your view of Captain Kidd leans toward the mythical or the historical, it's hard to resist the tantalizing legends of pirate gold and buried treasure. Many of these tales are linked to the state's Thimble Islands, just off the coast from Branford's Stony Creek, and local residents nurture the Kidd mythology. The residents of High Island, for example, refer to their home as Kidd's Island and enhance its piratical flavor by flying the skull and crossbones and painting their cottages black. And on Money Island, where Kidd is widely supposed to have buried some of his treasure in a cave, shovels and spades get a good workout every summer as people try to locate the buried booty.

The *Thimble Islands* were discovered in 1614 by Adrien Block and have been used for everything from farming to quarrying granite. Today, many of the islands play host to wealthy out-of-towners who have built opulent vacation homes on them. You can tour the islands on one of two boats that leave from the Stony Creek Dock on Indian Point Road (203–488–8905). The boats cruise the islands, delivering mail and supplies to island residents while the captains supply a lively running commentary about the area, past and present. Bird-watching cruises are also offered. Seal cruises began about fifteen years

## AUTHORS' FAVORITES

| | |
|---|---|
| Gillette Castle | O'Rourke's Diner |
| Goodspeed Opera House | Thimble Islands |
| Mashantucket Pequot Museum and Research Center | |

ago, when several varieties of migrating seals used the Branford shoreline as one of their resting places. The cruise schedule varies, depending on the seals'

migrating paths, but they usually run from December through mid-April. As many as forty seals—harbor, harp, hooded, and gray seals—have been spotted on the popular two-hour excursions. The regular island cruises start in mid-May. Call the *Volsunga IV* with Captain Bob (203–483–6659) or the *Sea Mist II* with Captain Mike (203–488–8905) for exact schedules. Or go to their Web sites. Captain Bob's is www.thimbleislands.com; Captain Mike's is www.seamistcruises.com.

One note: All the islands are privately held. Unless you're an invited guest, don't plan on getting off the boat to explore; uninvited guests are understandably not welcome.

If you're hungry for seafood after your cruise, try **Lenny's Indian Head Inn**, 205 South Montowese Street in Branford; (203) 488–1500. Lenny's offers lobsters fresh off the boat and fish and seafood so fresh it practically swims into the kitchen. It's a comfortable place with wooden booths and customers from all walks of life, from Creekers to tourists, looking for a real New England seafood place. Open for lunch and dinner, Tuesday through Saturday.

**The Stony Creek Market,** 178 Thimble Islands Road, is another local hangout. It's good for lunch or for picking up sandwiches and salads for an impromptu picnic. Open Tuesday through Sunday for breakfast and lunch. Call (203) 488–0145.

You can tell a lot about a town by its library, one reason why Branford is a special place. Not only is the **James Blackstone Memorial Library,** 758 Main Street, in downtown Branford breathtaking in design and decor, it's been lovingly restored, reflecting the justifiable pride town residents take in this unique building. A trip to the library may be a tough sell to vacationing kids, but it's definitely worth the trouble.

The Blackstone Library was built in 1896 at a cost of $300,000. The centerpiece is the octagonal rotunda, paved with a marble and mosaic floor. The

50-foot dome is decorated with large murals that provide a pictorial history of bookmaking, from *Gathering the Papyrus* to *The First Proof of the Gutenberg Bible*. The paintings are illuminated by an ornamental skylight that forms the eye of the dome. Medallion portraits of famous American authors, including Emerson, Hawthorne, Longfellow, Whittier, and Stowe, also adorn the room. The whole building is studded with elegant period detail, including wide marble staircases leading to the second floor and a large, inviting fireplace in the main reading room. Open 9:00 A.M. to 8:00 P.M. Monday through Thursday and to 5:00 P.M. Friday and Saturday. Call (203) 488–1441.

Across the street from the library is a spot that might be an easier sell for the kids. It's also a good place to go if you're looking for a souvenir and don't want to buy yet another mug or refrigerator magnet. **The Rock Garden** sells fossils, polished rocks, and other geological curiosities. They have many kits and arts and crafts projects. Kids can design their own Connecticut Shore memento, choosing from a wide assortment of beads and charms for stringing. The Rock Garden also sells all the equipment you need to create a custom-made necklace, bracelet, key chain, bookmark, or backpack

branfordtrivia

Salt produced in Branford was used to preserve meat for the Revolutionary army.

The hospice movement in America began in Branford in 1974.

fob, and the helpful staff is happy to offer advice and instruction. *NOTE:* They have a resident cat who sprawls out on the display cases pretending to sleep while watching customers' every move. Open 11:00 A.M. to 7:00 P.M. Monday through Friday and 10:00 A.M. to 6:00 P.M. Saturday. Call (203) 488–6699.

Are Connecticut residents hungrier than residents of other states, or are they just more food conscious? Scientific evidence is lacking, but anecdotal experience indicates that people in this state like to talk food a lot, and whenever they do, the talk quickly turns to pizza. Who makes the best crust? Best sauce? Most generous topping? The winner of the debate is often Branford's own **Born in America Restaurant and Pizza Kitchen,** a tiny, unassuming pizza place, tucked away into a pretty ordinary strip mall, Brushy Hill Plaza, 4 Brushy Plain Road. The eatery is divided into two parts: One half serves takeout, and the other half is a small sit-down restaurant. Chef Darrell Janis won the gold in the 1997 Pizza Olympics in Las Vegas. His creations range from the Full House pizza (white sauce, duck, portobello mushrooms, and spicy chorizo sausage topped with smoked gouda, mozzarella, roasted garlic, tomatoes, and scallions) to a few veggies, sweet and flavorful red sauce, and just a tad of mozzarella on the chewy and tender crust. Born in America also offers appetizers, salads, grinders, and daily specials. Open from 4:30 to 10:00

P.M Sunday, Tuesday, and Wednesday; 11:30 A.M. to 10:00 P.M. Thursday; and 11:30 A.M. to 11:00 P.M. Friday and Saturday. Closed for most major holidays. Operating hours seem to be somewhat sporadic, so call ahead before you visit: (203) 483–0211.

In Guilford, *Fair Street,* from the Boston Post Road (U.S. Highway 1, but called Route 1) to the green, offers a nice walk. It's less than a city block long, but in that short distance, you'll see a converted foundry and a former one-room schoolhouse, and homes representing a variety of architectural styles.

If sidewalks aren't your thing, Guilford has many scenic foot trails. The *Anne Conover Nature Education Trail* sits amid 235 acres of tidal wetlands that form the heart of the Guilford Salt Meadows Sanctuary. The 1-mile walking trail is a family-friendly outing and popular bird-watching location. Many educational displays are located along the trail, and guides are available at the trail kiosk. The WestWoods Trail System is the largest recreational area for hiking in Guilford. It contains 39 miles of trails featuring cave structures, waterfalls, salt marshes, and an inland tidal lake. For more information go to www.audubon.org. Parking is available.

Although the addition of upscale restaurants and trendy clothing stores has somewhat lessened the homey appeal of downtown Guilford, it's still a charming place to spend a lazy afternoon. The presence of a bygone-era bookstore and hardware store on the green has blunted the impact of gentrification, and the side streets off the green are studded with any number of interesting places well worth a leisurely poke.

North on Church Street at 411 is the *Guilford Art Center,* a small school of arts and crafts with a gallery that does about ten shows per year, and a shop that is open year-round. Open 10:00 A.M. to 5:00 P.M. Monday through Saturday, until 7:00 P.M. Thursday evenings, noon to 4:00 P.M. Sunday. Call (203) 453–5947.

On Whitfield Street, you'll find the *Henry Whitfield State Museum.* Built in 1639 as a combination minister's home, stronghold, and meeting hall, the Henry Whitfield House is reputedly the oldest stone house in New England. Today it's a showcase for seventeenth- and eighteenth-century antique furnishings. There's also a pretty fair herb garden on the grounds. Open 10:00 A.M. to 4:30 P.M. Wednesday through Sunday. Admission. Call (203) 453–2457.

If you like old houses or antique furnishings, there are also two other houses worth looking at in Guilford. Both are on Boston Street. The 1660-vintage *Hyland House* (number 84) is a classic colonial saltbox noted for its unusual woodwork and for no less than three walk-in fireplaces. The 1774-vintage *Thomas Griswold House* (number 171) is another saltbox that has been

Henry Whitfield State Museum in Guilford

turned into a museum of local history. In addition to the usual collection of furnishings, this house has some period costumes and a restored blacksmith shop. The Hyland House is open June through September, 10:00 A.M. to 4:30 P.M. Tuesday through Saturday and noon to 4:30 P.M. Sunday. The Griswold House is open 11:00 A.M. to 4:00 P.M. Tuesday through Sunday, as well as by appointment. Both charge a small admission. Call (203) 453–9477 for information on the Hyland House and (203) 453–3176 or (203) 453–3176 for information on the Thomas Griswold House.

For a beautiful water view, follow Whitfield Street south from the green to Guilford Harbor. You'll find some thoughtfully placed comfortable benches, just right for sitting a spell. If you're of a mind to see some more beautiful scenery, follow Mulberry Point Road (off Route 146) to its end. You can't park at the point, but you can see Faulkner Point Lighthouse off in the distance.

When you stand on the Guilford shore and gaze out at the beacon of Faulkner's Lighthouse, be grateful. If it weren't for the determination of the Faulkner's Light Brigade, you might not see anything but a slim strip of land. In the early 1990s, this historic lighthouse, located 3 miles off the Connecticut coast in Guilford, seemed doomed. A series of storms had worn away the island on which it stood. The structure was on the brink of toppling into the sea. But a coalition of local volunteers lobbied their legislators, and eventually Congress allocated more than $4 million to stabilize the island and save the lighthouse.

Faulkner's Lighthouse was built in 1802. In 1976 the keeper's house was destroyed by fire. The Coast Guard replaced the valuable Fresnel lens in the tower with a modern plastic optic and the lighthouse became automated. While that move toward modernity may have cost the lighthouse some of its romance, you can still see the old light faithfully announcing its presence from many parts of Guilford and adjoining towns, as well as on vessels navigating Long Island Sound.

The island is a refuge for the rare roseate and common terns who end their long flight from winter homes in South America and the Caribbean to nest and breed there. This means that Faulkner's is off-limits to the public, except for occasional "open houses" coordinated by the brigade. Even on those occasions, you need a small boat to get there.

*The Place* (901 Boston Post Road; Route 1) in Guilford has been serving excellent grilled food in the rough to legions of satisfied customers for the past twenty summers. If you've not been there, do stop by for the grilled seafood (or whatever). Steaks, chicken, clams, corn on the cob, lobster—they all get grilled over the same 18-foot firepit. Seating is outdoors at tables made from discarded telephone-wire spools, and the sound system is a boom box. For foul weather days, there's a tent. The owners invite you to "make your own dining statement" by augmenting all that good grilled stuff with your own alcoholic beverages, tablecloths, flowers, candles, or other embellishments; there are a couple of package stores close by. Open seasonally from May until about Columbus Day weekend. Open 5:00 to 11:00 P.M. Monday through Thursday, 5:00 to midnight Friday, noon to midnight Saturday, and noon to 10:00 P.M. Sunday. Call (203) 453–9276.

Something to ponder: Just when did ice cream become a gourmet dessert, with accompanying high prices to prove it? While mulling that over, forget such trendiness by capping off your seafood barbecue with a few scoops of the cold stuff at *Ashley's Ice Cream Cafe.* They've got all the flavors and toppings you've come to expect from a place that's raised ice-cream production to an art form, plus a few surprises. Ashley's is located just across the road from The Place, at 942 Boston Post Road (Route 1). Hours are 11:00 A.M. to 10:00 P.M.

guilford**trivia**

Guilford has the largest town green in New England.

While looking for something lost, have you ever muttered, "Now where in the Sam Hill is it?" And did you ever wonder who Sam Hill was? Well, he was a real guy, who lived in Guilford (1678–1752). Old Sam was the town clerk for thirty-five years, judge of the probate court for twelve years, and deputy to the general court for at least twenty-two sessions. He ran for so many offices that people used to say "running like Sam Hill" when they meant someone was persistent. Poor Sam's name—which had become known throughout the country and which sounds so much like the common name for the nether regions—eventually lost that connotation and became a polite euphemism for "hell."

Sunday through Thursday, 11:00 A.M. to 11:00 P.M. Friday and Saturday. During the summer Ashley's is open to 11:00 P.M. every night. Call (203) 458–3040.

Cider fanciers, don't leave the Guilford area without stopping at **Bishop's Orchards Farm Market** at 1355 Boston Post Road (Route 1). Started in 1910 as a produce stand, Bishop's has grown to a sizable cider mill and pick-your-own/cut-your-own farm with sidelines in Vermont cheeses, local honey and eggs, and fresh herbs. The cider mill makes splendid apple cider, but try the pear cider, too. It's a little thicker than apple cider and maybe a little sweeter, but the fresh pear taste is quite unusual and invigorating. Open 8:00 A.M. to 6:00 P.M. Monday through Saturday and 9:00 A.M. to 6:00 P.M. Sunday. Call (203) 453–2338 or log on to www.bishopsorchards.com.

The 1785 **Allis-Bushnell House & Museum** at 853 Boston Post Road in neighboring Madison is noted for the unusual corner fireplaces and original paneling that grace its period rooms. It's now home to the Madison Historical Society, which maintains collections of toys, dolls, costumes, kitchenware, and china. Modest admission. Open May through October 1:00 to 4:00 P.M. on Wednesday, Friday, and Saturday. Open other times by appointment. Call (203) 245–4567.

Another historic home in Madison comes complete with a family ghost. The 1685 **Deacon John Grave House at Tunxis Farm,** 581 Boston Post Road, was owned and occupied for 300 years by the descendants of Deacon John Grave. Open mid-June through Labor Day, 1:00 to 4:00 P.M. Wednesday through Saturday, and Labor Day through Columbus Day, 10:00 A.M. to 4:00 P.M. on Saturday and Sunday. For more information call (203) 245–4798.

Madison is also home to the **Meigs Point Nature Center,** located in **Hammonasset Beach State Park,** the largest of Connecticut's shoreline parks. Be forewarned: The beach is overrun with visitors in summer, making for heavy traffic and other hassles. Another option is to visit during the off-season when the park is much less crowded but no less enticing. The Meigs Point Nature Center gives visitors an introduction to the sealife found in Long Island Sound, including horseshoe crabs, lobsters, and a variety of fish. It also has some reptiles found in Connecticut, as well as some mounted animals, including a deer and a black bear. A calendar of family and children's activities is offered. Nature walks are held at 9:30 A.M. Tuesday through Saturday. Call (203) 245–8743. Open Memorial Day through Labor Day, 10:00 A.M. to 5:00 P.M.

A good place to stop to rest weary feet in Madison and catch up on the latest doings of the Royals is **Front Parlour at The British Shoppe,** 45 Wall Street, an English outpost in a 1690s colonial home, not far from the late twentieth-century sprawl that's the Boston Post Road. John and Barbara Jago-Ford from Devon, England, sell British teas and other comestibles at the British

Shoppe. The tearoom, located in the front of the house, is called the Front Parlour. The decor of the tea shop blends a certain rough-hewn colonial character with English Victorian charm. Tables are layered with dainty embroidered cloths, and your tea is served on flower-sprigged china, accompanied by whimsical butter spreaders and a host of spoons. Photographs of the royal family adorn the walls as does a letter acknowledging the Jago-Fords' sympathy on the death of Princes Diana. By the way, the Jago-Fords are happy to share their opinions on the Royals—just don't ask about Fergie unless you want a real earful! For your tea, you can have scones and cream, crumpets, or tea sandwiches, wispy little wafers with savory fillings, and desserts, including a lovely lemony cake. The tea is, as they say, strong enough to trot a mouse on. Robust lunches with offerings such as Cornish pasties or steak and kidney pie are also served. The shop is open 10:00 A.M. to 5:00 P.M. Tuesday through Saturday. The tearoom is open 11:30 A.M. to 4:00 P.M. Call (203) 245–4521 or (800) 842–6674 or visit www.thebritishshoppe.com for more information.

Take exit 63 off Interstate 95 to find a hidden jewel called **Chamard Vineyards,** 115 Cow Hill Road in Clinton. This operation certainly looks like a famous French winery, complete with an elegant tasting room and vine-wreathed entrance. But how good can the wine really be? As it turns out, really quite good. This is an artistic operation that focuses on a small but excellent line. The specialty is chardonnay, and in 1991, Chamard's chardonnay came in second to a much pricier French wine in a taste test conducted by *Cooks Illustrated*. The winery also produces good reds, including a merlot. Open for tours and tastings year-round, 11:00 A.M. to 4:00 P.M. Wednesday through Saturday. Call (860) 664–0299 or log on to www.chamard.com.

Chamard Vineyards, Clinton

## Sweet Treats

If you're looking for an interesting souvenir for the folks back home that won't break your budget—or if you just want a taste of Connecticut history—check out gourmet, candy, and souvenir shops throughout the state for these two regional sweet treats: Chocolate Lace candy and Rock Candy Mountain.

Chocolate Lace got its start in czarist Russia at the turn of the twentieth century, when a woman named Eugenia Tay made a magical candy that required a snowstorm. Her technique was to boil sugar and drizzle the hot syrup on the fresh snow, thus making delicate lacy patterns of caramelized sugar. When the substance hardened (almost immediately), the pieces of "lace" were brought indoors and dipped in chocolate. Hence the name Chocolate Lace.

When the Tay family fled Russia in 1917, they first settled in New York, where Eugenia Tay went into the candy business. Initially she used cold marble as a drizzling surface. Eventually, a machine, affectionately dubbed "Veronica Lace," was developed to automate the process of creating the lacy patterns. For around $9.00 for a seven-ounce box, you can present your nearest and dearest with a treat worthy of a Russian czar.

Everything old is new again. *Dryden & Palmer* makes old-fashioned rock candy. This treat is a revelation to many modern kids, but Dryden & Palmer has been turning it out since 1880. In addition to crystal-clear nuggets of rock candy, the company also manufactures rock candy swizzle sticks in bright jewel-tones and a variety of flavors. Great in fancy cocktails, the rock candy swizzle sticks never fail to charm young or old as stirrers for hot or iced tea or hot chocolate. A swizzle stick costs about 40 cents. Available in candy shops around Connecticut.

# The Connecticut River Valley

When the six men who formed the Company of Military Historians got together to do so in 1949, it is doubtful that any of them realized that one day it would be the largest international organization of military historians in the world. The organization has its offices in the *Military Historians Headquarters & Museum* in the old post office building on North Main Street in Westbrook. Here the organization has assembled the largest collection of American military uniforms and insignia in the country. Also on display is a collection of restored twentieth-century military vehicles, all in operating condition, ranging from the World War II–era M-29 Weasel to a Jeep from the Vietnam era. There's also a research library and a music room containing a display of bandsmen's uniforms and a collection of thousands of recordings of military music, which can be borrowed or copied. The hours of operation are sporadic, so it's best to call ahead: (860) 399–9460.

Crowded and touristy, **Lenny and Joe's Fish Tale Restaurant** (86 Boston Post Road in Westbrook) still has the best fried clams around, and the servings are huge. If you've never eaten whole-belly clams, this is a good place to start; but, be forewarned, you'll never again be satisfied with those sad little strips with which the rest of America gets stuck. Lenny and Joe's also has good lobster rolls, fresh coleslaw, and grand onion rings and fried zucchini. In the spring you can get a Connecticut River shad dinner. Be prepared to wait, though. Most days, there's a line. Open daily, 11:00 A.M. to 10:00 P.M. (until 11:00 P.M. on Friday and Saturday). Call (860) 669–0767. There's a second restaurant at 1301 Post Road in Madison. Call (203) 245–7289.

For a classic shoreline dining experience, visit **Edd's Place,** 478 Boston Post Road, Westbrook. Edd's offers paper-plate dining in an enclosed patio or an open courtyard overlooking a picturesque salt marsh. The atmosphere is shorts-and-sandals casual, with customers placing their orders at the counter inside what looks like a small barn. Edd's large and varied menu changes daily, but lobster rolls are the specialty of the house. They also serve grilled salmon, fresh local fish in season, crab cakes, clam chowder, lobster bisque, and an array of homemade pies, puddings, cakes, and cheesecakes. Edd's, which is listed in Zagat's, was named "best new restaurant" in 2002 by *Connecticut* magazine and was a winner in the shoreline's 2003 readers' poll. Customers are encouraged to bring their own beer and wine, and fishermen can bring their cleaned and filleted catch to be prepared by the pros. For $7.95, Edd's will cook their fish broiled, blackened, or teriyaki, served with potato and tossed salad. Open 9:00 A.M. to 8:00 P.M. Monday through Saturday, 9:00 A.M. to 6:00 P.M. Sunday. Call (860) 399–9498.

With one of the best anchorages on the Connecticut River, Essex has always had intimate ties with the river. The main street of Essex is called Main Street, and it still looks very much like its eighteenth-century counterpart. Clapboard houses, fan-shaped windows, and fences abound, and in the shops that line the street, pricey purveyors of antiques, clothing, and gifts ply their trade to tourists from around the world.

There used to be two shipyards in the town, and from 1754 there was a West Indies warehouse next to the town dock, where goods from Africa and the Indies were unloaded for redistribution across the state. It was next to that warehouse at the Hayden Shipyards that America built its first warship, *Oliver Cromwell,* in 1776.

It is therefore fitting that the Connecticut River Foundation's **Connecticut River Museum** is located at Steamboat Dock, 67 Main Street in Essex. The museum chronicles the history of Connecticut by tracing the evolution of the Connecticut River and of steam power. Among the exhibits is a gorgeous scale model of the Victorian pleasure ship, *City of Hartford,* which sank in the Connecticut River on March 29, 1876, after striking and carrying away the Middletown railroad bridge. A full-scale working replica of David Bushnell's 1775-vintage *American Turtle* is also on display. This is the first submarine ever constructed. One of the most interesting (and appropriate) exhibits is a model of the *Oliver Cromwell.* The museum also contains nautical paintings, shipbuilding tools, and memorabilia. Open year-round from 10:00 A.M. to 5:00 P.M. Tuesday through Sunday. Gift shop. Admission. The Research archive is open by appointment only. Call (860) 767–8269 or visit www.ct rivermuseum.org.

After looking at the exhibits in the Connecticut River Museum, you might want to actually spend some time on the water, maybe even see some of the eagles that inhabit the river's banks. If so, you are within a few yards of your embarkation point. During the winter eagle-spotting cruises along the Connecticut regularly depart from **Steamboat Dock** next to the Connecticut River Museum. Call the Connecticut River Museum for information, schedules, and prices. Lighthouse and tall-ship cruises are also offered.

If you've never visited the 1776-vintage **Griswold Inn,** don't leave Essex without doing so. People who know and love this place often call it the "Gris" (pronounced *Griz*). Located at 36 Main Street, about 100 yards from the river, the inn has fourteen rooms, three petite suites, and eight suites, all with private bath and telephone. The Garden Suite has two double beds and a full bath upstairs and a living room with a wood fireplace downstairs.

The Gris serves lunch and dinner daily Monday through Saturday, plus a Sunday brunch in the form of the justly famous Hunt Breakfast. This tradition goes back to the War of 1812, when officers of the British army, which was then occupying Essex, forcefully suggested that the establishment start serving a regular Sunday Hunt Breakfast. Today the Hunt Breakfast table groans with an array of food that includes fried chicken, lamb kidneys and mushrooms, and creamed ham and eggs over English muffins. It's almost, but not quite, enough to make you forgive the British for burning New London during the same war.

Griswold Inn

A number of the inn's downstairs rooms have been turned into dining rooms. You can, for example, eat in the book-lined library or in the Steamboat Room with its lifelike mural of steamboating on the river. No matter where you land, you'll have an interesting experience. Open throughout the year except for Christmas Eve and Christmas Day. Call (860) 767–1776 for hours and to make reservations.

If the river formed Essex's early history, the railroad had much to do with its later development. The ***Essex Steam Train and Riverboat,*** 1 Railroad Avenue off Route 154, was chartered in 1868. It still runs a steam train, with an optional riverboat ride, along the Connecticut River. Four or more trains per day make the 12-mile round-trip from Essex to Deep River, and all but the last train connect with the riverboat. Boats make a round-trip from Deep River to Gillette Castle and East Haddam. Before or after the excursion, guests can tour a variety of vintage train cars and visit the gift and snack shops (both in old railroad cars). The railroad runs a varying schedule from May through October and from Thanksgiving through Christmas. Tickets are available at the station in Essex. The Polar Express and Thomas the Tank Engine require reservations. Modest children's fares; somewhat steeper adult fares. Call (860) 767–0103 or (800) 277–3987 or log on to www.essexsteamtrain.com.

Essex used to be famous for manufacturing piano keys, and nearby Ivoryton was the center of the ivory trade that supported that industry. In fact the town's name derives from the fact that it used to import "ivory by the ton." Both the legal ivory trade of olden days and the local piano works have ceased to be. But a salute to music of a different sort can be found at the ***Museum of Fife & Drum*** (63 North Main Street in Ivoryton), where the Company of Fifes and Drummers is headquartered. Exhibits trace the development of military parades in America from the Revolutionary War to the present day and include many uniforms and musical instruments, including drums dating from 1793. There's a special display of Civil War–era musical instruments. This is the only museum in the world devoted to fife and drum, so don't miss it if you're in the area. Open weekends, 1:00 to 5:00 P.M., June 30 through Labor Day weekend or by appointment. The museum is closed the third weekend of July and fourth weekend of August. Admission. Call (860) 399–6519. Visit them on the Web at www.companyoffifeanddrum.org/museum.html.

*The Ivoryton Playhouse,* at 103 Main Street in Ivoryton, was the first self-supporting summer theater in the nation. Although cozy and unpretentious, the Ivoryton can boast some of the most famous names in American theater. Marlon Brando, Ginger Rogers, Carl Reiner, Groucho Marx, Helen Hayes, Jerry Orbach, Alan Alda, Mary Astor, and Gene Hackman all graced the playhouse's stage. Katharine Hepburn, who was born in Hartford and

essextrivia

David Bushnell, designer of the *American Turtle,* coined the word *submarine* to describe his invention.

lived in the Fenwick section of Old Saybrook, launched her career at the Ivoryton. The theater, which was completely renovated not long ago, still offers a summer program of theatrical entertainment. Call (860) 767–7318.

Ivoryton is also home to one of the state's better inns. Named for a spectacular 200-year-old tree that graces its front yard, the *Copper Beech Inn* at 46 Main Street (Route 9, exit 3) offers two styles of accommodation. For the traditional-minded, the elegant 1890-vintage main building boasts four guest rooms with antique and country furnishings. The refurbished carriage house in the rear has nine rooms with a mix of more modern amenities and traditional furnishings. The inn's award-winning country-French restaurant opens to the public for dinner Tuesday through Sunday starting at 5:30 P.M. Call (860) 767–0330 for reservations; (888) 809–2056 toll-free.

Settled in 1635 as part of Old Saybrook, the sleepy village of Deep River is known throughout the state as the site of the *Ancient Muster,* held the third Saturday of July. At that time the tiny village on the Connecticut River welcomes thousands of visitors who come to witness a historical pageant staged by a hundred fife and drum corps. Call the Central Regional Tourism District's Office at (800) 793–4480 for more information.

The rest of the year, not much happens in Deep River. History lives mainly in the *1840 Stone House* at 245 Main Street, where the local historical society maintains a small museum filled with such items as nineteenth-century furnishings, maritime memorabilia, locally made cut glass, and Indian artifacts. Open July and August 2:00 to 4:00 P.M. Tuesday, Thursday, and Sunday. Donation requested. Call (860) 526–1449.

Our grannies called armoires "clothespresses" or "wardrobes" and used them in place of closets. Today, armoires are hot properties for storing televi-

## The XYZ Bank Robber

This romantic Connecticut folktale reads more like a story from the Old West than old New England. On a mid-December day in 1899, four men tried to rob the Deep River Savings Bank. Unfortunately for them, but fortunately for the citizens of Deep River, the bank had been tipped that a robbery was likely. When the four robbers arrived at the bank, one of them tried to pry open a window. Capt. Harry Tyler, a bank guard, felled the would-be robber with one shot. His companions in crime turned tail and ran. The robber's body was carried to the local undertaker, where it was examined and photographed. No identification was found on the body and no one turned up to claim it.

After the news of the aborted robbery became known, Captain Tyler received an anonymous letter asking that the young robber be buried under a headstone marked XYZ. And so he was interred in Fountain Hill Cemetery. Every year for almost forty years, a woman, her identity shielded by a flowing black veil, arrived in Deep River to lay flowers on the grave. The citizens of Deep River, true to their mind-your-own-business Yankee heritage, never questioned her and let her carry out her sad duty without interference. The Deep River Savings Bank is now Citizens Bank.

sions, VCRs, DVDs, and computers, and we've never seen a better stock than at Doc Slater & Sons' *Irish Country Antiques,* at the intersection of Union Street and Route 154 in Deep River. The shop also stocks wooden hutches, farm tables, and kitchen chairs, in short, everything you need to furnish your house in country style. All pieces are imported; in fact, a huge container arrives from Ireland several times a year loaded with goodies. Prices are excellent, much better than most antiques stores. Open 10:00 A.M. to 5:00 P.M. Wednesday through Sunday and by appointment. Call (860) 526–9757.

Hardy souls have a New Englandy urge to visit the Shore in the winter when the crowds are gone. Unfortunately, most of the clam shacks and ice-cream stands close up in the off-season. That's why it's good to know that *Johnny Ad's,* 910 Boston Post Road in Old Saybrook, stays open year-round. Johnny Ad's is something of a shoreline landmark. In the summer it's a popular destination for tourists; in the winter the locals have it all to themselves. Depending on the season, you can eat inside in the restaurant or take your food outdoors to the picnic tables and fight the seagulls for it. The lobster roll is the genuine, butter-drenched Shore favorite and the fried whole-belly clams are crunchy and briny. Open 11:00 A.M. to 3:00 P.M. on Monday and Tuesday, 11:00 A.M. to 4:30 P.M. Wednesday and Thursday, 11:00 A.M. to 7:30 P.M. Friday and Saturday, 11:00 A.M. to 6:00 P.M. Sunday. Call (860) 388–4032 for information.

In Old Saybrook itself, there's an old building worth checking out. The *James Gallery and Soda Fountain* at 2 Pennywise Lane played host to General Lafayette in 1824, as the sign outside states. Besides its gorgeous marble counters, vintage tables and chairs, and luscious ice-cream creations, it is also notable for being a pharmacy and soda fountain once owned by Ada James, who, in 1917, became the state's first African-American female pharmacist. The soda fountain is open noon until 10:00 P.M. daily from mid-May through October. The soda fountain is next to the *Deacon Timothy Pratt B&B,* 325 Main Street, which has nine rooms and is open year-round. Call (860) 395–1229 for both.

Knowing how much kids love trains, we recommend a visit to *Pizzaworks* as a nice break from the hot dog/clam shack scene. Pizzaworks is located at the Old Saybrook Railroad Station, 455 Boston Post Road. The restaurant is literally next to the train tracks, so if you time your visit right, you'll be sure to see a train pull into the station. Pizzaworks capitalizes on its location with a railroad decor in the main dining room. The big attraction is two working model trains that weave their way through meticulously re-created miniature villages. Steps have been placed near the trains so kids can climb up and get a better look. This entertaining distraction keeps the kids happy and makes the wait for your meal much more relaxed. The menu features red and white pizzas, pasta dishes, and salads. The pizza is good and goes well beyond plain and pepperoni. Some of the more exotic toppings include Hawaiian (pineapple and Canadian bacon), shrimp and sun-dried tomatoes, Thai chicken, Tex-Mex, pesto mushroom, and clams casino. Open 4:00 to 9:00 P.M. Monday and Tuesday, 11:30 A.M. to 9:00 P.M. Wednesday, Thursday, and Sunday, and 11:30 A.M. to 10:00 P.M. Friday and Saturday. Call (860) 388–2218.

## oldsaybrooktrivia

The Ingram House in Old Saybrook is one of only a few octagonal houses still standing in Connecticut. It was purchased, prefab, from the Sears-Roebuck catalog and constructed on-site in about 1890. The Old Saybrook Chamber of Commerce offers a walking-tour booklet of many interesting sites in town, including the Ingram House. Stop by the chamber's office at 655 Boston Post Road to pick up a copy or call the chamber at (860) 388–3266 for more information. The Chamber of Commerce is open 9:00 A.M. to 5:00 P.M. Monday through Friday. Visit the Web site at www.oldsaybrookchamber.com.

The town of Chester is home to a four-star establishment widely considered one of the best French restaurants in the state. Specializing in French country cooking, *Restaurant du Village* (59 Main Street) has long been noted for quaint charm and quality cuisine. Its already outstanding reputation has been enhanced

## A Road Trip through the Connecticut River Valley's Past:
### Route 154 between Middletown and Deep River

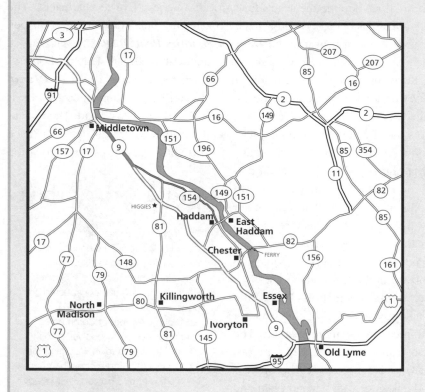

The sky-blue, Connecticut-shaped road sign reads SCENIC ROAD NEXT 9.2 MILES. For most of those miles, Route 154 winds through some of Connecticut's prettiest country. It's part of what gives the Coast and Country region its Country tag. In its

under owners Michel and Cynthia Keller. Michel does most of the cooking, while Cynthia manages the house, but both are noted chefs. The menu changes seasonally, with crusty fresh-baked breads, tasty soups, and to-die-for desserts as a constant. Michel has been adding to the menu unique variations on dishes from his native Alsace. There is also an excellent and surprisingly affordable wine list. Open for dinner 5:00 to 9:00 P.M. Wednesday through Saturday, and 5:00 to 8:15 P.M. Sunday. Call (860) 526–5301. There are two seatings an evening; reservations strongly suggested.

day the road has served as both a dirt path and a commercial turnpike, but today it lives its life as a quiet country road.

Heading south from Middletown toward Haddam, taking Route 9 to Route 154, you'll come upon a large rock set well back from the road. This is **Bible Rock** and its cleft marks the line between Middletown and Haddam. Look carefully because the rock is well back from the road and easy to miss when leaves cover the trees.

Located at 236 Saybrook Road about 0.3 mile from the junction of Routes 81 and 154 on Route 154 north of Higganum Center is a Connecticut institution called **Higgies** (also known as Higgies Roadside Eatery). This restaurant has been around since 1945 and has a reputation for the "best dogs and shakes" in the area. The owners pride themselves on using only top-quality products. The shakes must be pretty good because customers show up as regularly as clockwork. A shake, flanked by a couple of chili dogs topped with a homemade meat sauce made from a recipe that's more than forty years old, makes a perfect nostalgic lunch, but the steamed cheeseburgers and pulled pork sandwiches are also popular. The best way to enjoy a Higgies lunch is outside at a picnic table under the trees. Open daily 11:00 A.M. to 8:00 P.M. early April until late October. Call (860) 345–4403.

Continue south on Route 154 and you'll pass some beautiful Victorian, Beaux Arts, and Gothic Revival houses. About 2 miles out of Higganum Center, there's a former Catholic church, now a private residence, overlooking the Connecticut River, the perfect brooding realization of Gothic architecture.

Another local institution on Route 154 is the **Pilot House,** 1364 Saybrook Road, Haddam (860–345–8333). Its claim to fame is a secret relish served with sandwiches. This is one of those ramshackle drive-in restaurants to which families make annual pilgrimages. Open 11:00 A.M. to 8:00 P.M. Tuesday through Sunday from May through late October, although the hours vary depending on the season, so you might want to call ahead.

Stopping where the road ends at the **East Haddam Swing Bridge,** with the **Goodspeed Opera House** standing grandly on the opposite bank, ponder someone's engineering inventiveness. Thanks to basic old Yankee ingenuity, the bridge slowly swings parallel to the Connecticut River to allow boats to pass, then just as slowly swings back to allow cars to cross.

If driving through the Connecticut River Valley has whetted your appetite for shad roe, then head for **Me & McGee Restaurant,** 40 Saybrook Road (in the Higganum section of Haddam). It's one of the few places we know that still takes time to prepare this Connecticut springtime food. You can have your shad roe cooked in the traditional method with bacon or served with a piece of shad, cooked with lemon, garlic, and white wine. When shad isn't in season or if you aren't a shad fancier (we aren't), Me & McGee offers plenty of country-cooking delights. Breakfasts are approximately the size of Ohio. Try Emilie's

Casserole, a toss of cheese, eggs, sausage, and home fries—all the bad-for-you breakfast stuff people adore. Lunch dishes are equally generous and interesting. Open for breakfast and lunch from 6:00 A.M. to 2:30 P.M. Monday through Saturday. Call (860) 345–3777.

**Sundial Gardens** on Hidden Lake Road in Higganum is actually a collection of formal gardens, including a seventeenth-century knot garden, an eighteenth-century-style garden, and a topiary garden with a fountain. There's also an herb shop and tearoom on-site, and on Sunday the owners offer "tea talks" that include a tour of the gardens followed by tea and dessert. Open for tea and garden tours by reservation. The shop is open January though mid-October, 10:00 A.M. to 5:00 P.M. Friday and Saturday. Call for Christmas shop hours. The gardens are open for browsing from mid-May to mid-October, 10:00 A.M. to 5:00 P.M. Friday and Saturday. Call (860) 345–4290 or visit them on the Web at www.sundialgardens.com.

**O'Rourke's Diner** at the end of Main Street by the bridge in Middletown is a popular place that's been owned by the same family for more than fifty years. The building at 728 Main Street has been a diner since the early 1920s and is listed on the National Register of Historic Places. The original establishment started life as a Mountain View dining car, the 223rd made, in an era when Mountain View was building some of America's most stylish diners.

portland**trivia**

Portland supplied so much brownstone for Manhattan town houses that it was called the "city that changed the face of New York City."

The current owner, Brian O'Rourke, started working in the diner, helping his uncle, when he was ten years old. Brian is a self-taught cook, which may be an advantage. The food here is plentiful and cheap as you would expect, but it's also quite imaginative. One newspaper has listed O'Rourke's Diner as one of the top ten places in the United States to get a good meal for under $10.

The lunch menu usually features half a dozen homemade soups. Entrees include such diner staples as meat loaf; if you know and like diner food, you'll probably have a pretty good idea of what to order. Weekends, Brian does special breakfasts. Each month there's a new omelette; in July, for example, it's smoked salmon and asparagus topped with Hollandaise. There's also a different pancake special each week, like double blueberry (blueberry pancakes with blueberry syrup). O'Rourke's also does its own jams, breads, and muffins, including magnificent Irish soda bread and a terrific banana chocolate chip muffin. [Note: At press time, O'Rourke's was closed due to a fire, but in the

## The Legend of the Leatherman

He sounds like a literary character dreamed up by Charles Dickens or Washington Irving, but the Leatherman was real, and he called Connecticut "home" for much of his rambling life. This nineteenth-century wanderer could not speak except to say "tonk" (perhaps "thanks" for the scraps of food he received). His moniker comes from the outfit he always wore: a handmade patchwork leather suit. According to legend, the Leatherman was first spotted in Harwinton in 1858. Later, observers pieced together his circuit, a regular 350-mile route through Connecticut and New York. He walked about 10 miles a day, completing his loop every thirty-four days. He followed the same path for three decades, surviving on the food given to him by hundreds of people along his route. The only time he'd change course was if someone tried to talk to him, then he wouldn't return.

The Leatherman avoided densely populated areas, preferring the countryside, where he would sleep in caves. He walked along roads such as Route 1 in Madison and Clinton; and through parts of Milford, Woodbridge, Orange, Stratford, Bridgeport, New Fairfield, Greenwich, and many other Connecticut towns. As the years wore on, people along his route began to notice the Leatherman was ill. Cancer was eating away his chin and mouth. A few Samaritans actually succeeded in getting him to a hospital in Hartford, but the Leatherman escaped and hit the road again. Despite his extensive wanderings in Connecticut, his final resting place is in Ossining, New York, at the Sparta Cemetery. But his legend remains woven tightly into the fabric of Connecticut.

process of raising money to rebuild. Visit www.orourkesdiner.com for information about when the diner will reopen.]

Don't leave Middletown without stopping at the **Middlesex Fruitery,** 191 Main Street. This is an old-fashioned, family-run greengrocer with primo produce. Not only do the owners personally select your produce for you, but they carry it out to your car. Open 8:30 A.M. to 5:30 P.M. Tuesday through Saturday. Call (860) 346–4372.

For the past quarter of a century, **Mazzota's Restaurant & Bakery,** 650 South Main Street in Middletown, has been a place to go for hefty portions of good Italian food, friendly service, and reasonable prices. It's been such a mainstay on the local scene that regular customers might have taken it for granted by now. First-timers must avoid temptations of the dessert case on their way to the dining room. Any of the traditional Italian menu offerings are good choices. One standout is a Sicilian orange and onion salad composed of thinly sliced sweet oranges, purple onions, and black olives tossed with a light vinegar-and-oil dressing. The pastas are marvelous, especially the veggie lasagna. For lighter fare, opt for a small pizza or hot oven grinder. And then there's dessert. Scan the cannoli selections, but don't pass up the Italian cookies or rum cake. All of the desserts go well with the house cappuccino or espresso. Open 8:00 A.M. to 8:00 P.M. Tuesday through Saturday and 8:00 A.M. to 1:00 P.M. Sunday. Call (860) 346–6735.

## a killingworth gravesite

Hugh Lofting, the man who gave the world the character Dr. Dolittle, rests in a little cemetery in rural Killingworth, unseen by virtually all who pass by. Lofting was a native of England but moved to tiny Killingworth in 1928 at the height of his popularity as the author of a series of books about a kindly, eccentric veterinarian who could talk to animals. According to a town historian, Lofting wrote some of his books while living here, in a house on River Road. He died in 1947. Lofting's grave is in Evergreen Cemetery, across the street from his house, now privately owned by another family. The cemetery is on Green Hill Road, and Lofting's tombstone is in the back right-hand corner.

South and east of Middletown at the junction of Routes 66 and 147 in the village of Middlefield is another of our favorite stops for road food. With its rural surroundings, *Guida's Drive-in* (pronounced *GUY-das*, not *G-WE-das*) is just about a perfect place for a springtime hot dog lunch. The claim to fame here is the "10-inch pedigreed hot dogs," which come sizzling from the grill, nestled in a toasted bun. The accompanying chili sauce is hot, spicy, and vinegary and just right with mustard and onions. The shakes are honest, luxuriously thick, and made from hard ice cream the way God intended. Open 6:00 A.M. to 8:00 P.M. Monday through Saturday and 8:00 A.M. to 8:00 P.M. Sunday. Call (860) 349–9039.

East Haddam is the heart of the lower Connecticut River Valley's resort country and was once a mecca for New Yorkers seeking to avoid the crowding closer to the shore. It isn't as popular as it once was, but the area is still liberally sprinkled with holiday camps, lodges, gift shops, antiques stores, and similar establishments.

East Haddam is the only town in the state to occupy both sides of the Connecticut River, and as you approach the eastern part of the township from across the river, you pass over the longest swinging bridge in New England. This uncommon bridge actually pivots sideways to open a path for passing boats. The first thing you see on the other side is a glorious three-story American Gothic palace that looks like a wedding cake and dominates the East Haddam skyline. This symphony in gingerbread is the *Goodspeed Opera House.* Founded by William Goodspeed more than a century ago, the Goodspeed is widely known as "the birthplace of the American musical," thanks to the number of Broadway hits that received their first tryouts there. An extended summer season—from April through December—of professional theater is still offered in this renovated structure. You can also enjoy the view from the Good-speed's porch bar. Call (860) 873–8668 for details. Visit them on the Web at www.goodspeed.org.

While you're in East Haddam, stop by **St. Stephen's Church** in the center of town. The church bell up in the belfry was cast for a Spanish monastery in A.D. 815 and is probably the oldest bell in the New World. Behind the church is the **Nathan Hale Schoolhouse,** a one-room establishment where Hale taught in 1773–74. Originally called Union School, it was renamed for Hale after he became an acknowledged American hero. Today the schoolhouse is a museum containing Hale possessions and displays of artifacts relating to local history. The church and school are open noon to 4:00 P.M. weekends between Memorial Day and Labor Day. Admission. Call (860) 873–9547.

The real name of the **Merchant House,** 1583 Saybrook Road in Haddam, is Ye Olde Tyler Merchant House, but you're welcome to call it Arts and Crafts Heaven. In that rarified category of antique furniture, the Stickley reputation looms large. But pick any name from the Arts and Crafts and Mission movements and you'll most likey find high-quality reproductions at the Merchant House. You might eye an oak Harvey Ellis writing desk or perhaps Prairie settles. There's too much on display to do justice to the overall selection, so just drop by to browse and drool. Besides the glorious furniture, the Merchant House displays a lot of gift items like potpourri and fragrant lotions, creams, and potions. The Christmas shop carries some of the most interesting and unusual orna-ments and decorations around. Stuff from the Christmas shop starts flying off the shelves in early October, so come early. Take a minute to peruse the watercolors of historic and well-known Connecticut attractions; they make wonderful souvenirs or presents to commemorate special occasions. You'll see drawings of lots of the places described in this book. Open 10:00 A.M. to 7:00 P.M. Monday through Saturday, 10:00 A.M. to 6:00 P.M. Sunday. Call (860) 345–4195 or (800) 613–0105.

## goodspeedtrivia

The Goodspeed Opera House was the birthplace of these famous American musicals: *Man of La Mancha, Annie,* and *Shenandoah.*

During World War I a militia unit was posted in the Goodspeed to guard the East Haddam Swing Bridge against possible U-boat attacks!

On opening night, October 24, 1877, the premier production at the Goodspeed Opera House was a comedy, *Charles II,* and two farces, *Box and Cox* and *Turn Him Out.*

East Haddam old-timers whisper that the Gelston House, built in 1853, which today serves as an elegant restaurant for theatergoers at the Goodspeed, was once a hideout for rum runners during Prohibition.

Historians don't agree on how the **Devil's Hopyard** in East Haddam got its name, but they do agree that there are a lot of fascinating legends surrounding the 860-acre state park outside of the town of East Haddam. The most lurid one has Satan himself playing in the house band while the locally renowned Black Witches of Haddam held sabbat in the area. According to this legend, Mister Scratch would sit on a rock near the 60-foot cascade of Chapman Falls in the center of the park and play while his minions cavorted.

Nutmeggers' Yankee forebearers were kind of obsessed with Satan, and the sabbat origin certainly *seems* reasonable. Sadly, the origin of the park's strange name is probably more commonplace than legend admits. There are those who maintain that a local farmer and noted bootlegger named Dibble once cultivated a hopyard along Eight Mile River and brewed his harvest into a particularly potent moonshine. According to this version, the park's name began as Dibble's Hopyard, which later evolved into Devil's Hopyard.

Whatever the true origin of its name, there is no denying that this isolated, heavily forested, and reputedly haunted park is a truly spooky place at night. During daylight, though, the Devil's Hopyard is one of the most popular picnic spots in this part of Connecticut, and the big rocks around Chapman Falls are especially nice for spreading a blanket and whiling away a summer's afternoon. For a daytime visit, take Route 156 (Hopyard Road) and follow the signs. There are some picnic shelters scattered around the park, but most people just lay out a spread near the falls. The park is open from 8:00 A.M. until sunset. Call (860) 873–8566.

The granite structure that is Hadlyme's **Gillette Castle** (67 River Road, off Route 82) was built over a five-year period from 1914 to 1919 as the retirement home of the famous actor William Gillette, who designed the edifice, including its unique, hand-carved interior furnishings and appointments. Built on 122 acres, the twenty-four-room mansion is now a museum, kept almost as it was when Gillette lived there. Among the actor's possessions on display is his collection of more than one hundred scrapbooks filled with pictures of cats. Gillette's best-known stage role was as British detective Sherlock Holmes, and Gillette Castle also houses the largest collection of Holmesiana in the world, including a complete re-creation of Holmes's sitting room at 221B Baker Street.

Gillette specified in his will that the property not "fall into the hands of some blithering saphead who has no conception of where he is or with what he is surrounded," thus Gillette Castle is now owned by the state of Connecticut. While there is ample parking, the facilities are generally modest, and the rustic beauty of this spot has been well preserved. The view down the Connecticut River from the castle's broad terraces is one of the best in the state. In late winter and early spring, before the facility opens for the season, you can stand on the main terrace in splendid isolation and watch eagles soar above the river.

In addition to his many other passions, Gillette was a train enthusiast. He had two small working trains that used to make loops around the castle grounds, but they long ago fell into disuse. They are now being refurbished, and the hope is that they will be displayed soon.

Gillette Castle was closed for three years while it underwent an ambitious $11 million restoration. It

Gillette Castle

is now open to the public again from 10:00 A.M. to 5:00 P.M. from the Saturday of Memorial Day weekend through Columbus Day. There is a modest admission fee for the castle tour, but none to picnic or walk the grounds, which are open 8:00 A.M. until sunset. A snack bar and gift shop are also located on the grounds. Call (860) 526–2336 for more information.

To enhance the old-world charm of the experience, we recommend approaching the castle from across the Connecticut River in Chester. Just follow Route 148 to the river and take the ***Chester-Hadlyme Ferry.*** This is the second oldest continuously operating ferry in the United States (after the Glastonbury–Rocky Hill Ferry). It runs 7:00 A.M. to 6:45 P.M. Monday through Friday and 10:30 A.M. to 5:00 P.M. weekends between mid-April and mid-November and can accommodate up to eight cars at a time. There's a minimal charge. Call (860) 443–3586.

***Allegra Farm*** on Town Street (Route 82) in East Haddam calls itself a "living history museum." In fact, horses and carriages from Allegra Farm were featured in the movie *Amistad*. The museum, located in a post-and-beam carriage house and livery stables, is chockful of carriages, sleighs, coaches, and any other horse-drawn vehicle you can imagine. Once you've taken in the vehicles, go outdoors and check out the creatures that draw them as well as some chickens, sheep, and a llama. Horse-drawn carriage, sleigh, or hayrides are available on reservation. All the horse-drawn rides provide refreshments that vary with the seasons, from iced mint tea to hot chocolate served by a campfire. In the spring and summer, carriages from Allegra Farm are a familiar sight carrying wedding parties throughout the Connecticut River Valley. The museum is open by appointment. You'll find Allegra Farm on Route 82, about 2 miles from Gillette Castle and just past Ye Old Christmas Shop. Call (860) 537–8861 for information and reservations.

Moodus, near Mount Tom, is the site of another curious phenomenon steeped in legend. At more or less regular intervals, loud noises like the voices of the damned can be heard throughout the town. These are the famous *Moodus Noises.*

Native Americans said these noises were the voice of an evil spirit who lived on Mount Tom. Early colonists believed the noises were the result of an ongoing battle between the Good Witches of East Haddam and the feared Black Witches of Haddam. According to this myth, when the battle between good and evil goes on too long, a benevolent spirit, Old Machemoodus (for whom the town of Moodus is named) awakes and waves his sapphire wand, clearing away the evil witches and ending the battle. The Black Witches of Haddam then gather their powers once again, and the battle is rejoined, causing more Moodus Noises.

According to geologists, the true cause of the noises is the rubbing of tectonic plates against each other along a fault line, a phenomenon known to generate earthquakes. In fact in 1791 Moodus was shaken by two quakes, which were felt as far away as New York and Boston. A future quake is expected sometime during the next few centuries, and there have been predictions that some day Moodus will be swallowed up by the fault and disappear into the earth forever.

The *Florence Griswold Museum,* 96 Lyme Street in Old Lyme, isn't a particularly large museum, but it's one of the nicer ones in Connecticut. Back in the nineteenth century, Florence Griswold turned her ship-captain father's 1841 house into a boardinghouse and salon for painters. The light is supposed to be particularly good in this part of the state, due to its proximity to large bodies of reflective water; the shore is very near, and the Lieutenant River runs behind the house. Anyway, a community of artists ended up boarding at the Griswold home, where they worked, played, and inspired each other to greater efforts.

The doors and woodwork throughout Florence Griswold's home came to be decorated with original paintings by the likes of Willard Metcalf, Henry Ward Ranger, and Childe Hassam. The vast Griswold collection, including the works of some 110 local artists, is on public display inside the Griswold home. The museum is open year-round from 10:00 A.M. to 5:00 P.M. Tuesday through Saturday and 1:00 to 5:00 P.M. Sunday. Admission. Call (860) 434–5542. Visit them on the Web at www.flogris.org.

The word *impressionism* generally conjures the revolutionary work of French masters Monet, Renoir, and Degas, but Connecticut was where American Impressionism began. From 1885 to 1930, American painters were drawn to Connecticut's picturesque landscape. They painted scenes of bucolic beauty and community life in a distinctive style characterized by vivid colors and broken brush strokes. Connecticut is home to nine museums, including the Florence Griswold Museum, that display the work of some of the artists who played leading roles in the American Impressionism movement. These museums, along with five other museums and historic sites, comprise the ***Connecticut Art Trail***, a self-guided tour of the diverse art collections within the state. For a complete list of the museums and more information about the trail, visit www.arttrail.org.

After driving 4 miles east from the Griswold Museum, you'll reach Old Saybrook, then continue down Main Street to southernmost Saybrook Point, where the Connecticut River flows into Long Island Sound. This is ecologically protected National Conservancy topography, and the perfect place for lodgings that rank high up among coastal New England's most appealing. Namely: ***Saybrook Point Inn*** at 2 Bridge Street, in business since 1989. The layout includes a dock and marina (big enough for 125 moorings) as well as a spa for fitness workouts, massages, a whole slew of sophisticated beauty treatments, and indoor/outdoor swimming-pool plunges. All 80 guest rooms are tastefully furnished (Chippendale and Queen Anne styles predominate), with sizeable bathrooms, fluffy robes, ample storage space, and vintage lithographs adorning

## Baa-d to the Bone

OK, visiting ***Sankow's Beaver Brook Farm,*** 139 Beaver Brook Road in Old Lyme, is one of those times when carnivores hang their heads in shame. It's hard to reconcile the sight of sweet, gamboling spring lambs with the succulent rack of lamb we order in restaurants. The farm does sell its lamb meat (and very good lamb meat it is), but you might never have the heart to buy it. Instead, we covet their incredibly fluffy and luxurious sheepskins (wonderful baby gifts) and their all-natural woolen clothing, such as vests, hats, and very cute sweaters finished with pewter farm-animal buttons—all made from the farm's own sheep. Farm owner Susan Sankow is happy to show you her flock, and farm tours are available by reservation. Occasionally Susan teaches classes on spinning. Starting at Thanksgiving, things turn festive with visits by Santa and hayrides through the fields. The farm is also a working dairy, selling ice cream and cheese. It is open daily from 9:00 A.M. to 4:00 P.M. Call (860) 434–2843 or (800) 501–WOOL for information about farm tours, wool products, special events, and classes.

the walls. If you'd like romantic intimacy and feel willing to "spend extra," choose between either of the two suites that are nestled inside the marina's mini-lighthouse.

Chef Jim Gallagher and his staff are the brains behind the Terra Mar Grille's fine cuisine offerings, augmented by an extensive wine list. Dinner menus feature such temptations as Colorado rack of lamb, cioppino seafood stew, and Kansas City strip steak. Dark wood-grain paneling, thick brocade draperies, and English bone-china dinnerware set the tone. Wraparound windows provide water-and-landscape panoramics, with Fenwick Point's lighthouse and mansions in view. Looking over that way, Jake, our waiter, told us how to spot Katharine Hepburn's former waterfront estate. Sunday brunch is a major production, served from 11:00 A.M. to 2:00 P.M. Make reservations by calling (860) 388–1111.

One of the nicest off-the-beaten-path places we've found lately has the added advantage of being free. The **Connecticut Department of Environmental Protection Marine Headquarters,** Ferry Road, Old Lyme, offers a way-cool boardwalk with the added allure of that universal kid favorite, trains. This is a wonderful, out-of-the-way destination for parents and kids. (Don't be put off by the DEAD END sign on Ferry Road. Just go all the way to the end, and turn into DEP marine headquarters; the parking lot is beyond the main building.)

The boardwalk meanders along the river and ends at a marsh. At the marsh you'll find an elevated platform, ideal for bird-watching or just watching the river flow. Markers along the walk identify the different animals you might see. The fisherfolk who congregate along the river are more than willing to tell tales to willing little ears of the big one that got away.

The boardwalk also rambles under a railway bridge that gives you a very unusual view of speeding trains: Underneath! Free. The best time of year to visit is spring through fall. Trains cross the bridge mornings (about 9:30 A.M. to 1:00 P.M.) and afternoons (around 4:00 to 6:30 P.M.). The site offers free parking, is wheelchair accessible, and has well-maintained picnic tables and restroom facilities. The park closes at sunset.

If you are dedicated to sleuthing out the places that "only the locals know," take our suggestion by following their trail to **Flanders Fish Market and Restaurant,** 22 Chesterfield Road (Route 161) in East Lyme. It is a place you probably wouldn't find on your own, but once found, it becomes a regular on your "always-eat-here-when-at-the-Shore" list. It's an unpretentious place, where good food and friendly service are more important than tricky vertical presentations or whatever other food nonsense is in vogue these days. On the menu you'll find not only Shore perennials like lobster bisque and oyster stew, but

# OTHER ATTRACTIONS WORTH SEEING IN COAST AND COUNTRY

**Clinton Crossing,**
Premium Outlet Mall,
exit 63 off Interstate 95;
(860) 664–0700.
An open-air shopping complex of
70 top-shelf stores.

**Essex Saybrook Antiques Village,**
345 Middlesex Turnpike,
Old Saybrook;
(860) 388–0689.

**Kidcity Children's Museum,**
119 Washington Street,
Middletown;
(860) 347–0495.
Hands-on fun and learning for
children ten years old and under.

**Old Bank Antiques,**
66 Main Street,
East Hampton;
(860) 267–0790.
A multidealer shop.

**Richard D. Scofield Historic Lighting,**
104 Main Street,
Ivoryton;
(860) 526–1800.
Handmade reproductions.

**Mohegan Sun,**
1 Mohegan Sun Blvd.,
Uncasville;
(888) 226–7711.
Casino, moderate-to-expensive restaurants, shops, cabaret, expensive high-
rise hotel.

**Sunbeam Express,**
Captain John's Sport Fishing Center,
15 First Street,
Waterford;
(860) 443–7259;
www.sunbeamfleet.com
The lighthouse cruise is a five-hour tour
of eleven Long Island Sound lighthouses, including a narrated history of
each. The 100-foot boat, which can
accommodate 6 to 149 passengers, is
also available for private charter and
open party boat fishing.

**Thankful Arnold House,**
intersection of Hayden Hill
and Walkley Hill Roads,
off Route 154,
Haddam;
(860) 345–2400;
www.haddamhistory.org
Unusual architectural features
and gardens; 1795 house.

**Wesleyan Potters,**
350 South Main Street,
Middletown;
(860) 344–0039.
Prestigious craft gallery.

also the increasingly rare clear, broth-based clam chowder. Worth mentioning, too: their clam fritters, the hot lobster roll, and the blackened swordfish. The side dishes, sometimes forgotten in fish places, are especially good, including the Flanders fries and the sweet potatoes, either fried or baked. For dessert, try

the crisp of the day. The restaurant knows not all kids like fish, so a peanut-but-
ter-and-jelly sandwich and a milk shake are also on the menu. On nice days, it's
fun to take your food outside and eat in the picnic area. If you liked your lobster so much you want to share it with the folks back home, they ship lobsters
anywhere in the United States. Lobster line: (800) 242–6055 (in Connecticut);
(800) 638–8189 (nationwide). Open 8:00 A.M. to 9:00 P.M. Sunday through Thursday and 8:00 A.M. to 10:00 P.M. Friday and Saturday. The restaurant is admittedly
a bit tricky to find, so try these directions: exit 74 from I–95, take a left at the
end of the exit, go through the traffic light and watch for restaurant on the left.
Call (860) 739–8866 or (800) 242–6055 or visit www.flandersfish.com.

You don't have to be a book lover to spend many contented hours at the
**Book Barn,** 41 West Main Street, Niantic. To call this place a used bookstore
is like calling the Grand Canyon a neighborhood park. The Book Barn is a
compound of six buildings, each overflowing with volumes and, luckily, meticulously arranged by subject—so, for example, one building houses fiction and
poetry, while another is devoted to science and history. There is also an area
dedicated exclusively to children's books. Best of all, the proprietors *want* you
to stay as long as possible. Chairs, benches, and couches are strategically
placed throughout the complex to entice you to linger. There are also picnic
tables, gardens, and a play area, including a playhouse, for children. Kids will
also be delighted and distracted by all the animals that have made the barn
their home. At last count there were two dogs, three goats, twenty-four cats,
and some goldfish. Plans are under way to install a fountain and memorial garden for a beloved resident Labrador retriever who died not long ago.

If all that doesn't convince you to make an afternoon of it, there's also free
coffee, doughnuts, biscuits, and juice. Checkers and chessboards are set up for
anyone who has the time and urge to play. Paperbacks cost $1.00 and hard-
cover novels run about $4.00 to $5.00. The Book Barn is open daily from 11:00
A.M. to 9:00 P.M. Call (860) 739–5715, or log on to www.bookbarnniantic.com.

The Book Barn's inventory was getting so massive that a few years ago the
owners opened **Book Barn Downtown,** at 269 Main Street in downtown
Niantic. But even this store has a large collection of more than 20,000 volumes
focusing on nautical themes, food, nutrition, and health. There is also a wide
variety of mass-market paperbacks and a children's room featuring books and
videos. It is open daily from 9:00 A.M. to 9:00 P.M.; (860) 691–8078.

A few doors down, at 279 Main Street, is the **Niantic Cinema,** considered
by many to be the best independent movie theater in the area. The five-screen
theater shows first-run movies as well as independent films you won't find at
your mall multiplex. Ticket prices are reasonable, and the popcorn is actually
affordable. Call (860) 739–9995.

# Mohegan Country

The **Sands World Wide Games Factory Outlet,** 75 Mill Street in Colchester, has a stupendous selection of puzzles, games, and related items ranging in sophistication from kiddie games (ages five and up) to heavy-duty adult strategy games, from Lego blocks to Dungeons & Dragons. For those who refuse to let their kid side show, there are even some beautifully crafted chess sets, chess being an acceptably "adult" form of play. There is also a selection of new and discontinued arts-and-crafts items. Most of the inventory is of American invention, but there are also some interesting foreign products on display.

Most products are discounted 30 to 40 percent, with seconds discounted up to 60 percent. The store also sells some first-quality current games at retail prices. Open 8:00 A.M. to 8:00 P.M. Monday through Friday and 8:30 A.M. to 1:00 P.M. Saturday. Call (860) 537–2325.

Located off Route 16, the 1872-vintage **Comstock Bridge** (now honorably retired) is one of Connecticut's three remaining covered bridges. It is now used mainly by fishermen and folks just watching the river flow. The wheelchair-accessible area was designed by Peter Reneson, a polio victim who grew up in Colchester. Call (860) 267–2519.

The town of Lebanon and the Jonathan Trumbull family are practically synonymous. Trumbull was the only colonial governor (1769–1784) to support the American War of Independence. He organized George Washington's supply line almost single-handedly, and it was largely thanks to Trumbull that Connecticut came to be called the Supply State. Today there are at least three buildings in Lebanon associated with the Trumbulls and the governor's historic efforts to support the Revolution. All three are located very near each other on West Town Street (Route 87) on the green.

The 1735 **Jonathan Trumbull House,** 169 West Town Street, was once the governor's home. Today it is furnished with period furniture and administered by the Daughters of the American Revolution. Also on this site is **Wadsworth Stable.** George Washington didn't sleep there, but his horse did. It is open 1:00 to 5:00 P.M. Wednesday in mid-May through mid-October. Finally, the property also contains the home of Dr. William Beaumont, the "father of physiology." The **Beaumont home** houses a display of surgical instruments. Open 1:00 to 4:00 P.M. Saturday mid-May through mid-October. Adult admission. Call (860) 642–6579.

The 1769-vintage **Jonathan Trumbull Jr. House,** 780 Trumbull Highway, is a center-chimney farmhouse with eight intricately carved corner fireplaces and a gorgeous original cherry staircase with a molded rail. Today it is furnished with both reproductions and period antiques. Open Memorial Day through Columbus Day, Saturday and Sunday, noon to 4:00 P.M. Adult admission. Call (860) 642–6100 or visit www.jtrumbulljr.org.

Built in 1727 as the Trumbull Family Store, the *Revolutionary War Office,* 149 West Town Street, was where the Council of Safety met to plan the logistical effort that kept Washington's army in the field during the Revolutionary War. Open 1:00 to 4:00 P.M. Saturday and Sunday, Memorial Day through Columbus Day. Adult admission. Call (860) 642–7558.

Located at the confluence of the Yantic and Shetucket Rivers, Norwich was founded in the second half of the seventeenth century. By 1776 it was the second-largest city in Connecticut, and it was a major Patriot stronghold during the Revolutionary War. Among Norwich's sons who fought in that war was Benedict Arnold, the talented American general who tried to turn West Point over to the British and who later burned New London. *Benedict Arnold's birthplace* at 299 Washington Street can still be seen today.

A block from Arnold's birthplace is the *Christopher Leffingwell House* (348 Washington Street), a unique restoration of two small saltbox houses joined together to form a single home. The oldest portion dates from 1675. In 1701 Ensign Thomas Leffingwell opened a tavern on the premises, and there his son entertained George Washington in 1776 when the general was on his way to Lebanon. Open April 1 to December 1, 1:00 to 4:00 P.M. Friday, Saturday, and Sunday or by appointment. Admission. Call (860) 889–9440.

There must be a dozen other historic buildings scattered along Washington and Town Streets, most within easy walking distance of each other. One with an interesting history is the *Samuel Huntington House* at 34 East Town Street. Samuel Huntington was Norwich's most prominent citizen after Benedict Arnold; he signed the Declaration of Independence and presided over the signing of the Articles of Confederation. There's also the *Joseph Carpenter House,* which dates from the 1770s, when it was home to one of New England's most successful silversmiths. The homes are private and can be viewed only from the street.

Norwich also contains several sites of interest to fanciers of Native American lore. Over on Yantic Street by Yantic Falls is *Indian Leap.* After the Battle of East Great Plains in 1643, the Mohegans pursued a band of fleeing Narragansetts into this gorge, forcing them to jump to their deaths. And on Sachem Street you'll find the *Royal Indian Burial Ground,* the last resting place of Uncas, the Mohegan chief who gave Europeans the land on which the settlement of Norwich was constructed. President Andrew Jackson laid the cornerstone of Uncas's monument in 1833.

The *Slater Memorial Museum and Converse Art Gallery,* 108 Crescent Street, on the campus of the Norwich Free Academy, doesn't have the romantic lure of some of Norwich's historical attractions, but it's well worth a visit, especially if you've never been able to get to the Louvre or any of the other great European sculpture galleries. This imposing three-story Romanesque structure was built in 1888 to house a truly impressive collection of plaster casts of famous Greek, Roman, and Renaissance sculpture. The casts are still the main attraction; but in addition to that collection (one of the three finest in the United States), the museum also has displays of antique American and European furniture, Native American artifacts, textiles, and various fine art, including one of the best collections of Hudson River art in America. Open September through June, 9:00 A.M. to 4:00 P.M. Tuesday to Friday, 1:00 to 4:00 P.M. weekends. Open July and August, 1:00 to 4:00 P.M. Tuesday through Sunday. Modest admission. Call (860) 887–2506.

Early in the seventeenth century, a Pequot subchief named Uncas formed a new tribe, the Mohegans. During the Pequot Wars of 1638, Uncas and his people sided with the British, beginning a century of intimate involvement in the affairs of European settlers. The Mohegans and Pequots eventually united under Uncas's leadership, and they became a powerful force in southwestern Connecticut. The first major American novelist, James Fenimore Cooper, recounted part of their story in his 1826 sensation *The Last of the Mohicans,* one of his famous *Leatherstocking Tales.*

Actually, the Mohicans (Mohegans) didn't quite die out in the manner that Cooper suggests. There are about 600 of them left, including 35 in Connecticut. In 1931 John Tantaquidgeon, a direct descendant of Chief Uncas, founded the ***Tantaquidgeon Indian Museum*** on the Norwich–New London Road (Route 32) in Uncasville. Here the culture and history of the Mohegans and other New England Indians are presented in a series of displays featuring artifacts of stone, wood, and bone made by Indian craftsmen, living and dead. Artifacts from other tribes of the Southeast, Southwest, and Plains are housed in their own sections. The hours are sporadic, depending on the availability of volunteers, so it's advisable to call ahead: (860) 862–6403. Donation requested.

There are several other points of interest related to the Mohegans in Montville. Just 200 yards from the Tantaquidgeon Indian Museum is the ***Mohegan Congregational Church,*** an 1831 meetinghouse that is still in use. West of Mohegan Hill, off Raymond Hill Road, is ***Cochegan Rock,*** the site of secret meetings between Uncas and his councilors (and said to be the largest boulder in Connecticut). Farther north, near the village of Mohegan, is ***Fort Shantok State Park,*** which contains an old Indian fort and a Mohegan burial ground, among other points of interest.

Montville also offers an attraction that is sure to delight the younger explorers in your party: ***Dinosaur Crossing and Nature's Art,*** 1650 Route 85.

Visitors enter the park by walking under a life-size brachiosaurus, which stands over 40 feet tall. They will encounter several more prehistoric surprises while on their woodland exploration of three trails showcasing creatures that roamed the earth millions of years ago. There is also a picnic area, children's playground, and ice-cream shop. Open daily mid-June through Labor Day, 9:30 A.M. to 7:00 P.M.; reduced hours before and after the peak season. Last ticket to park sold one hour before closing. Admission. Call (860) 443–4367. After you finish with the dinosaurs, stroll over to Nature's Art, an interactive science, nature and shopping experience. Activities include digging for gems and crystals or panning for "gold," keeping all the treasures you find. Unearth a dinosaur skeleton, make a craft, or select a geode that is millions of years old and have it cut open. The fossil gallery features life-size dinosaur skeletons and minerals and crystals from around the world. There is also a cafe, gift shop, and fossil gallery. Call for hours: (860) 443–4367.

Back on the shoreline, nestled in Niantic is an absolutely awesome children's museum, the ***Children's Museum of Southeastern Connecticut,*** 409 Main Street. Frequently children's museums overflow with activities for kids over five, but fall short for those under five, so this interactive educational center is a real discovery. The exhibits and activities are designed to appeal to, but never talk down to, kids and are engaging enough to capture the attention of adults, too.

Nursery Rhyme Land is a wonderful place for toddlers to explore, as is Kidsville, a kids-size town. The Discovery Room, best for kids six and up, brings the wonders of science to life. In one such activity youngsters get serious when they "play doctor" and bandage and splint up each other or mom and dad. Throughout the year, the museum features a number of exhibits, field trips, seminars, and musical performances of interest to kids, including a respected summer camp program that focuses on the environment, science, and the arts. Admission. Open 9:30 A.M. to 4:30 P.M. Tuesday through Saturday, Friday until 8:00 P.M.; noon to 4:00 P.M. Sunday. Open Monday during summer and school holidays. A picnic area is available. Admission; kids under two, free. Call (860) 691–1111 or log on to www.childrensmuseumsect.org.

## The Eastern Shore

If you're planning a trip to Connecticut, you probably know as much as we do about Mystic, Mystic Seaport, and other Mystic attractions. After all, this is just about the most popular tourist destination in the state, and the folks at Mystic do a wonderful job of getting the word out about this attraction. All we'll say here is that Mystic Seaport is a grouping of some sixty buildings and four vessels from all over the New England coast that re-create life in an old Yankee seaport. The admission is steep, but one ticket is good for two consecutive days. Open April through October, daily 9:00 A.M. to 5:00 P.M.; November through March, daily 10:00 A.M. to 4:00 P.M. Call (860) 572–0711 or visit www.mystic seaport.org or www.visitmysticseaport.com.

A neat place to stay in Mystic is the *Red Brook Inn,* 2750 Gold Star Highway. Its description sounds lovely but pretty typical for a high-end B&B in a tourist spot. Guest rooms are in two historic colonial (1756) buildings on a beautifully landscaped, seven-acre property. Some of the ten antiques-filled

## Eating in Mystic

Mystic has its share of formal dining, but its more relaxed family places are appealing, too. Number one on most lists for travelers to Mystic is *Mystic Pizza,* 56 West Main Street. Until the movie *Mystic Pizza* came out, this was just another small-town pizza parlor. Now it's a movie-trivia-buff pilgrimage. Everyone wants to see where a young Julia Roberts served up pies—even though she was actually on a set in nearby Stonington Borough. Movie buffs will have a good time with all the movie memorabilia on the walls (and for sale) in the restaurant. The pizza's pretty good, but let's face it, the charm comes from the film connection. Serves lunch and dinner daily from 11:00 A.M. to 11:00 P.M. Call (860) 536–3700 or visit www.mysticpizza.com.

Next to the drawbridge at 2 Main Street you'll find *Mystic Drawbridge Ice Cream,* a cute ice-cream parlor that locals claim has the best ice cream around. The Kona-coffee flavor, made from Hawaiian coffee ground on the premises, and the Barbados buttered rum come highly recommended. It's open 11:00 A.M. to 9:00 P.M. weekdays and 11:00 A.M. to 10:00 P.M. weekends. Call (860) 572–7978. By the way, that cute drawbridge is called a *bascule* (French for seesaw), and you'll have plenty of opportunity to contemplate its rare beauty because car traffic along Main Street goes into gridlock when it's raised to allow boats to pass.

*Kitchen Little* at 81½ Greenmanville Avenue, near Mystic Seaport, has been lauded in more travel guides and articles than you can shake a stick at. As you'd guess from the name, this is a small restaurant. In fact, the breakfasts are almost bigger than the restaurant itself. Size and fame conspire to draw crowds, so be prepared for a short wait. Eggs—any way, shape, or form—are big here, but you might prefer the French toast or ham-and-cheese-stuffed pancake sandwich. Lunch offerings are equally good and generous; prices are beyond reasonable. Open 6:30 A.M. to 2:00 P.M. weekdays and 6:30 A.M. to 1:00 P.M. weekends for breakfast only; (860) 536–2122.

You'll find the *Sea Swirl* at the junction of Route 1 and Route 27. When food pundits compile their "Best of" lists, the Sea Swirl is a perennial on the Best Fried Clams list. Without a doubt, this tiny drive-in is the best place in Connecticut for fried whole-belly clams. The other fried seafood offerings are similarly stellar. Open daily April through October from 11:00 A.M. to 8:00 P.M. Call (860) 536–3452.

rooms have fireplaces and whirlpools. Unlike other inns, though, the Red Brook Inn has a ghost or two. Over the years, guests and staff have reported cold spots that move throughout the inn and the sound of voices where no voice should be heard. Moderate to expensive. Call (860) 572–0349.

## mystictrivia

Mystic derives its name from the Pequot Native American word *Mistuket.*

If you've come to Mystic, there's a good chance you arrived with children. That being the case, your best bet for lodging is probably the **Hilton Mystic,** 20 Coogan Boulevard; (800) HILTONS (445–8667). It's close to the aquarium, the seaport, and Old Mystick Village. Best of all, they know what kids like, and the staff seem to genuinely like children. There are a plethora of child-oriented activities, such as face painting, magic shows, and kids' barbecues. Lots of amenities for big people, too. The restaurant, The Mooring, offers excellent seafood and desserts. Open year-round; moderate to expensive. Call (860) 572–0731.

## mystictrivia

The Hoxie Scenic Overlook between exits 89 and 90 on the northbound side of Interstate 95 offers a postcard view of Mystic Seaport. To the east, you can see the seaport, home port to the *Charles W. Morgan* whaling ship, the *L.A. Dunton,* and the square-rigged *Joseph Conrad* among others. The bluff on the right is where the Pequot Indian War was fought.

A nice alternative to the hustle and bustle of Mystic is Stonington. There's a lot to enjoy in this small town, and all of it at a quieter pace than Mystic.

The town of Stonington is perched on a mile-long peninsula so narrow that you can stand on some cross streets and see the ocean on either side. Were it not for the town's protected harbor, it is unlikely that anyone would ever have chosen to build in such a confined space. That harbor, however, made Stonington a center of New England's whaling and sealing industries in the first half of the nineteenth century. It also helped make Stonington an important railroad terminus. In the early days of railroading, before rail bridges crossed the state's major rivers, Stonington was on the most direct route between Boston and New York, and seventeen separate tracks once converged on the town. In those times, passengers arriving by rail from Boston had to board steamboats in Stonington Harbor for the trip to New York.

At the height of Stonington's fortunes, the town's two main streets were packed cheek by jowl with commercial buildings and the fancy homes of wealthy merchants. When whaling and sealing fell off, the railroad moved on, and Stonington, which lacked the real estate to expand into a bedroom community, was left frozen in the mid-nineteenth century. Most of the beautiful Federal and Greek Revival homes are still there, only now they're B&Bs, restaurants, antiques stores, and crafts shops.

The town dock on Pearl Street (1 block west of Water Street and 1 block north of Grand Street) is an exception to Stonington's Brigadoonish aura; it's still a working fishing dock. In fact, Stonington has the only active fishing fleet left in Connecticut. Stonington's annual June **Blessing of the Fleet** is a festive event. You can get information and a free calendar of events by calling (800) TO-ENJOY (863–6569). And by the way, it was from this harbor that Capt. Nathaniel Palmer embarked on the 1820 sailing trip that resulted in the discovery of Antarctica.

You can visit Palmer's home, the **Captain Nathaniel B. Palmer House,** at 40 Palmer Street. In addition to his discovery of Antarctica, Palmer is remembered as the designer of the first clipper ship. His home, which has been designated a National Historic Landmark, has a permanent exhibit that traces the Palmer family's role in the maritime history of Connecticut. Changing exhibitions relate to Palmer, Stonington, and maritime history. The house was built in the late Federal style. It has fourteen rooms and a cupola that looks out over the shipyard and lighthouse. The worn floorboards of the lookout tower are a testament to how often worried family members paced the floors watching for sea captains returning from their trips to China. A restored outbuilding with an icehouse and workshop is located on the grounds, along with a genealogy library and a collection of oil portraits. The home is bordered by water on three sides, and the property has been naturalistically landscaped. Visitors are encouraged to stroll the grounds and bring a picnic lunch. The Palmer house is open May through October, 1:00 to 5:00 P.M. Thursday through Sunday. Admission. Call (860) 535–8445.

**Cannon Square,** toward the south end of Market Street, marks the site where the Stonington militia successfully fought off the British in August 1814. It and the surrounding streets are the center of Stonington's historic district. Stroll up Main Street from the square (away from the Point) and admire the architecture of the 1827-vintage **Old Customs House** and the elegant 1780-vintage **Captain Amos Palmer House,** both worth more than a passing glance. A tidbit of town trivia: James MacNeill Whistler, who painted *Whistler's Mother,* spent part of his boyhood in this house.

Down at the end of Water Street (at number 7) is an especially popular local landmark, the **Old Lighthouse Museum.** Constructed in 1823, it was moved to its present location in 1840 to protect it from erosion. It is now a museum housing six rooms of exhibits, whaling and nautical displays, a

Old Lighthouse Museum, Stonington

collection of pre-1835 pottery made locally, an ice harvesting exhibit, and the popular lighthouse display, featuring a fourth-order Fresnel lens and photography of the lighthouses of Long Island Sound. There is also a children's room with an antique dollhouse. If you care to climb the stone steps to the top of the lighthouse, you'll be rewarded by a stunning view of Long Island Sound, including Fisher's Island. Open daily 10:00 A.M. to 5:00 P.M. May to November. Admission. Call (860) 535–1440.

If you're at the museum around day's end, linger a while to see a spectacular sunset over Stonington Point.

***The Mashantucket Pequot Museum and Research Center,*** 110 Pequot Trail on the Mashantucket Pequot Reservation in Mashantucket, is, without a doubt, one of the most beautiful, stunning, and moving museums in all of Connecticut. Mashantucket Pequots invested $135 million of the monies earned from the nearby Foxwoods Casino in building this state-of-the-art museum and research center. The museum brings to life the story and history of the Mashantucket Pequot people, a history spanning 20,000 years from the last Ice Age to today, and that of other Native American tribal nations.

The life of woodland Native Americans is portrayed in stunning detail with dazzling multisensory dioramas and exhibits. Based on years of scholarly research and the works of Native American artisans, you'll see re-creations of life in a sixteenth-century Pequot village, a seventeenth-century Pequot fort, and an eighteenth-century farmstead. You can hunt caribou along simulated glacial crevasses—complete with howling winds and the sounds of creaking ice. When you visit the village, you'll hear the sounds of children playing and women working and smell the smoke of many campfires. The detail of each diorama is magnificent, especially the life-size, hand-painted Indian figures, cast from living Native Americans. In a specially designed theater, you can watch a thirty-minute film called *The Witness,* which recounts the 1637 massacre of 600 Pequot people at the Mystic fort.

Don't miss the 185-foot stone-and-glass observation tower, which gives you a sweeping view of the area. In fall this is one of the best places in the state to take in the brilliant reds and golds of a New England autumn. It's best to visit the tower before going through the museum. Somehow seeing the sweep of the Pequots' homeland makes the exhibits and dioramas all the more meaningful.

The museum is open daily 9:00 A.M. to 5:00 P.M. (last admission is at 4:00 P.M.). Closed major holidays. Fairly stiff admission charge, but worth it. Call (800) 411–9671 for information about tours and special events. And be sure to visit www.mashantucket.com.

Stepping into **Randall's Ordinary** on Route 2 in North Stonington is like returning to an earlier century. The wide floorboards, the flickering firelight, and the rich tang of wood smoke mingled with cooking odors emanating from the fireplaces all conjure images of the distant past. The Randall family's original clapboard inn dates to 1685, with additions made in 1720 and 1790. There's a lot of history in this structure, which is now a landmark on the National Register of Historic Places. Be sure to check out the heavy shutters that were hung for protection from Indian attacks during the colonial period. Also ask to see the trapdoor used to conceal escaped slaves when the inn was a station on the Underground Railroad in the 1830s.

Secluded on twenty-seven acres of rolling woodlands, the inn is a calm retreat from the hustle and bustle of twenty-first-century life. Arrive early enough to take a stroll through the grounds.

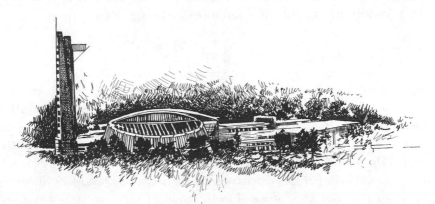

The Mashantucket Pequot Museum and Research Center

Food here is cooked the way the Randalls did: over an open hearth. Cooks and servers also dress much the way the first owners did, in authentic colonial garb. Dinner is served seven days a week starting at 5:30 P.M. The pan-roasted Nantucket scallops are the boffo dish, along with the bread basket that includes spider bread (corn bread baked in a "spider," aka a cast-iron skillet). Dessert is usually a sampling of traditional New England desserts such as Indian pudding, long baked, molasses-spiked, and served with a dab of ice cream, and straw-berry fool, strawberries blended with softly whipped cream.

Open for breakfast, lunch, and dinner year-round. A continental breakfast is included in the price of a room. Breakfast is served daily from 7:00 to 11:00 A.M.; lunch is from noon to 3:00 P.M. If you plan to take dinner at the Ordinary, be certain to make reservations well in advance. Call (860) 599–4540.

If B&Bs are more your style—or if you just like old things—then you might try North Stonington's **Antiques and Accommodations** (32 Main Street). The four guest rooms, one three-bedroom suite, and all the public rooms in this restored 1861-vintage Victorian home are lovingly furnished with formal antique furniture and odd accessories. What makes this place truly one-of-a-kind, though, is that many of these gorgeous furnishings are for sale to the guests. Do you like that Victorian bureau in your room or the four-poster bed you slept in last night? For a modest fee added to the purchase price, you can have them shipped home. Did your significant other fall in love with that sil-ver brush set on the dressing table? You can give a gift that will always have special meaning. Even if you don't see anything that tickles your fancy, you'll enjoy your stay at this elegant little B&B. Everything done here is carried off with taste and style. From the fresh-cut flowers and decanter of sherry that greets new arrivals to the breakfasts served by candlelight, every element has that small touch of class that makes for a memorable experience. Lunch and dinner are served daily. Breakfast on Friday, Saturday, and Sunday. Call (860) 535–1736 or (800) 554–7829 for reservations and exact times.

# The Southeast Shore

Groton is the birthplace of the atomic submarine and the site of the nation's largest submarine base. This history is commemorated at the **USS Nautilus Memorial** on the U.S. submarine base off Route 12. In addition to touring the world's first nuclear sub, you can spend hours in the 12,000-square-foot **Historic Ship Nautilus and Submarine Force Museum** adjacent to the sub base. The museum includes extensive exhibits tracing the history of America's submarine fleet and offers a pair of top-notch multimedia shows in two differ-ent theaters: one tracing the history of the submarine force and one dealing specifically with *Nautilus.* Open May 15 through October 17. The museum is free and open daily May 15 through October 31 from 9:00 A.M. to 5:00 P.M. except for Tuesday, 1:00 to 5:00 P.M. Call (860) 694–3174 or (800) 343–0079.

Groton's **Fort Griswold Battlefield State Park** commemorates the warfare of a different era. Located at Monument Street and Park Avenue, the park is the site of a 1781 massacre of American troops at the hands of a force of 800 British soldiers under the command of the traitor Benedict Arnold. At that time Yankee privateers based in New London were a thorn in the side of the British in New York, and Arnold came to burn the town, which he did, destroying 150 buildings. The part of his force that advanced up the east bank of the Thames suffered heavy casualties assaulting Fort Griswold, which was held by a force of 150 militia under the command of Col. William Ledyard. When Ledyard finally surrendered, he was murdered with his own sword, and eighty of his men were slaughtered.

grotontrivia

The first diesel-powered submarine was built in Groton in 1912.

Many of Fort Griswold's old emplacements remain, and there are some interesting historical displays. The 134-foot monument tower provides a nice view of the coast. The park is open year-round. The museum and monument are open from Memorial Day through Labor Day, 10:00 A.M. to 5:00 P.M. Wednesday through Sunday. The fort is open until sunset daily. After Labor Day, call ahead for hours: (860) 449–6877.

This is just our observation, but kids are generally bloodthirsty little monsters. Tell them you're taking an environmental cruise, chances are you'll get yawns; hum the theme song from *Jaws* and mention sharks and they're in the car in a New York minute. For budding Cousteaus and their parents, **Project Oceanology,** 1084 Shennecossett Road, Groton (Avery Point), makes an interesting and educational day trip (don't forget to hint at the possibility of shark attacks). You'll cruise the waters off Groton to learn about the environment and marine life in ways you never could at an aquarium. The boats, *Enviro-Lab II* and *III,* are oceanographic research vessels, staffed by marine research scientists and teachers. They really communicate their love for the sea and give kids a chance to participate in lots of hands-on adventures such as catching lobsters and taking and analyzing samples

coastandcountry trivia

When you're in Southeastern Connecticut, call the Thames River the *Thamz* (rhymes with James), not the *Timz* like the one running through London.

from the ocean using oceanographic sampling instruments. It's so engaging you can probably drop the shark patter about five minutes after boarding. Meanwhile, *you* can kick back and enjoy some beautiful ocean views, including a slice of the southeastern Connecticut coastline and some postcard-pretty lighthouses. Admission. Cruises run mid-June through Labor Day. The *Enviro-Lab* cruises run daily at 10:00 A.M. and 1:00 P.M. Children under six are not allowed. The lighthouse cruise runs Tuesday, Thursday, and Saturday at 4:00 P.M. Both cruises take two and a half hours. Call (860) 445–9007 or (800) 364–8472 for cruise schedules.

Some places *belong* in the movies. **Norm's Diner,** at 171 Bridge Street, is one of them. It's down near the shoreline with its smokes and mists and is the sort of venue where, on foggy nights, you expect hard-boiled detective Philip Marlowe to burst through the door and pistol whip some bad actor to his knees under the steely gaze of the approving clientele. Despite this film noir quality, so far all we've encountered at Norm's are nice, quiet guys who look like retired machinists from Electric Boat.

The slightly battered exterior of this 1954-vintage metal-sided Silk City features a handsome barreled roof, adorned with the requisite neon sign proclaiming its name to the world. The interior is done up in shades of green and pink. The counter is a pale green. The Formica tables are salmon pink. Green vinyl adorns the booths and stool seats. The rims of the stools are shiny metal with alternating stripes of bright candy pink. This is definitely 1950s decor.

Norm's is a good place for a late-night breakfast. The cheesecake is locally famous and made on-site from a top-secret recipe. Open twenty-four/seven except for Christmas Eve and Christmas Day. Call (860) 445–5026.

One of the best places in the world to eat lobster is **Abbott's Lobster in the Rough** (117 Pearl Street), down by the shipyards in Noank. You have your choice of eating indoors in the dining room or outdoors at picnic tables scattered around the lawn and pier. Take your food outdoors; on good days, you can see three states. The view of the sea and the passing trawlers and sailboats is worth the small loss of comfort.

## lobstertrivia

A lobster tidbit: It takes between five and seven years for a lobster to reach salable weight. Want to pick the very freshest live lobster? Easy, just pick the friskiest one with its tail curled tightly under its body.

During the summer Abbott's serves thousands of pounds of lobster a day, so just assume they wrote the book on cooking crustaceans. Your lobsters come steamed fresh from the pot, the way nature intended, with butter, coleslaw, and chips on the side. Nothing fancy, but you came to Abbott's for lobster, and lobster is what you get. Try it the way connoisseurs do: Order

# Norm's Texas Beef Stew

1 to 1½ pounds cubed stewing beef

2 tablespoons oil or butter

1 onion, chopped fine

2 stalks celery, chopped fine

2 carrots, chopped fine

1 16-ounce can pinto beans, drained and rinsed (You can substitute an equal amount of diced raw potato, but the pinto beans bring out the "Texas" in the stew.)

1 28-ounce can tomatoes, diced with liquid (or an equal amount of diced raw tomatoes)

2 to 3 cups beef stock (either homemade or canned, low salt)

1 cup fresh or frozen corn

1 cup fresh or frozen green peas

1 cup fresh or frozen green beans

(You can omit any of the vegetables or double up on the ones you like and leave out the ones you don't.)

1 cup barbecue sauce (Norm's recommends Bullseye brand.)

Heat oil in large pan (Dutch oven or something with a lid) over medium heat.

Dry beef well and sauté in oil until very brown.

Add the beef stock and the tomatoes and simmer covered for about one hour until about half done. Stir frequently.

Add the chopped onion, carrots, celery, and pinto beans to beef mixture.

Continue to simmer over low heat, stirring often, for about 45 minutes or until beef is very tender.

Add corn, peas, beans, and barbecue sauce. Continue to simmer until vegetables are tender, maybe about 15 minutes.

Cook stew and then refrigerate overnight. Reheat and serve.

Serves 6–8.

a large lobster (2 ½ pounds or more, depending on your lobster obsession) to split and fixings for two dinners. That way, you'll get more lobster and less shell for your money. The lobster rolls at Abbott's are a lazy person's way to get around the cracking, picking, sucking, and lip-smacking that go with demolishing a whole lobster. Each lobster roll consists of a quarter pound of premium butter-soaked lobster on a toasted bun. Abbott's also serves a classic shore dinner with steamers, cooked shrimp, and clam chowder in addition to the lobster.

However you take your lobster, be prepared to wait. This is a very popular place. Open noon to 9:00 P.M. Memorial Day through Labor Day; noon to 7:00 P.M. weekends from Labor Day to Columbus Day. Call (860) 536–7719.

Although Hammonasset gets most of the press, **Rocky Neck State Park** (exit 72 off I–95 in Niantic) is the better location, especially for off-season picnics. If you like things historical, be sure to check out the pavilion, constructed as a Works Progress Administration project. For picnics, though, walk out to the end of the rocky point, where you have the waters of Long Island Sound on three sides. This is a beautiful and peaceful place to pitch a blanket and share a meal. Be sure to bring some stale bread or a couple of anchovy pizzas for the gulls; they seem to expect it. The park has a picnic area and a place to cook. Open daily from 8:00 A.M. to sunset. Parking rates Memorial Day through Labor Day: $7.00 for Connecticut vehicles and $10.00 for out-of-state vehicles on weekdays; weekends and holidays, $9.00 for Connecticut vehicles and $14.00 for out-of-state vehicles. Mid-April through Memorial Day and Labor Day through the end of September, parking is free weekdays and $7.00 for Connecticut vehicles and $10.00 for out-of-state vehicles on weekends. A season pass is $40.00. Call (860) 739–5471.

Ledyard Township, north of Groton, is the site of the eleven-acre **Ledyard Powered-Up—Powered-Down Sawmill** (Iron Street; Route 214), an unusual restored 1860-vintage water-powered vertical sawmill. The park also has a working blacksmith shop, a restored gristmill with a two-acre mill pond, an 1878 "Lane" Shingle Mill, ice-harvesting equipment, and a picnic area. The park staff includes a working blacksmith. The saw operates Saturday from 1:00 to 4:00 P.M. during April and May and from mid-October to November. Call (860) 464–7678.

At its founding in 1876, the original name of the **U.S. Coast Guard Academy,** 15 Mohegan Avenue, New London, was Revenue Cutter School of Instruction. Today visitors are welcome year-round to tour the academy. Tours are free and self-guided. Full-dress reviews, held at Washington parade field, happen most Fridays at 4:00 P.M. in the spring and fall. USCG sweatshirts and other souvenirs are for sale at the gift shop. The campus is open daily from 9:00 A.M. to 5:00 P.M.; the visitor center is open May to October daily from 10:00 A.M. to 5:00 P.M. The museum is open 9:00 A.M. to 4:30 P.M. Monday through Friday, 10:00 A.M. to 5:00 P.M. Saturday, noon to 5:00 P.M. Sunday. In the summer the academy offers some wonderful band concerts of patriotic and popular music; call for concert schedule. When in port, the three-masted training barque *Eagle* is open to visitors 1:00 to 5:00 P.M. Friday through Sunday. Pets must be on a leash and cameras are permitted. There are no picnic facilities at the academy, but you can spread a blanket at Riverside Park, next to the academy. Much of the parking is restricted or reserved; park at the visitor center or next to the museum. Call (860) 444–8270.

Though often crowded to the point of distraction, downtown New London has so much going for it that it would be a shame to miss the experience if you are anywhere in the vicinity. We recommend a fall or spring walking tour, including the **Captain's Walk** and **Whale Oil Row.** Points of interest include **Ye Ancient Burial Ground** and the **New London County Courthouse,** built in 1784 and still in use. In late July New London hosts America's longest-running polka festival. Come prepared to eat and dance the day and night away. Admission. The festival is held at Ocean Beach Park from noon to midnight.

Energetic walkers may want to head all the way down to Bank Street to see the granite-walled 1833-vintage **Custom House Maritime Museum,** 150 Bank Street. This is the oldest operating custom house in America, and the only one in Connecticut. The front doors were assembled from planks taken from the frigate USS *Constitution (Old Ironsides)*. Open 1:00 to 5:00 P.M. Tuesday through Sunday. Suggested donation. Call (860) 447–2501.

British soldiers led by Benedict Arnold burned New London in 1781, and just about every structure in the city today postdates that episode. The exception is the 1678-vintage **Joshua Hempsted House** (11 Hempsted Street), the home of a famous Connecticut diarist and now the oldest surviving house in New London. One of the interesting features of this home is that it is insulated with seaweed. Open noon to 4:00 P.M. Thursday through Sunday from May 15 to October 15 and by appointment. Admission varies. Call (860) 443–7949.

Our favorite walk is down Whale Oil Row, with its flanking of 1832-vintage Greek Revival houses built by the leading figures in the whaling industry. New London was the center of the whaling industry in Connecticut. During the years 1784–1907, it was home port to 196 whaling vessels, over twice as many as ventured from all other Connecticut ports combined. The men who ran this business were the OPEC of their age, and New London was their Riyadh. The industry peaked in 1846 and died off rapidly thereafter, but Whale Oil Row still carries some of the aura of those days when Connecticut whale oil helped light the lamps of America.

New London has another—literary—side that's every bit as fascinating as its seagoing heritage. Eugene O'Neill, arguably America's greatest playwright, spent part of his childhood in **Monte Cristo Cottage** (325 Pequot Avenue) in New London. Named for O'Neill's actor father's best-known stage role, Monte Cristo Cottage is a pretty little gingerbread structure that looks like it should be filled with light and laughter. Alas, the years O'Neill and his brother Jamie spent there were more like one of the Grimms' darker fairy tales. Both father James and brother Jamie were heavy drinkers. O'Neill's mother, Ella, addicted to morphine from O'Neill's birth, battled her own demons throughout his childhood. Ella is said to haunt the tiny cottage. The Tyrone family in *Long Day's Journey into Night* is a reflection and expression of the misery of O'Neill's summers at the cottage. The comedy *Ah! Wilderness,* also set in Monte Cristo, portrays a life that O'Neill never knew except as an outsider; he based his happy and slightly zany characters on the McGinleys, the family of a childhood friend.

## newlondontrivia

The grinder sandwich was supposedly invented by Benny Capablo in New London in 1926. Despite our proximity to the sub base at Groton, Nutmeggers stick with the handle "grinder." Submarine sandwich is really a Pennsylvaniaism. Other names for the same over-stuffed sandwich: hoagies, poor boys, wedgies, and bombers.

Huddled beneath the eight-lane Gold Star Bridge is Ye Olde Towne Mill (860–447–5250), the nation's oldest industrial power plant (1650).

New London's Shaw Mansion is considered the cradle of the American navy. It was Connecticut's naval office during the Revolutionary War.

The cottage where O'Neill's dark dreams were born is a conglomeration of small buildings, all wrapped up in the Victorian pseudogentility of gingerbread, wraparound verandas, and turrets. Inside, especially on the second floor, the rooms are grim, claustrophobic cells. The first floor of the cottage is fully restored and furnished. In a room adjacent to the living room, a short multimedia show narrated by the late actress Geraldine Fitzgerald describes O'Neill's life in New London in the early 1900s. Open Memorial Day through Labor Day, 10:00 A.M. to 5:00 P.M. Tuesday through Saturday and 1:00 to 5:00 P.M. Sunday. Moderate admission. Call (860) 443–0051.

The **Lyman Allyn Art Museum** at 625 Williams Avenue in New London is one of Connecticut's lesser-known gems and a delight for kids. There's a wonderful roomful of Indian artifacts and a collection of antique dollhouses and toys. In addition the museum has collections of Egyptian, Roman, medieval, and Greek artifacts as well as various changing exhibits. The small museum shop is a real find, offering both antiques and reproductions. Also located on the museum grounds is the historic Deshon-Allyn House, a nineteenth-century mansion that was home to whaling captain Lyman Allyn; the first floor is furnished and open to visitors. The museum has a noncirculating reference library of art and art history books available for use during museum hours. Open July through Labor Day, 10:00 A.M. to 5:00 P.M. Tuesday through Saturday and 1:00

to 5:00 P.M. Sunday; closed major holidays. Admission; kids under eight, free.
Wheelchair accessible. Wheelchairs and
ASL interpreter available by reservation. Call (860) 443–2545 or visit
www.lymanallyn.org.

**Ledge Lighthouse** in New London Harbor is haunted by a ghost
named Ernie. Some believe Ernie was
a lighthouse keeper who, depressed by
marital problems, cut his own throat
and then jumped off the structure.
Some reports say the ghost is a tall
bearded man dressed in a slicker and
rain hat. The prankster ghost has been
known to untie boats, hide coffee cups
and radios, and slam doors. The Ledge

New London Ledge Lighthouse

Lighthouse is atop a 65-foot, three-story square building in the water at the
meeting of the Thames River, Fisher's Island Sound, and Long Island Sound in
New London Harbor.

Despite spooky legends, there are no ghosts at New London's **Lighthouse
Inn.** Originally a 1902-vintage mansion called Meadow Court, the building at 6
Guthrie Place in New London became the Lighthouse Inn in 1928. The exterior
suggests Spanish Moorish influences, but the interior is elegant Victorian and best
described as opulent and unique. Many of the furnishings are antiques, rescued
from flea markets; most of the rest are quality reproductions. The three formal
dining rooms offer a good view of the green lawns that roll down to Long Island
Sound. Service is excellent, and the food is well prepared. The seafood, especially the famous clam bisque, gets high marks for both preparation and fresh-
ness. Open for lunch 10:30 A.M. to 3:00 P.M. Monday through Saturday. Open for
dinner daily 5:00 to 9:00 P.M.; 5:00 to 10:00 P.M. Friday and Saturday. Sunday
brunch, 10:30 A.M. to 3:00 P.M. The inn's 1902 Tavern features entertainment five
nights a week. Call (860) 443–8411; www.lighthouseinn-ct.com.

## Places to Stay in Coast and Country

**B & B at Roseledge Herb Farm,**
418 Route 164,
Preston;
(860) 892–4739.
A 1720 B&B with canopy-topped high featherbeds.
Moderate.

**House of 1833 B&B,**
72 North Stonington Road,
Mystic;
(860) 536–6325 or
(800) FOR–1833.
An elegant and romantic Greek Revival mansion.
Moderate to expensive.

**Madison Beach Hotel,**
94 West Wharf Road,
Madison;
(203) 245–1404.
Beautiful gray-shingled beach resort/hotel.
Moderate (includes breakfast).

**Old Lyme Inn,**
85 Lyme Street,
Old Lyme;
(203) 245–0005;
www.oldlymeinn.com.
Thirteen rooms, all with private baths.
Expensive.

**Tidewater Inn,**
949 Boston Post Road,
Madison;
(203) 245–8457.
www.thetidewater.com.
A former stagecoach stop, offering nine guest rooms.
Moderate to expensive; off-season rates are more reasonable.

## Places to Eat in Coast and Country

**Al Forno,**
1654 Boston Post Road,
Old Saybrook;
(860) 399–4116.
Fine Italian cuisine, also pizzas.
Moderate to expensive.

**Cafe Routier,**
1353 Boston Post Road,
Westbrook;
(860) 399–8700.
One of the best French bistros in the state.
Expensive.

**Dock & Dine,**
Saybrook Point,
Old Saybrook;
(860) 388–4665.
Where the Connecticut River meets Long Island Sound.
Moderate.

**Hallmark Ice Cream,**
Route 156,
Old Lyme;
(203) 434–1998.
Inexpensive.

**It's Only Natural,**
386 Main Street,
Middletown;
(860) 346–9210.
Award-winning natural food.
Inexpensive.

**Niantic Diner,**
26 West Main Street,
Niantic;
(860) 739–2975.
Pleasantly informal.
Inexpensive.

**Pat's Kountry Kitchen,**
70 Mill Rock Road East,
(junction of Routes 1 and 154),
Old Saybrook;
(860) 388–4784 (restaurant).
Moderate to expensive.

**Paul's Pasta Shop,**
223 Thames Street,
Groton;
(860) 445–5276.
You can take away prepared food or buy your own pasta and sauce.
Inexpensive.

# The Quiet Corner

East of Hartford is an area the state's tourism promoters have nicknamed the Quiet Corner. Bounded on the north by Massachusetts and on the east by Rhode Island, the Quiet Corner encompasses the lightly populated, slightly bucolic uplands of Tolland and Windham Counties. It is an area of peace and tranquillity that has escaped both the bulldozers of the state's developers and the attention of the chic set. In truth the Quiet Corner has such an air of serenity that in many places you can easily imagine that this is the way all of Connecticut looked 350 years ago. Fertile farmland abounds. There are country inns that wouldn't be out of place in France. Herb and flower gardens are among the region's most popular attractions. With some exceptions, the antiques here are neither quite as antique nor nearly as pricey as those sold in the trendier stores across the state in Litchfield County. And if other regions have more to offer the casual traveler, for the patient, the Quiet Corner has its own rewards.

## Nathan Hale Country

You can easily miss the turn onto Silver Street from U.S. Highway 44 in Coventry. But, hard as it is to find, *Caprilands* is,

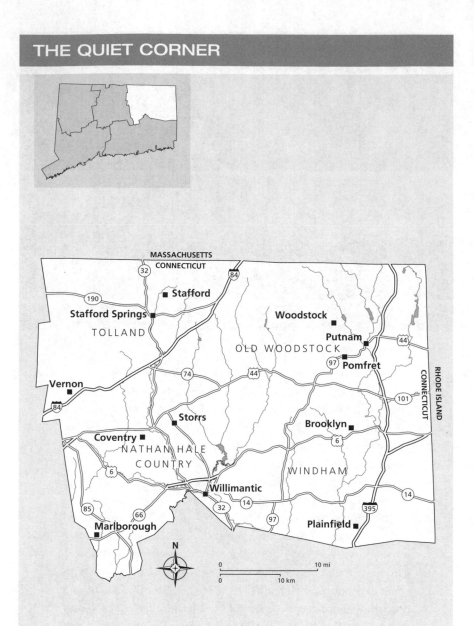

for many people, the crossroads of the world. Visitors flock to the fifty-acre herb farm at 534 Silver Street from the far corners of the earth, and the guest book is as likely to contain the names of visitors from distant New Zealand as from nearby Hartford.

Part of the lure of Caprilands was its famous mistress. Adelma Grenier Simmons, the farm's owner and the grande dame of American herbalists, was famous for her lectures on herbs and for her herb-spangled lunches, which varied with the season. The eccentric Ms. Simmons, who died in 1997, often dressed in swirling cloaks, odd hats, and exotic jewelry and liked to describe herself as "the Agatha Christie of the herb world." Adelma Simmons's husband and family are determined that Caprilands will continue exactly as its famous mistress wished.

Caprilands' main attractions are its thirty-one theme gardens filled with more than 300 varieties of herbs, spices, and wild grasses. Visitors are free to wander among these little worlds at their own pace, and each is a unique delight. Sundials in the identification and eighteenth-century gardens will get you thinking about ages past, when people looked at time in terms of the rhythms of nature rather than as a driving force in its own right.

You might think that spring and summer would be the best times to visit Caprilands, but every season is special, and each offers something new and different to see, smell, and taste. Christmas is celebrated with style at Caprilands, but so are even older festivals, such as Lammas in August.

The herb farm is open daily from 9:00 A.M. to 5:00 P.M. year-round, and herbal luncheons (including a tour of the gardens, a lecture, and a five-course meal) are offered on Saturday, April through October. Christmas dinners are served in December. High tea is served April through October on Sunday at 2:00 P.M. Reservations are absolutely essential. Call (860) 742–7244; www.caprilands.com.

Near Caprilands, at 2224 Boston Turnpike (the junction of US 44 and Route 31 north), is *Memory Lane Countryside Antique Center.* Gail and Gene

## AUTHORS' FAVORITES

Antiquing in the Northwest

Caprilands

Golden Lamb Buttery

Memory Lane Countryside Antique Center

Prudence Crandall House Museum

UConn campus, Storrs

Dickson's multidealer shop consists of a house, a large barn, and several sheds full of antiques. Two dozen different dealers have items on display here, so a wide variety of styles and tastes are represented. The large, airy barn is mostly furniture, organized into a dozen or so separate displays, including some of the better nineteenth-century oak furniture in the area. The house also contains some quality furniture and a raft of smaller items: jewelry, glassware, tools, and the like. There's one whole room given over to some of the best estate, antique, and plain old costume jewelry in the state, most of it very reasonably priced. Don't leave without saying "hey" to the kitties who preside over the premises. Open 10:00 A.M. to 5:00 P.M. Wednesday through Sunday. Call (860) 742–0346.

Next door to Memory Lane is **Memories, Too,** another antiques coopera-tive worth a gander. It isn't affiliated with Memory Lane, but the two shops don't consider themselves competitors either. Call (860) 742–2865.

Seeing a small cluster of picturesque shops around a pond at 45 North Main Street in Marlborough means you've reached the **Marlborough Country Barn.** Actually, it's several barns and outbuildings. This is the place to shop for country furniture, including beautiful kitchen tables made in Pennsylvania Dutch Country. Giftwares are displayed, too. The people who work at the com-plex are patient and knowledgeable, always willing to help solve decorating problems.

You'll find everything from woodstoves to Christmas ornaments to penny candy for sale. There's always something to pique your interest in the beauti-fully decorated room settings. The Christmas Shop is open year-round and car-ries lovely ornaments and Yuletide accessories. Take a tip and hit the Christmas Shop early—around Labor Day—because after Veterans Day things get awfully crowded and boisterous. Special events are held throughout the year: antiques shows, for instance, plus summer and fall crafts shows and guest appearances. Open 10:00 A.M. to 5:30 P.M. Tuesday through Sunday, Friday until 8:00 P.M., and noon to 5:00 P.M. Sunday. Call (860) 295–8231 or (800) 852–8893. Visit the Web-site at www.marlboroughbarn.com.

Take a break from shopping with breakfast, lunch, or dinner at **Sadler's Ordinary,** 61 North Main Street, a low-ceilinged old tavern. If you come in winter, ask to sit near the fireplace, and savor such New Englandy dishes as chicken pot pie and salmon cakes. You will be equally pleased with the bread baskets, full of sweet quick breads and warm-from-the-oven sunflower bread, crunchy with sunflower seeds. For dessert, try the old-fashioned creamy tapi-oca pudding covered with freshly whipped cream, or cream cheese–pecan pie. Or grab a quick snack in the bakery in front of the restaurant, then settle down at one of the picnic tables to rest your feet and relax. Open 11:00 A.M. to 8:00 P.M. Tuesday through Thursday, to 9:00 P.M. Friday and Saturday, and 8:00 A.M. to 7:00 P.M. Sunday. Call (860) 295–0006.

Here's a "secret" recipe for cream cheese–pecan pie that produces a pie almost as good as Sadler's.

## Almost as Good as Sadler's Ordinary Cream Cheese–Pecan Pie

### Ingredients

1 9½-inch deep-dish pie shell, unbaked (your own recipe or a premade crust)

1 8-ounce package cream cheese, at room temperature (Light cream cheese works just fine.)

1 egg

1 teaspoon vanilla

⅓ cup sugar

¼ teaspoon salt

3 eggs

¼ cup sugar

1 cup light corn syrup (Karo)

1 teaspoon vanilla

1¼ cup whole pecans (or chopped pecans)

Preheat oven to 375 degrees.

In a small bowl, combine cream cheese, 1 egg, 1 teaspoon vanilla, ⅓ cup sugar, and salt. Mix until all ingredients are well combined. (If little lumps of cream cheese remain, that's OK.) Set aside.

In another small bowl, beat 3 eggs. Mix in ¼ cup sugar, corn syrup, and 1 teaspoon vanilla. Blend well.

Spread cream-cheese mixture over the bottom of the unbaked pie shell. Sprinkle with chopped pecans. Carefully pour the corn-syrup mixture over the pecans.

Bake at 375 degrees for 35 to 45 minutes or until center is set. Refrigerate until firm.

Best served cold with small dollops of lightly sweetened whipped cream.

Serves 8–10.

Hint: Rely upon a half-and-half blend of light and dark corn syrup to concoct a proper pecan pie. You can gild the lily by adding 1 cup (8 ounces) semisweet chocolate chips to the corn-syrup mixture.

Nathan Hale is Connecticut's official state hero, and there are Nutmeggers who feel about him kinda the way Tennesseans feel about Elvis. Hale (Yale class of 1773) was a fervent patriot who left his position as a local schoolmaster to join the rebellion against the British as soon as word arrived of the doings up at Lexington and Concord. He fought with the Continental army through most of 1776. In September of that year, he slipped into New York to gather information on British strength and deployments. After being caught (possibly as a result of being betrayed by a cousin), Hale was hanged by the British for spying. He was just twenty-one. Our history books always reported his last words as "I only regret that I have but one life to lose for my country." However, the recently revealed diaries of British captain Frederick MacKenzie, who witnessed Hale's execution, report young Nathan's final remarks as "It is the duty of every good officer to obey any orders given him by his commander-in-chief." Evidently, the spinmeisters were at work even then.

The ***Nathan Hale Homestead*** at 1199 South Street, Coventry, was once Hale's home, which is sufficient to make it some sort of landmark. Hale himself might not recognize the house in which he grew up: It was rebuilt in the then-fashionable Georgian style the year he died. He'd probably recognize the surroundings, though. The house sits in the middle of the 1,219-acre Nathan Hale State Forest, a wooded setting not too dissimilar from the surroundings of Hale's boyhood 300-acre farm. Today the farmhouse is preserved much as it was when the Hale family lived there. On display inside the building is a collection of colonial antiques, including many of the personal possessions used by two generations of Hales. Open daily May 15 through October 15, 1:00 to 4:00 P.M. Wednesday through Sunday. The homestead is the site of an encampment and muster in July and a corn maze the first week in August. September features the annual Nathan Hale Day celebration. Admission. Call (860) 742–6917.

By the way, while the nearby ***Nathan Hale Cemetery*** on Lake Street is a nice enough old graveyard, the great man isn't buried there. After they hanged

Nathan Hale Homestead, Coventry

## A Day in the Country

The Bolton watershed area is actually a collection of wilderness areas in the Bolton Notch and Valley Falls area, including Bolton Notch Park, Valley Falls Park, Freja Park, and the Shenipisit Trail. You'll find several marked trails through the woods, perfect for hiking, and streams just right for a little canine swim. Be careful on the trails, however, as the marking isn't quite ready for prime time. Autumn seems to be the best time to see the area in all its glory, but we like late spring walks. Remember whatever you carry into Connecticut state parks, you must carry out, including trash and garbage. The Bolton watershed area is located off exit 5 off Interstate 384. Take a left at the exit to the commuter parking lot at the junction of U.S. Highways 6 and 44. Park in the commuter lot. Enter the watershed area just south of the parking lot. The area is open during daylight hours.

In recent years there's been heated debate around the state over whether dogs should be allowed off their leashes in public parks. This dog fight is far from settled, so if your canine companion comes along, throw a leash in the backseat, just in case. Then, when you get to the park, check the leash policy, which will surely be posted at the park entrance.

him, the British dumped his remains in an unmarked grave that now lies somewhere under Sixty-sixth Street and Third Avenue in Manhattan.

Connecticut tourists almost never have the campus of the **University of Connecticut** at Storrs on their itinerary, but they should. The UConn campus is home to more than students. It also houses some attractions that leave many more heavily promoted facilities in the dust.

Added to the UConn campus in 2001, the **Connecticut State Museum of Natural History** has more than two million holdings and includes a top-notch Archaeological Center. Displayed on a rotating basis, the collections provide fascinating insights into Native American cultures, birds of prey, sharks, minerals, even honey bees. At 2019 Hillside Road; (806) 486–0827; www.cac .uconn.edu. Hours are 9:00 A.M. to 4:00 P.M. Monday through Friday and 1:00 to 4:00 P.M. Sunday.

Also on campus is the **Ballard Institute and Museum of Puppetry** (Willimantic Cottage, Weaver Road), a collection of more than 2,000 puppets. More than half the puppets were created by Frank Ballard, puppetry wizard and professor emeritus of dramatic arts. Puppets and puppet lore dominate the museum's three rooms. Some of the puppets are beautiful and charming; others are dark and disturbing; all are exquisite. Regarding marionette origins, legend has it that Saint Francis of Assisi made small jointed figures to dramatize the Nativity. He

## Great Scoops at UConn

With all the attention showered on UConn's famed basketball program, it's easy to forget that UConn is also widely known for its excellent agriculture department. An offshoot of that department's activity is the *UConn Dairy Bar.* The Dairy Bar has been around since the 1930s, and it has been scooping up fountain treats at the current location—3636 Hill Road Extension (exit off Route 195)—since the early 1950s. Every day about twenty-five flavors of frozen treats are on the menu, with old favorites such as chocolate, vanilla, strawberry, and coffee. Specialty flavors such as Jonathan Supreme (named for the school's mascot), which is peanut-butter-swirled vanilla with chocolate-covered peanuts, show up from time to time. According to more than one pistachio ice-cream fanatic, the Dairy Bar is one of the few places in Connecticut that still churns up his favorite flavor with real pistachios, instead of green-dyed almonds. Servings are colossal. Open 10:30 A.M. to 5:00 P.M. Monday to Friday, noon to 5:00 P.M. Saturday and Sunday. Call (860) 486–2634.

called them "little Marys" or "marionettes." Open noon to 5:00 P.M. Friday, Saturday, and Sunday. Admission. Call (860) 486–4605 for information about special exhibits and events.

A short distance from the busy UConn campus at Storrs, the Natchaug River rumbles through a shallow gorge and pours over a small waterfall into a clear pool at the center of a secluded, sun-dappled clearing. Winding over, under, and around the tumbled boulders on either shore are a handful of gentle walking trails. This is ***Diana's Pool,*** and it is a secret picnic ground used mainly by local fisherfolk and UConn students.

Diana's Pool isn't easy to find, but it's worth the effort. Take U.S. Highway 6 and look for signs directing you to South Chaplin or Sherman Corners. Turn right onto Diana's Pool Road. This is a dead end, but about 100 feet up the road there's an unmarked parking area on the left (look for a NO SWIMMING sign). From there walk about 100 feet down the trail; it branches a couple of times, and if you're not sure which branch to follow, walk toward the sound of the water. At the end of the trail you'll find yourself in a sylvan glade so perfect you'll expect to see dryads and fauns frolicking. If you want to picnic, you'll have to do without picnic tables, but the sun-warmed rocks above the pool are a great place to spread a blanket and watch the play of sunlight and shadow on the water. Diana's Pool is relaxing at almost any time of the year. Cool autumn temperatures kill off the mosquito population and the fall foliage is in full color. Be sure to wear boots or high-top sneakers for walking and rock climbing.

Continuing west along US 44, you'll wind up in the quaint community of Ashford, home to a wonderfully thrifty, only-in-New England version of recycling: a library in the old town dump! It's a metaphor for the regional motto: "Use it up. Wear it out. Make it do or do without." Which makes this "library" at the Ashford Transfer Station such a practical idea. It happened this way. A few years back, folks began remarking that a lot of perfectly good books were being sent to the dump, so the people down at the town's **Babcock Public Library** put their heads together to come up with a way to get some more mileage from these castoffs. What they came up with was an "annex" of the library at a central location—the, er, dump—where people could drop off or pick up used books free of charge.

So the **Ashford Transfer Station,** where everybody takes their recyclables and trash, gained a plywood shed with simple plank shelving. Now, when residents drop off their recyclables, more often than not, they stop by the "annex" to browse the shelves and pick up a couple novels. The arrangements are simple. Books are divided into broad categories such as "mysteries," "westerns," or "romance," with titles running the gamut from those of Stephen King and Tom Clancy to books of philosophy and children's books; drop off what you've read and take as many other books as you want. People from outside of Ashford—such as yourself—are welcome to use the library, but trash serv-

## Movies under the Stars

Like other states, Connecticut has a proud history as the one-time home of many drive-in movie theaters. There were at least thirty of them during the peak years of the 1950s. But, as has happened in the rest of the country, the drive-ins have gone dark town by town, leaving just two survivors. They're worth the trip.

*The Pleasant Valley Drive-in,* at 47 East River Road, Barkhamsted, is a vintage site that feels almost like the year it was built: 1947. You will be treated to bonus cartoons and get a chance to feast on hot dogs, fries, and pizza at the concession stand. The price for a double feature is just $7.00. The movies start at dusk, April to September (Thursday to Sunday during spring and fall). Call (860) 379–6102.

The state's other perennial is the *Mansfield Drive-in,* 228 Stafford Road, Mansfield Center. Going strong since 1954, it features three screens, all with double features. Tickets are $8.00 per adult, and carloads can get in on Wednesday night for $16.00. Mansfield is open April through October, weekends only during spring and fall. Call (860) 423–4441.

Regardless of which of these drive-ins you choose, plan on arriving early. On some nights they're packed.

ices are for Ashford residents only. The transfer station "library" (232 Upton Road; 860–429–3409) is open 2:00 to 8:00 P.M. Wednesday, 8:00 A.M. to 4:00 P.M. Saturday, and 10:00 A.M. to 4:00 P.M. Sunday.

Tiny Franklin has a surprising number of attractions. At the **Blue Slope Country Museum,** 138 Blue Hill Road, city slickers can get acquainted with farm implements and tools housed in a Pennsylvania Dutch–syle Amish barn. The museum offers educational programs and demonstrations relative to the importance of farming in this country. Special events in October. Call (860) 642–6413 for information and hours.

## Franklin's Cursed Apples

The quiet little hamlet of Franklin in the far southern reaches of the Quiet Corner has always been a farming community. One of Connecticut's most famous pieces of folklore is about dark doings and murder in this peaceful village.

In spring 1693 when Franklin's apple orchards were in blossom, an old pack peddler named Horgan spent a successful day in the village, selling his wares to the goodwives of Franklin. He asked one of the farm wives for a place to stay for the night and was directed to Micah Rood's farm. Rood often made his spare room available for travelers.

Micah Rood might have had room in his house, but throughout the village, he was known as a man with no room in his heart. He was a miserly skinflint who delighted in scaring the children who crept into his apple orchards hoping to make away with a piece of fruit. Horgan made his way to the Rood farm, where Micah agreed to put him up for the night. It's said that dinner conversation revolved around how much gold and silver the peddler had taken in that day.

The next morning, villagers were stunned to find Horgan's battered and bloody body beneath an apple tree in Rood's orchard. Micah Rood was questioned about the murder, but with little evidence, Horgan's death went unpunished. As spring came on, the townspeople noticed that the white apple blossoms on the tree beneath which Horgan had met his fate were splashed with red. Later when the fruit of the tree matured, the apples' sweet white fruit was stained with dark drops of red. The townspeople whispered the old peddler had, with his dying breath, cursed Rood and his trees. Mr. Rood never picked the fruit from that tree and later was found dead, sitting in a chair staring out at his orchard. Franklin's bloody apple tree continued to thrive and bear fruit until it was blown down in the 1938 hurricane. Today, you can still see traces of Franklin's blood-stained apples when you pick apples at some of the neighboring orchards.

Franklin is located on Route 169, one of the most scenic roads in Connecticut.

# Tolland

As a rule, Nutmeggers understand deli about as well as New Yorkers understand chowder. Which is to say that neither understands the other very much at all. The pleasant exception is ***Rein's Deli-Restaurant*** at 435 Hartford Turnpike (Route 30) in Vernon. This is a large, noisy place, with brisk service and small tables that would be right at home in Gotham. The only reminder that you're still in Connecticut are the signs making witty references to New Yorkish things and places (with the restrooms naturally located in Flushing).

But never mind the decor. What counts is the authentic deli food you wouldn't be surprised to find at Manhattan's famed Carnegie. The half-sour pickles are crisp and briny. The firm, fat chips arrive smoking hot. The turkey, pastrami, and corned beef are eminently respectable; same for the combo sandwiches. And the Reubens rival the ones you get at the Manhattan deli from which that sandwich gets its name. If your taste doesn't run to deli meats and sandwiches, don't worry. The menu here is huge, and everything on it seems to be available all day. No matter when you stop by, you can get anything from blintzes to bagels, to lox and eggs, to a full dinner, to a diet plate. And all of it has that special deli touch. If you've ever wondered why New Yorkers rave about deli, here's your chance to find out without having to actually go to New York. So what more could you ask for? Open daily, 7:00 A.M. to midnight. Call (860) 875–1344.

The lights are on, but nobody's home at the ***Daniel Benton Homestead*** on Metcalf Road in Tolland. A ghostly figure in a military uniform seems to appear at the front door. Footsteps echo through the east wing and then gradually trail off into silence. Occasionally the whole house shakes without making a sound.

A spokesman for the Tolland Historical Society, which acquired the Benton Homestead in the late 1960s, enigmatically notes that an old house plagued by a flying squirrel "can produce a lot of noise" but refrains from speculation on the subject of the supernatural. The society prefers to concentrate on the house's unusual architectural details, original paneling, period furnishings, and the facts that it is the ancestral home of former U.S. Senator William Benton and was used to house Hessian prisoners during the Revolution.

Area ghost watchers, on the other hand, have an abiding interest in the place and eagerly place the blame for certain strange goings-on at the homestead squarely on the shoulders of one Elisha Benton. In 1777 patriot Benton contracted smallpox while being held in a British prisoner-of-war camp. Sent home to Tolland to die, he was nursed by his seventeen-year-old sweetheart, Jemina Barrows. A little more than a month after Benton died in this house,

Jemina succumbed to the same disease. Their graves lie 48 feet apart on the west lawn of the homestead.

During the years since this incident, the Benton Homestead is said to have played host to various ghostly activities. A member of the household staff claimed to have seen a weeping apparition in a white dress; a guest once reported having heard inconsolable sobbing at midnight; a common story has a uniformed figure wandering the house with arms outstretched as if pleading.

The Benton Homestead is open 1:00 to 4:00 P.M. daily, May through October. Donation appreciated. Call (860) 872–8673.

Two other antique buildings in Tolland have a less lurid past. In colonial times the **_Hicks-Stearns Museum_** at 42 Tolland Green was first a tavern, then a private home. It was later made over in the Victorian style, a form that it retains today. The building now houses a collection of Victoriana, including faux bamboo furniture and a collection of children's toys. The museum also sponsors a summer concert series, a Victorian Christmas open house, and a Victorian fall evening walking tour. The house is open from mid-May through mid-October by appointment. Donation appreciated. Call (860) 875–7552.

The 1856-vintage **_Old Tolland Jail Museum_** on the green at the junction of Routes 74 and 195 housed prisoners until 1968. Today the intimidating iron-and-stone structure houses the Tolland Historical Society's collection of antique manufactured goods, farm implements, furniture, and Indian artifacts. The museum is open mid-May through mid-October 1:00 to 4:00 P.M. on Sunday or by appointment. Call (860) 870–9599.

Continuing north and east, you'll come to Stafford Springs. Once upon a time, the springs drew crowds to take their healthful waters. Today the remnants of life in a former Victorian spa-cum-mill town can still be seen in many of the beautiful Queen Anne and Gothic Revival houses that crowd the town's hilly streets. Stafford Springs is also home to a raceway and a perfectly wonderful little enthusiasts' museum called **_Gasoline Alley Automotive Museum_** at 58 Buckley Highway (Route 190).

In the collectors' lexicon, we're not sure what comes after "car nut," but whatever the word is, Don Passardi fits it to a T. He collects everything connected with the car industry from vintage gasoline pumps and oil cans to restored autos such as a 1946 Ford Sportsman, one of only 743 manufactured. In danger of being squeezed out of his living quarters by his "collection," Don did what any sensible person in the throes of passionate collecting would do: He built a 4,800-square-foot building next to his house and christened it the Gasoline Alley Automotive Museum. Admission to the museum is by appointment only, so call (860) 684–2675.

# I Scream . . .

You didn't think they keep all those cows just for pretty did you? The Quiet Corner is home to some of the most sinful, homemade ice cream in the state. Besides UConn's Dairy Bar, here are some more super scoopers to check out.

*D. Fish Family Dairy Farm,* 20 Dimock Lane (off Route 85), Bolton. Here's your chance to show the kids each step in the ice-cream-making process, starting with petting the calves. Well, OK, that's not really an official step, but it's a nice fringe benefit. Milking occurs twice each day (5:30 to 6:00 A.M. and 4:00 to 5:00 P.M.). Bottling is more or less constant. Ice-cream making happens on Monday. All of these activities are open for viewing. Of course, the big treat is sampling the ice cream. The dairy store at the farm sells milk; very rich, very creamy ice cream; fresh organic produce; and locally made jams and jellies. Pony rides and other special events are offered from time to time. The dairy store is open 8:00 A.M. to 8:00 P.M. Monday through Saturday. Ice cream is scooped noon to 8:00 P.M. Call (860) 646–9745 for information about tours or special events.

*Salem Valley Farms,* 200 Darling Road, Salem (near junction of Routes 11 and 85). Rich is the word for Salem Valley Farms' ice cream. Rich and, well, eccentric. How else would you describe an establishment that peddles outrageous flavors like ginger and espresso fudge? Actually, the menu features plenty of familiar flavors as well as an ever-changing menu of innovative items. Open noon to 9:00 P.M. daily; shorter hours in cooler months; closed January and February. Call (860) 859–2980.

*We-Lik-It,* Route 97, Pomfret. Nestled in a nineteenth-century cider mill, this ice-cream shack comes complete with farm critters and the occasional movie star. Paul Newman, whose Hole in the Wall Camp for terminally ill children is just down the road, has been spotted indulging in We-Lik-It's ultra-rich frozen confections. Open 11:00 A.M. to 9:00 P.M. daily. Call (860) 974–1095. (For those who like to star gaze, we have it on very reliable authority that when Mr. Newman is at the Hole in the Wall—usually in the summer—he often can be spotted picking up his Sunday *New York Times* at the Cumberland Farms in Ashford.)

***Buell's Orchard*** at 108 Crystal Pond Road in nearby Eastford is a century-old farm stand par excellence. Starting in June with strawberries, the stand sells fresh produce throughout the growing season. August brings fresh peaches. Apples appear during the fall and can last well into the winter, depending on the size of the apple crop. The stand also sells cider, Vermont cheese, and pumpkins. The caramel apples are made with a special caramel sauce into which are dipped "firm late apples." We guarantee that they are among the best you've ever tasted. The season for caramel apples starts about Labor Day and ends around Halloween. On Columbus Day weekend, the Buells celebrate the harvest with an open house that includes hayrides and free cider and

## Gentlemen, Start Your Engines

If the death of car racing legend Dale Earnhardt in 2001 taught us anything, it's that you don't have to live in the heartland or south of the Mason-Dixon Line to care a lot about NASCAR racing; it's a hugely popular spectator sport nationwide. Here in Connecticut it also offers a welcome alternative to all the scenic vistas, quaint shops, historic homes, and nautical lore. In addition to Lime Rock, the racetrack that attracts the biggest names both on the track and in the stands, there are three other cozy, family-friendly NASCAR tracks in Connecticut that offer weekly schedules of qualifying rounds, featured races, and special events:

**Stafford Motor Speedway,**
55 West Street,
Stafford Springs.
Racing every Friday on paved, semi-banked half-mile oval track, April through September.
Call (860) 684–2783.

**Waterford Speedbowl,**
1080 Hartford Road,
Waterford.
Saturday evening races.
Call ahead: (860) 442–1585.

**Thompson International Speedway,**
205 East Thompson Road,
Thompson.
Racing on ⅝-mile banked oval track.
Thursday evening, April through October.
Call (860) 923–2280.

doughnuts. Open 8:00 A.M. to 4:00 P.M. weekdays, 8:00 A.M. to 3:00 P.M. Saturday, and 1:00 to 5:00 P.M. Sunday. Call (860) 974–1150.

North of Stafford, hard by the Massachusetts line, is Connecticut's smallest town, the diminutive settlement of Union (population 620). Most travelers pass it by, but for bibliophiles, it's a standard stop en route to Massachusetts. For here resides one of the state's unique eateries, the *Traveler Restaurant* on Route 86 (Interstate 84, exit 74). The Traveler is first and foremost a place for good, home-style cooking. Full-tilt-boogie turkey dinners and turkey pot pies at very moderate prices are the specialties here, and the Traveler reputedly serves twelve tons of the big bird a year. What we like though is one special little twist. Not only can you order a decent meal here, but customers are invited to pick out a book from the shelves lining the walls, read it while eating, and then take it home. That's right, buy a meal, get a book. Children are well treated, and the supply of kids' books is great. If your one free book isn't quite enough, there's an excellent little used book shop on the lower level. There's also a cute antiques store on the property. Make sure you ask for a window table, so you can look out at the pond. Open daily from 7:00 A.M. to 8:00 P.M. The Traveler does breakfast, lunch, and dinner. Breakfast is served until 11:00 A.M., but omelettes and lighter fare are available all day. Call (860) 684–4920.

Like Union, the town of Willington, south of Stafford Springs, is one of those places most travelers pass by unknowingly. Don't you do so. For located on Route 32 (½ mile east of the junction with Route 195) in Willington is a little slice of heaven. *Willington Pizza,* with its small-town setting and decor running to carousel horses, may seem country quaint, but the pizza selection is definitely big-city sophisticated. There's a broad selection of pies and toppings, including some low-fat pies for people watching their cholesterol. But the reason most people make the pilgrimage to Willington is for the delicious Red Potato Pizza. This was the pie that gained nationwide attention on the *CBS Morning News*. Although pizza pros in New Haven would disown it, the crunchy crust, garlicky roasted potatoes, and sour cream topping make for a rich and different pie that needs to be judged (repeatedly) on its own merits. You're always liable to come across picky pizza-pie mavens who claim that the only way to eat a Red Potato Pizza is with a side-dish of iced caviar for topping each yummy slice. Open daily from 11:00 A.M. to 11:00 P.M.; midnight on Friday and Saturday. Call (860) 429–7433.

# Old Woodstock

*Christ Church* in Pomfret is definitely not the traditional white New England church with pointed steeple. Instead, this is a stone-and-brick building with a certain Byzantine influence. The interior, decorated in what one might call "high Victorian camp," makes an ideal backdrop for six extraordinary stained-glass windows, designed by famed Arts and Crafts designer Louis Comfort Tiffany early in his career and installed in the church in 1882.

Tiffany, a native of nearby Killingly, created the windows before moving to New York City, and all but one is an original Tiffany design. It is believed that Tiffany copied the Saint George window from an original Venetian design. Interestingly, the dedications and inscriptions in all six windows are rendered in lead, not in the more common paint, and the glass used is chunkier and more faceted than later Tiffany efforts. The themes here aren't normal to Tiffany, either. Instead of the common Tiffany floral and pastoral compositions, these items feature religious subjects. Besides Saint George, there are two crosses, one with a stylized peacock, of all things. There's also a window depicting the Parable of the Wise and Foolish Virgins and one depicting the Parable of the Talents, with the inscription, "Well done my good and faithful servant." Finally, there is a rose window depicting Ezekiel and the wheel. Visit about one hour before sunset to get the full effect of sunset through the rose window. Call (860) 928–7026 for information. Ask at the church office for a tour. Make sure you take a good look at the church's interior. It's a haven of gorgeous Arts and Crafts wood carving and tile work.

**Still Waters** at the junction of US 44 and Route 198 in tiny Eastford (about 7 miles west of Pomfret) is one of those shops antiques hounds, particularly lovers of clothing that was fashionable in bygone decades, dream about but rarely find. The vintage attire—especially the hats, costume jewelry, and coats—is glorious and in prime condition. And the prices aren't just right, they are a downright steal. You might luck into a gorgeous, hand-tailored alpaca swing coat from the '50s for practically the price of a department-store sweater. The owner, a helpful and pleasant woman, promises customers "many eclectic surprises," and she's right. Visit Still Waters and be surprised. Open 10:00 A.M. to 5:00 P.M. Thursday through Saturday, 11:00 A.M. to 5:00 P.M. Sunday. Call (860) 974–3500.

If you decide to stay in the Pomfret area, you can't do much better than **Celebrations Inn** at 330 Pomfret Street (US 44 and Route 169). Quartered in the old Pomfret Inn, this is a beautiful little B&B, with five rooms and suites, some with private baths. Lots of fireplaces and choice antiques punctuate the spacious rooms, most of which are charmingly decorated with floral patterns, giving them an airy English-garden quality. This is one of only a few accommodations in the state that welcome not only your children, but your pets. Just let them know you're bringing a furry friend when you make your reservation. At Celebrations the breakfast included in the room rate isn't just coffee and a roll; you get the full spread, well prepared and served with much warmth and style. Call (860) 928–5492 or visit www.celebrationsinn .com.

Route 169 weaves south from Woodstock through Pomfret, Brooklyn, and Canterbury and has been

## won'tfadeaway

The **Bara-Heck Settlement** at the junction of US 44 and Route 97 in Pomfret is another of those abandoned villages that just won't go away. Founded by two Welsh families in 1780 and abandoned in 1890, stories persist that somewhere in time, the town still lives. Visitors to this abandoned spot have reported hearing the sweet silver laughter of children, cows mooing, dogs barking, mothers calling children in from play, and wagon wheels creaking along unpaved tracks. The sounds reportedly appear most prevalent near the town's old cemetery and some of the cellar holes. Some visitors have also reported seeing the ghosts of a bearded man and a small child. Take Route 97 north to the side road just north and to the left of Mashomoquet Brook, then follow the dirt road about ¼ mile to the settlement.

officially dubbed one of the ten most outstanding scenic byways in the United States. This section of the book wouldn't be complete without making adequate reference to Pomfret's favorite hangout, the **Vanilla Bean Café.** Housed in a renovated nineteeth-century barn, this is one irresistible place for lunch, dinner, or a midafternoon cup of cocoa. The soups here are fabulous—nothing fancy, just deliciously prepared simple blends. The tomato Florentine, paired with a

## woodstockand pomfrettrivia

During the mid-to-late nineteenth century, Woodstock and Pomfret were dubbed "inland Newports" due to their popularity with the rich and ostentatious, who trained up from New York or down from Boston to build lavish summer "cottages" in the Quiet Corner.

salad, is ideal for summertime weather. When winter comes, go for a warmer-upper, such as cheese-topped chili with beef or a vegetarian alternative. Their sea-bass cakes will erase memories of school-cafeteria fish cakes. The turkey sandwiches taste like the best of part of Thanksgiving dinner, day-after leftovers. The Vanilla Bean is run by Barry Jessuruns, and chances are you'll run into him when you visit. Unless you wind up being too full for dessert, the homemade ice cream really hits the spot after a chili lunch. In the evenings patrons are often treated to entertaining poety readings, folk concerts, and poetry slams. (The UConn campus at Storrs is close by, so creative talents abound.) Open from 7:00 A.M. to 3:00 P.M. Monday and Tuesday, until 8:00 P.M. Wednesday and Thursday, until 9:00 P.M. Friday, 8:00 A.M. to 8:00 P.M. Saturday and Sunday. Call (860) 928–1562.

Called by *Travel + Leisure* magazine "a Caprilands for the '90s," **Martha's Herbiary,** 589 Pomfret Street (Route 169 at the junction of US 44 and Route 97) is a sweet-smelling treasure snuggled in the carriage house and servants' quarters of an eighteenth-century house. The gift shop is packed to the rafters with potpourri, soaps, essential oils, cooking herbs, and lotions. Cooking demonstrations and classes take place in the kitchen in the back. Outside, the gardens overflow with perennials, heirloom vegetables (vegetables grown from old strains of the plant, many dating back to colonial times), edible flowers, fish ponds, a sunken garden, and row upon row of herbs. Classes are offered throughout the year on a variety of topics such as making cordials, natural cosmetics, and drying herbs. Classes are by reservation only. Call (860) 928–0009 for operating hours and class schedules.

The **Brayton Grist Mill and Marcy Blacksmith Shop Museum** on US 44, at the entrance to Pomfret's Mashamoquet Brook State Park, showcases two establishments that in 1857 made an agreement to jointly support a dam and flume on Mashamoquet Brook.

## Follow the Vine

While you might think you need to travel to the south of France, a Tuscan village, or California's Napa Valley to visit a working vineyard and partake of its flavorful offerings, don't call your travel agent just yet. Connecticut has twelve vineyards open for tours and tastings. The wineries have been organized into the **Connecticut Wine Trail,** a three-day tour that takes you through some of the state's most picturesque and historic towns. The tour, which is marked by blue signs, starts in the Housatonic Valley, with stops in the Litchfield Hills, the coastal area, and Norwich before ending in Pomfret, in the Quiet Corner. For more information contact the Connecticut Wine Trail, 74 Chester Maine Road, North Stonington 06359, or call (860) 535–0202.

The four-story Brayton Grist Mill is a reminder of long-ago days when every town on a river or creek had a water-powered mill to shell corn and grind grain. The gristmill on Mashamoquet Brook was operated by William Brayton from 1890 until his death in 1928. The equipment on display includes the turbine, the millstone, and a corn sheller patented in 1888.

The Marcy Blacksmiths also plied their trade in a shop along Mashamo-quet Brook; in fact, the area became known as Marcy Hollow. In 1830 Orin Marcy of Pomfret opened the shop, which used a water-powered bellows and triphammer. The next two generations of Marcys prospered, perfecting their craft. Darius, Orin's son, won a first prize for his horseshoes at the Chicago World's Fair in 1893. There are a number of antique tools displayed at the blacksmith shop; some are farrier's tools, others are wheelwright's tools. Several tools are specially made and stamped "O. Marcy."

The museum doesn't have a telephone, but it is open 2:00 to 5:00 P.M. weekends, May through September. Admission is free.

Merchant and publisher Henry Chandler Bowen had two great obsessions: roses and the Fourth of July. He indulged both at his summer residence in the center of the town of Woodstock, in the northeastern corner of Connecticut. There, in 1846, he built himself a board-and-batten-sided, gingerbread-encrusted Gothic Revival palace. Outside he planted a rose garden, and inside he uphol-stered much of the furniture in pink. The house itself he painted a fashionably subdued light lavender, but it was later repainted pink with green shutters and dark green and red trim, reminiscent of the flowers that Bowen loved. He named this classic Victorian "painted lady" **Roseland Cottage,** but today most folks in Woodstock just call it "the pink house."

It was at Roseland, during the latter half of the nineteenth century, that Bowen held the most extravagant series of Fourth of July celebrations that America had ever seen. On the day before each celebration, prominent guests from all over the country would arrive by train in neighboring Putnam, whence they would be transported by carriage to Woodstock for an evening reception that featured (what else?) pink lemonade. The next day a huge American flag, would be displayed on one side of the house. The guests would then parade down Route 169 to Roseland Park, where they would amuse the public and each other with exchanges of high-flown rhetoric until it was time to return to Roseland for further diversions of a nonalcoholic nature.

Roseland Cottage

(Bowen was a temperance man.) What makes all of this so remarkable is that no less than four U.S. presidents—Benjamin Harrison, Ulysses S. Grant, Rutherford B. Hayes, and William McKinley—participated in these shenanigans, two of them—Harrison and Grant—while in office, the others while they were congressmen.

Today Roseland Cottage and its grounds and outbuildings are open to the public. Everything is much as it was in the glory days. The rose garden is still there, along with an 1850s-vintage maze of boxwood hedges, and so is most of the original Gothic Revival furniture. The famous flag is displayed in its traditional location each Fourth of July. Even the bowling alley out in the barn, thought to be the oldest such facility in a private residence in America, is still as it was. One can almost imagine Ulysses Grant—who seems to have coped well at Roseland despite the fact that he was most definitely not a temperance man—bowling his famous strike there during his July 4 visit.

Roseland Cottage is open 11:00 A.M. to 4:00 P.M. Friday through Sunday, June 1 to mid-October. Admission. Call (860) 928–4074.

***The Christmas Barn,*** 835 Route 169 in Woodstock, is more than just a red barn full of Christmas paraphernalia. The year-round display of Christmas decorations upstairs is balanced by displays of country furniture, crafts, lace curtains, curios, collectibles, quilts, craft supplies, and Victoriana suitable for all seasons. Besides, owners Joe and Kris Reynolds are that rare breed of people who seem able to keep the Christmas spirit alive all year. Open June through December, 10:00 A.M. to 5:00 P.M. Tuesday through Saturday, noon to 5:00 P.M. on Sunday. Call (860) 928–7652.

When you venture off the beaten path in Connecticut, one of the first things you'll notice is the labyrinth of stone walls that snake across the landscape. Some were built with the precision of Egyptian pyramids; others look like day-care projects. Whatever the level of construction skill, the origin of these natural building blocks is yet another reminder of the limitless power of Mother Nature. Glaciers, which inched their way across the region close to 20,000 years ago, scraped the earth as they went, carrying tons of rocks and boulders with them. Farmers had to remove this debris so they could till the soil and plant their crops. The mortarless stone walls you see throughout the area were originally built to make use of the rocks that had been liberally deposited everywhere and to mark field boundaries. Today, they serve as elegant property accents, adorning many of the state's most opulent homesteads. Craftsmen who have mastered the ancient art of stone wall construction are well compensated for their work these days.

## noclothes,no kidding

*Solair Recreation League,* (860) 928–9174, Woodstock, is what our mothers in their most shocked voices used to call a nudist camp. It's been around since the '30s and offers 300 acres of wooded solitude. Amenities include a lake, rental cabins, pool, tennis and volleyball courts, and a social hall. Visitors are welcome provided you make reservations in advance. If you're feeling frisky, you can get a couples-only one-day trial membership for a small fee. You'll find the Solair Recreation League off English Neighborhood Road in Woodstock. Before just dropping in, call for directions, hours, more information, and reservations. Open from mid-April through late October (when it gets a bit nippy to be running around sky-clad!). Don't forget the sunscreen.

Originally constructed in 1814 as a stagecoach tavern, **White Horse Inn** on Route 193 in Thompson (east of Woodstock and Interstate 395) was used throughout the nineteenth century for various purposes. One of its last incarnations was as a tavern owned by Capt. Vernon Stiles, a distinguished, if slippery, local politician.

Located near the Rhode Island and Massachusetts borders, Captain Stiles's establishment was a hole-in-the-wall for fugitives fleeing neighboring states and runaway lovers, who used Captain Stiles's good offices to join in the bonds of holy matrimony. Newlyweds became such a common presence that the tavern's kitchen routinely baked a wedding cake every Sunday.

Unlike so many venerable New England establishments, the White Horse Inn doesn't claim that Washington slept or dined there. In fact, it claims that Washington selected a rival inn in 1775 and pronounced the accommodations "not good." The Marquis de Lafayette did, however, dine and sleep here in 1824. Call (860) 923–9571 for current hours. Last we checked, the tavern was open to the public only for Sunday brunch, 11:00 A.M. to 2:00 P.M.

## gloriousfalldrive

In the Quiet Corner, there's no prettier fall drive than Route 169 north. Start at the intersection of Rocky Holly Road in Lisbon and head off to Woodstock and points north.

You know you've found *Zip's Dining Car* when you see the neon sign that towers over the building advertising with commendable brevity: EAT. Located at the junction of Routes 101 and 12 (exit 93 off I–395) in Dayville, Zip's is an original O'Mahoney diner, built in 1954.

The diner is actually a New England invention. Its progenitor, the lunch wagon, was invented by Walter Scott in 1872 in Providence, Rhode Island. More improvements followed, and in 1906 the Worcester Lunch Car Company was born. It soon was the primary popularizer of the art deco, neon-crowned, nickel alloy (later stainless steel) structure that we now associate with the American diner.

Zip's is one of the last of the original stainless steel diners still in operation and is especially notable for its pristine condition. The quilted and beveled stainless steel and the blue-accented chrome just gleam. This isn't some embalmed cultural icon, though. It's an honest-to-goodness working diner owned by local boy Thomas Jodoin, whose father managed the forerunner of the current Zip's in Danielson back in the 1940s. Thomas's brother Robert is the head chef; his son, Michael, also works in the kitchen. Brother James is the general manager. It's that kind of place. Truckers really do eat here. So do the locals, who call the place "Town Hall North."

Zip's menu is diner classic, featuring freshly prepared food, most of it made from scratch. The roast turkey with all the trimmings and the Yankee pot roast are both big dinner favorites. For lunch hoist a huge Zip burger (an especially good cheeseburger on a bulky roll) or a turkey club (made with freshly roasted turkey); these examples of the sandwich-making art are as well executed as you will find anywhere. But what Zip's is really famous for are its desserts, especially its homemade puddings and custards and the strawberry shortcake made with a flaky biscuit—all topped with real whipped cream, beaten with a wire whisk. It takes something special to stand out in this crowd, but the one dish that manages to do so is the Grape-Nuts pudding, a

## danielsontrivia

In 1855 R. R. Jones of Danielson became the country's first woman dentist.

# Zip's Own Grape-Nuts Pudding

¾ cup Grape-Nuts cereal

2 cups milk and 1 cup light cream (or 3 cups milk)

½ cup sugar

4 eggs, at room temperature, beaten

dash salt

good splash of vanilla (about 1½ to 2 teaspoons)

cinnamon and freshly grated nutmeg mixed together for topping (about ½ teaspoon cinnamon and ¼ teaspoon nutmeg)

soft butter or nonstick cooking spray for greasing the baking dish

Preheat oven to 325 degrees.

Generously butter a 1½- or 2-quart baking dish. (Or spray with nonstick cooking spray.)

Line the baking dish with the Grape-Nuts. Just dump them in and shake the dish around until the bottom and sides are coated with a thin layer of the cereal.

Mix the milk, eggs, sugar, salt, and vanilla together.

Pour the egg-sugar-milk mixture over the Grape-Nuts in the baking dish and then sprinkle with cinnamon-nutmeg mixture.

Bake at 325 degrees for about one hour or until a knife inserted in the center comes out clean. (Ovens vary; start checking at 45 minutes.)

Serve slightly warm with freshly whipped cream.

Serves 8.

house specialty. Open daily 6:00 A.M. to 9:00 P.M. No credit cards. Call (860) 774–6335.

Head south from Zip's on Route 12 and you'll hit *Logee's Greenhouse* at 141 North Street. With the revival of all things Victorian, violets have never been more popular, and the best place to see and buy violets is Logee's. The business has been a family operation since 1893, so when it comes to plants, they speak gospel truth. The eight greenhouses have the feel of Victorian conservatories with their displays of orchids, jasmine, ferns, and a dazzling variety of begonias. Logee's publishes a mail-order catalog that's available at a small charge. Logee's is open year-round; 9:00 A.M. to 5:00 P.M. Monday through Saturday, 11:00 A.M. to 5:00 P.M. Sunday. Call (860) 774–8038 for information.

# Windham

Mention the **Golden Lamb Buttery** in a roomful of Connecticut foodies, and chances are that the initial reverent silence will shortly be followed by exclamations of "Isn't it just the best!" With all due respect to Farmington's Apricots, this woodsy eatery at Brooklyn's Hillandale Farm, 499 Wolf Den Road (off Route 169), just may be the most romantic restaurant in the state.

Owners Jimmie and Bob Booth (cook and host, respectively) do know how to set a scene. During the warmer months, cocktails are served on a tractor-drawn hay wagon that carries you to the restaurant through the opalescent summer twilight. During northeastern Connecticut's chilly winters, dinner is served by a roaring fireplace. The pieces of eclectica scattered about, the vintage Jaguar, the telephone box, the country-costumed waitresses, tell you that you're in for a memorable dinner from the time you enter the barn.

Dinner starts with soup, always seasoned with fresh herbs from the garden and always a knockout. There's usually a choice of several entrees. Duck is a perennial, but lamb and beef are common, and there's almost always some kind of fish or seafood. Veggies, lots of them, are served family-style with the meal; marinated mushrooms always seem to be on the menu, and other vegetables ebb and flow with the output from the farm's garden. Everything is fresh, and it's all cooked without salt or preservatives. The desserts here are endearingly homey, especially the cakes.

Dinner is prix fixe and is served at 7:00 P.M. Friday and Saturday; there's one seating only, and you *must* have a reservation. Tuesday through Saturday the restaurant also serves lunch from noon to 2:30 P.M. (without the stage dressing, but still quite wonderful). Dinner seatings are booked months in advance; lunch is easier to get into. The restaurant is closed from January through April. No credit cards. Call (860) 774–4423.

Creamery Brook Road in bucolic Brooklyn is bordered by the usual Quiet Corner collection of quaint stone walls and verdant pastures. That's as expected. What's completely unexpected is the herd of shaggy bison. After all, Connecticut isn't exactly known as the home where the buffalo roam. Except that they do now. Austin and Deborah Tanner started out buying one bison for their dairy farm and ended up with a small, shaggy herd of American bison on their **Creamery Brook Bison Farm,** at 19 Purvis Road (I–395, exit 91).

The Tanners offer a forty-minute tour of their working farm, including a visit and petting session with Thunderbolt, their enormous, but gentle, show bison. Farm tours also include trying your hand at churning butter or ice cream. The Tanners and their employees will happily teach you about the healthful qualities of lean, red bison meat, and you can purchase various cuts of bison meat and souvenirs at the farm store. The Tanners suggest bison burgers are a good way to start. Tours are held July through September at 1:30 P.M. on Saturday. Also, visitors can partake of buffalo burgers on the grill and wagon rides. Admission. Call (860) 779–0837 for tour information or store hours.

If you're into fishing, consider putting Plainfield on your itinerary. The modern **Quinebaug Valley Trout Hatchery** on Hatchery Road in the township's Central Village is one of the largest hatcheries in the East, producing

## OTHER ATTRACTIONS WORTH SEEING IN THE QUIET CORNER

**Connecticut Audubon Society Center,**
189 Pomfret Street,
(Route 169),
Pomfret;
(860) 928–4948.

**Diamond A Ranch,**
975 Hartford Turnpike,
Dayville;
(860) 779–3000.
Trail rides, Wild West cookouts,
riding lessons, campouts.

**Eastern Connecticut Flea Market,**
Mansfield Drive-in,
228 Stafford Road,
(junction of Routes 31 and 32),
Mansfield;
(860) 456–2578.
Eastern Connecticut's largest weekly outdoor flea market.

**Freudenwald Antiques,**
26 Route 87 (1 mile from Route 6),
Columbia;
(860) 228–1245.
Americana, folk art, and pottery.

**Goodwin Conservation Center,**
Goodwin State Forest,
23 Potter Road (Route 6),
Hampton;
(860) 455–9534.

**Marlborough eagle,**
Route 66 between Route 2
(Marlborough) and Route 85 (Hebron).
A stunning piece of road art.

**New England Center for
Contemporary Art,**
7 Putnam Place,
Brooklyn;
(860) 774–8899.
Free.

**Special Joys Antique
Doll and Toy Shop,**
41 North River Road,
Coventry;
(860) 742–6359.
Also a cozy bed-and-breakfast.

**Theatre of Northeastern Connecticut
at the Bradley Playhouse,**
30 Front Street,
Putnam;
(860) 928–7887.

**Wright's Mill Farm,**
63 Creasey Road (Route 6),
Canterbury;
(860) 774–1455.
Sports facilities, hiking trails, ponds, five antique water-powered mill sites; horse, carriage, and wagon rides; hayrides.

280,000 pounds of trout annually. The operation is open to the public year-round, and visitors can view the hatchery through a big glass wall. The state allows restricted fishing in the nearby waters weekends from March through Memorial Day. Open daily, 9:00 A.M. to 3:30 P.M. Call (860) 564–7542.

Keep driving west from the Plainfield area on Route 14A until you're almost in Rhode Island. There, in the hamlet of Oneco (where Route 14A is known as Pond Road), you'll find something called ***River Bend Mining Attraction and Gem Stone Panning*** (41 Pond Street). We're not sure what to call this place. Maybe a "Dude Mine"? In any event, while you won't exactly find the treasure of the Sierra Madres here, children can don miners' hats and delve into an above-ground man-made mine in search of gemstones, fossils, or shells, or try their luck panning the sluice. Open 10:00 A.M. to 5:00 P.M. Tuesday through Thursday, 10:00 A.M. to 5:00 P.M. Friday, 10:00 A.M. to 5:00 P.M. Saturday, and 10:00 A.M. to 5:00 P.M. Sunday. Open early April through mid-October. Admission. Call (860) 564–3440 for information.

In 1832, at the request of the community, Prudence Crandall opened an academy on the Canterbury Green to educate the daughters of local wealthy families. The school flourished until the following fall, when Crandall admitted Sarah Harris, a twenty-year-old African-American woman. Outraged parents withdrew their daughters, forcing the school to close. But Crandall reopened it as a school for the education of "young ladies and little misses of color." The state responded by passing the "Black Law," which made it illegal for Crandall to run her school. Crandall was arrested and spent one night in jail. She was taken to court, but the case was dismissed for lack of evidence. Despite her legal victory, the school closed after it was attacked by a mob. Although Crandall's school was open for less than two years, it stands as a powerful symbol in the fight for racial equality and civil justice.

Prudence Crandall House Museum in Canterbury

## Antiquing in the Northeast

Woodbury may boast Connecticut's "Antique Avenue," but in **Putnam** you've got a whole Windham County town full of antiques shops. OK, some carry merchandise that's somewhere just above "tag-sale stuff" on the antiques food chain, but most are chockablock with high-quality, well-maintained furnishings, collectibles, and jewelry.

When its main industries quite literally went south, the community and its citizens could have held a pity party and thrown in the towel. Instead, they transformed Putnam into one of the hottest antiques shopping districts in New England. Now more than 400 dealers do business here; most are scattered throughout the Main Street area in a former mill, the old courthouse, and an 1880s Victorian department store.

The anchor attraction is the four-floor **Antiques Marketplace** at 109 Main Street, in what used to be the C. D. Bugbee Department Store. Jerry Cohen, a transplanted Californian, accomplished the changeover. Head up to the second floor's Mission Oak Shop, stocked with authentic Gustav Stickley furniture, reproduced circa-1910 Van Erp lamps, and Arts and Crafts–style pottery from Woodstock, New York. The place isn't just for big stuff, though. There's lots of good collectible jewelry, china, and glassware, plus vintage Christmas ornaments. The entire antiques district is open from 10:00 A.M. to 5:00 P.M. daily. Call (860) 928–0442.

The 1805-vintage building in Canterbury where Miss Crandall's academy was housed is preserved as the **Prudence Crandall House Museum,** a site for both permanent and changing exhibits on the history of black Americans in pre–Civil War Connecticut. There are also exhibits dealing with the life of Prudence Crandall and the development of Canterbury. The museum has a gift shop and a research library. You'll find the facility at the junction of Routes 14 and 169. Open April through December 14, 10:00 A.M. to 4:30 P.M. Wednesday through Sunday; December 15 through March 31 by appointment. Call (860) 546–7800.

**Cackleberry Farm Antiques** at 16 Lisbon Road in Canterbury is a piece of inspired goofiness located just off Route 14. For the uninitiated, "cackleberries" are eggs. You'll wonder which came first, the chicken or the egg cup, when you visit this homey antiques store. Run by Robert Forrest and his wife, Barbara, with crafts supplied by their daughter Jackie, Cackleberry Farm is fantasy land for collectors of country crafts and a mecca for fanciers of *Gallus gallus* (chickens to you and me).

Barbara Forrest has a private collection of more than 2,000 egg cups, and you'll discover egg cups galore at Cackleberry Farm. But you'll rarely see the

Other browsing-worthy stores include:

***Arts and Framing,*** 112 Main Street; (860) 963–0105. For antique mirrors and frames, custom hand-gilding, and glass as well as some antique furniture and accessories.

***Jeremiah's,*** 26 Front Street; (860) 963–8989. Large, multidealer shop, with an ever-changing display of estate jewelry, china, and glass in addition to Victorian and country-primitive furniture.

If all that walking has left you a tad peckish, central Putnam offers a modest selection of handy eateries for lunch and light noshing. A recommendable luncheon choice, with homemade soups and a selection of artful sandwiches, is the ***Courthouse Bar & Grille,*** 121 Main Street; (860) 963–0074. Open daily, 11:30 A.M. to 10:00 P.M.

If you tend more toward a snack, try ***Mrs. Bridges Pantry,*** 136 Main Street, featuring food, teas, and British gifts. You'll also find such "Brit stuff" as tea cosies, lemon curd, and imported cards. One of the owners is a cat fancier, so cute kitties abound. You can order a mini-luncheon consisting of scones, a "cuppa," or a complete teatime meal with sandwiches and desserts. Their low-fat ginger scones and ginger-peach iced tea make for a refreshing pick-me-up after a long afternoon of serious antiquing. The tearoom is open 11:00 A.M. to 5:00 P.M. daily except Tuesday. Call (860) 963–7040.

egg cups displayed there for the use that God intended them. Instead, Barbara and Robert show off their treasures in unexpected and unique ways. The Forrests also have other chicken-related collectibles in their store. If chickens aren't your thing, there are also lots of country craft items (soft sculpture dolls, place mats, and the like) for sale. Open by chance or by appointment; Barbara says they're around most of the time, but call ahead (860–546–6335).

When we think of collections, what usually comes to mind are coins, stamps, dolls, antiques, and such small easily displayed items. The Yaworski family has bigger ideas. Their ***Haul of Fame*** is a collection of antique trucks! Inside a 21,000-square-foot warehouse at 133 Packer Road in Canterbury, T. A. Cox, the curator, keeps fifty-seven antique vehicles and a collection of antique toys and models of heavy equipment (made by prison inmates) in tip-top shape. One of the jewels of the collection is a 1917 Mack truck. Probably the most famous item is a 1939 FK Model Mack truck, which, during World War II, hauled 70-foot 16-inch-bore cannons for coastal defense emplacements from Maine to Virginia. If your tastes run to flash, take a gander at the 1953 LTL Model Mack truck with buttery soft leather upholstery and exquisite hand-painted decals, which Cox modestly calls the most "dressed-out truck in the collection." So how does a museum like this get started? Yankee thrift, of course. The Yaworski family simply wanted to see the old trucks cared for and appreciated, not cast aside like junk. They plan on adding more space to the warehouse and upping the number of trucks in the collection to an even hundred.

## quietcornertrivia

The tiny settlement of Sterling near Canterbury in the Quiet Corner is named for a doctor who reneged on his promise to build the village a library if they named the town after him. Guess it was too much trouble to change the town's name yet again to Piker.

The museum keeps a pretty low profile. A lot of Canterbury residents don't even know it exists. So if you have problems finding it, go to the post office for directions. (By the way, this getting-directions technique works just about everywhere in New England.) Open 9:00 A.M. to 4:00 P.M. weekdays and 8:00 A.M. to noon Saturday. Closed Sunday and holidays. Call (860) 546–6733.

Willimantic (Willi to locals) is home to the largest thread mill in America and is sometimes called the "thread city." So where else would you locate a museum dedicated to the history of the textile industry? The **Windham Textile and History Museum** at 157 Union/Main Street.

The museum occupies two 1877-vintage buildings inside the mill complex of the old Willimantic Linen Company on Main Street. Dugan Mill is a two-story brick building housing a factory setting re-creating conditions of a century ago.

## Independence Day, Willi-Style

On July 4, Willimantic, like most towns in New England, celebrates Independence Day with a patriotic parade. Nothing very off-the-beaten path about that, except Willimantic's parade is a Boombox Parade. That's right, thousands of marchers all bopping along, boomboxes held high, all tuned into the town's radio station, WILI–AM. The radio station obliges by playing stirring patriotic marches and music. Anyone can join in as long you obey a few simple rules: wear red, white, and blue; tune your box to WILI; and be prepared to have a heck of a good time and not take anything too seriously. Aside from those few simple rules, your costume is limited only by your imagination (and good taste). Marchers costumed as George and Martha Washington, rocket ships, snowmen, and frogs (Windham is nearby) are regular participants. No preregistration is necessary. Participants usually assemble in downtown Willimantic, and the area is well marked with signs. The Willimantic Recreation Department can usually answer questions about this year's parade. Call (860) 465–3046.

There's a fully equipped shop floor with a spinning frame, carding machine, loom, and 1880s cast-iron proof printer. Overlooking the shop is an 1890-vintage overseer's office.

The museum's three-story main building houses a re-creation of the company store that once occupied the site; it's now set up as a gift shop. The museum also offers re-creations of a nineteenth-century mill owner's mansion and a mill worker's home. The Dunham Hall Library, on the third floor, contains a one-of-a-kind collection of books, photographs, and manuscripts, including a collection of old textile industry pattern books. Open 1:00 to 4:00 P.M. Wednesday through Sunday. Groups by appointment. Admission. Call (860) 456–2178 to find out about the Mill Mystery Tour and other special events.

Is **Moosup** (pronounced *MOOSE-up*) Connecticut's most patriotic town? Come visit them on the Sunday closest to August 14 (V-J Day, the day Japan surrendered) and find out. It always warms our hearts to see those brave veterans honored. The whole town turns out for its "Victory over Japan" parade— sadly, the last of its kind in the country. You'll see flags, brightly costumed marching bands, and baton twirlers, but the day really is for the vets. You'll probably have to brush away a tear or two as you watch these brave men, some wearing chestfuls of beribboned medals, walking in the parade or lining the sidewalks. The marchers parade from North Main Street to Prospect Street. The parade starts at 1:01 P.M. (the time Japan surrendered) and lasts until around 3:30 P.M. The parade is free; come early and bring your own lawn chairs. Call (860) 564–8005.

If you head west on US 6 out of Willie, you come across the **Hurst Farm** at 746 East Street in Andover. If your kids have never seen livestock up close and personal, then we suggest a visit. The farm boasts forty-five gardens, hayrides, and a country store. You'll also find lots of standard farm critters such as cows, goats, and lambs, as well as some of those exotic chickens with the punk-rocker hairdos. Big people will probably find more than enough to interest them at the food shop with James Hurst's own salsas, jams, and dried herb blends, and lots of "only in Connecticut" food products. In the fall there are pick-your-own pumpkin and dig-your-own chrysanthemums patches. Call ahead (860–646–6536) for hours and information about special events such as the hayrides.

In the springtime the swamps and woodlands of Connecticut are splashed with color from the wild rhododendrons that thrive in these parts. The beauty of these showy shrubs belies the brutality of the legend surrounding them. In 1637 the Pequot Indians were all but obliterated in a bloody massacre. British militiamen, aided by warriors from the nearby Narragansett tribe in Rhode Island, surrounded the Pequot village and set it afire. Men, women, and children were burned or speared to death. Captives were beheaded or sent into slavery. A leader of the bloody raid declared triumphantly, "We had sufficient light from the word of God for our proceedings." After the massacre a handful of survivors regrouped in the nearby cedar swamp, and tribal legend has it that the rosebay rhododendrons that still grow wild there and elsewhere bloom red in remembrance of that bloody confrontation.

Wild and cultivated rhododendrons are still plentiful across Connecticut, but one of the best places to view this beautiful bush is at the 23,000-acre rhododendron sanctuary in **Pauchaug Forest,** Route 49, Sterling (Voluntown). Call (860) 376–4075.

The sleepy village of Windham isn't well known these days. Two centuries back, however, the **Windham Frog Pond** was famous throughout England and her colonies. During the long hot summer of 1754, war and drought endangered Windham. As that summer drew to a close, ponds and streams across Connecticut were almost dry; a catastrophe for an agricultural community. That year, though, Windhamites had other worries. With the French and Indian War in full swing, they could expect especially ferocious Indian raids at the end of summer. One hot night worried residents heard an uproar coming from a marshy pond outside the village. It sounded, they thought, like the chanting of hundreds of Indians working themselves up to an attack. Some even thought they heard someone utter the words "Colonel Dyer and Elderkin, too." Dyer and Elderkin were the community's leaders.

All night long the sound continued as the town marshaled its defenses. In the last hour before dawn, the noise rose to a crescendo before dying out at first light. Their nerves drawn taught as bowstrings, the desperate colonists prepared to fend off the expected attack. But it never came. After a while, a

Windham Town Seal

scouting party crept through a swamp to the pond from whence the startling noises had come. There, they found not the expected French and Indians, but the corpses of thousands of dead bull frogs choking in the shallow waters of the pond. No one could explain what had happened, but it was a wonder and no mistake. Some speculated that the night-long noises were the sounds of the frogs fighting for territory in the restricted waters, but it was only speculation.

The Frog War story eventually became well known in Europe, so much so that it was made into a popular operetta that brought notoriety, if not fame, to the small town of Windham. As recently as thirty years ago, schoolchildren in Ohio still performed the operetta. In honor of the frogs, the town renamed the site Frog Pond. Windham Frog Pond can be seen today about a mile east of Windham Center on the Scotland Road (Route 14); the pond is on your left as you cross Indian Hollow Brook.

A few years ago, Windham announced that it was adopting a new town seal. The winning entry featured—you guessed it—a frog.

## Places to Stay in the Quiet Corner

**Bird-in-Hand B&B,**
2011 Main Street,
Coventry;
(860) 742–0032.
Moderate.

**Chickadee Cottage B&B,**
70 Averill Road,
Pomfret;
(860) 963–0587.
Moderate.

**Inn at Woodstock Hill,**
94 Plaine Hill Road,
Woodstock;
(860) 928–0528.
Fine dinners.
Moderate to expensive.

## Places to Eat in the Quiet Corner

**Golden Lamb Buttery,**
499 Wolf Den Road,
Brooklyn;
(860) 774–4423.
Expensive.

**Vanilla Bean Café,**
Route 169,
Pomfret;
(860) 928–1562.
Moderate.

**Zip's Dining Car,**
Junction Routes 101 and 12,
Dayville;
(860) 774–6335.
Inexpensive.

# Appendix: Annual Events

No one volume could do justice to all of the annual festivals, fairs, shows, garden and tag sales, and town hall dinners that make up Connecticut's yearly calendar. Connecticut's regional tourism offices all publish calendars of special events, and you can get on their mailing lists with a phone call. Dates, times, and events change from year to year, so call close to the announced date to confirm information. Throughout this book we've scattered information on events we especially enjoy. In addition, we've listed some of the larger events here.

## JANUARY

**Woodbury Winter Carnival,** Woodbury. Almost anything you'd want to do on the snow—snowboarding, tubing, skiing. Good events for kids. Call (203) 263–2203 for more information.

## FEBRUARY

**Connecticut Flower & Garden Show,** Connecticut Expo Center, Hartford. Just when you think spring will never come, this fabulous show reminds you it's just around the corner. Call (860) 844–8461.

**Eagle Watch Cruises,** Essex, from early February to mid-March. What more spectacular way to see America's national symbol than with a cruise along the Connecticut River? Bring binoculars, dress warmly, and be prepared to be dazzled. Call (860) 662–0577 for reservations and more information.

## MARCH

**Connecticut Spring Antiques Show,** at the Connecticut Expo Center, Hartford, 265 Reverend Moody Overpass. Call (207) 767–3967.

## APRIL

**The River Run 5k & 10k Races,** Iron Horse Boulevard, Simsbury. Call (860) 651–5917.

## MAY

**Civil War Battles and Reenactment,** Hammonasset Beach State Park. Union and Confederate reenacters re-create Civil War battles, encampments, period music, vintage fashions, and children's games. Call (860) 245–2785.

**Dogwood Festival,** Greenfield Hill Congregational Church, 1045 Old Academy Road, Fairfield. Stroll amid drifts of dogwood and welcome spring. Lots of good stuff to see and do, including garden tours, arts and crafts, a plant and garden sale (very good prices), historic walks, tag and rummage sales, picnic lunches, and an indoor luncheon (reservations required). Call (203) 259–5596.

**Lime Rock Grand Prix,** Lime Rock Park, 467 Lime Rock Road, Route 112, Lakeville. Spend Memorial Day weekend at the largest race in North America. The racing world is well represented with some of the best drivers from the International Motorsports Association (IMSA) and the Sports Car Club of America (SCCA). Auto-racing-related booths, souvenirs, and food. For the best view, forsake the stands and sit on the slopes overlooking the track. Call (800) RACE–LRP.

**Lobsterfest,** Mystic Seaport, 75 Greenmanville Avenue, Mystic. Outdoor lobster bake on the banks of the Mystic River. Lobster as you like it, along with all the family entertainment Mystic does so well, such as sea chanteys, demonstrations, entertainment, and food. Call (860) 572–5315.

## JUNE

**Taste of Hartford,** Alumni Park, East Hartford. If it's the best to eat, drink, or listen to in the Hartford area, you can sample it at the Taste of Hartford. Call (860) 291–7100.

**The International Festival of Arts and Ideas,** New Haven. Two weeks of free and ticketed events throughout the city, featuring some of the finest entertainers and most provocative thinkers from around the world, plus lots of kids' events. Call (888) ARTIDEA (278–4332) or visit www.artidea.org.

## JULY

**Riverfest,** Hartford and East Hartford. A celebration of the Fourth of July and the Connecticut River with show-stopping fireworks over the Connecticut River. Call (860) 525–4451.

**Buick Championship,** formerly the Greater Hartford Open (GHO), Tournament of Players Club, River Highlands in Cromwell. One of the crown jewels on the PGA tour. A great chance to see your favorite links guys up close. The Pro-Am contest before the actual tournament offers wonderful chances for photographs and autographs. Call (860) 522–4171.

## AUGUST

**Litchfield Jazz Festival,** Goshen Agricultural Society Fairgrounds, Route 63, Goshen. Spend some of Connecticut's hottest summer nights enjoying one of the coolest jazz scenes around. This festival is a real showcase for up-and-coming jazz talent. Music, art, and photography shows, and lots of yummy food (or bring your own picnic). Call (860) 567–4162.

**SoNo Arts Celebration,** Washington and South Main Streets, Norwalk. For three days the heart of SoNo (South Norwalk)—site of innumerable boutique shops, galleries, and neat restaurants—turns into one huge block party alive with outdoor arts, entertainment, and food. Call (203) 866–7916.

**Brooklyn Fair,** Route 169 and Fairgrounds Road, Brooklyn. The oldest continuously active agricultural fair in the United States. A real old-fashioned fair with oxen and horse pulls, home-and-garden exhibits, livestock displays, entertainment, and carnival attractions. Call (860) 774–7568 or (860) 779–0012 during the fair.

**Goshen Fair,** Goshen Agricultural Society Fairgrounds, Route 63, just south of Goshen Center. There are lots of old-fashioned touches, such as blue ribbons for the best corn relish, homemade quilts, and young 4-H kids exhibiting their sheep, cows, and pigs. Lots of midway action to occupy the kids and enough junk food to keep Drew Carey and Mimi happy. Call (860) 491–3655.

## SEPTEMBER

**Woodstock Fair,** Route 169 and 171, Woodstock. Connecticut's second oldest agricultural fair complete with livestock shows, food-and-garden contests, midway, entertainment, and petting zoo. Labor Day weekend. Call (860) 928–3246.

**Norwalk Oyster Festival,** Veteran's Memorial Park, Norwalk. Honoring Norwalk's seafaring past and present, this event features oyster shucking and slurping contests, tall ships, adult and kid entertainment, and a nice fireworks display. If you prefer to savor bivalves under less competitive conditions, you'll find plenty of oysters at the food court. Call (203) 838–9444 or (888) 701–7785.

**Mum Festival,** Bristol. It's mum-madness throughout the whole town, late September to mid-October. Beauty pageants, parades, arts and crafts, antique car show, and of course, mums for sale. Call (860) 584–4718; www.bristolmum festival.org.

**Ferry Park Family Festival,** Ferry Park, Rocky Hill. Food, carnival, steamboat rides on the Connecticut River, arts and crafts, exhibits, musical entertainment. Call (860) 258–2772 for details.

**Grandparents' Day at the Beardsley Zoo,** Bridgeport. Special programs about animal families with crafts for the kids. Call (203) 394–6565 for schedule and details. Free admission for all seniors accompanied by a paying child (age three and older).

## OCTOBER

**Open Cockpit Day,** New England Air Museum, just off Route 75, at Bradley International Airport in Windsor Locks. Your chance to visit the museum and, most important, climb into the cockpits of some of its coolest planes. This is a very popular event, so expect to spend some time waiting in line. Call (860) 623–3305; www.neam.org.

**Highland Festival,** Edward Waldo Homestead, Waldo Road, Scotland. Scottish festival. Bagpipe bands, dancing, athletic competitions, folk music, kid stuff, Scots wares and clothing, and ethnic food but, alas, no haggis. Call (860) 485–2692.

**City-Wide Open Studios,** New Haven. Visitors can stroll from studio to studio, as more than 40 artists open their doors to show off their work and offer a glimpse into the creative process. Call (203) 772–2709.

**Apple Harvest Festival,** on and around town green, Southington. Southington is Connecticut's Apple Town, and on this weekend the whole area turns out to celebrate the apple harvest. Apples, apple pies, apple cider, cider-glazed doughnuts, just apples galore as well as a carnival, arts and crafts fair, a foot and bed race, and entertainment. Call (860) 276–8461.

**Antiques Show,** Connecticut Expo Center, 265 Reverend Moody Overpass, Hartford. One of the country's best shows for American antiques. Dealers transform the center into elegant rooms full of decorative furnishings and art. There's usually some excellent food catered by one of the area's best caterers or restaurants. Call (207) 767–3967.

**Walking Weekend,** Northeast Quiet Corner. Historic, cultural, natural history, and scenic guided walks through twenty-five towns in Connecticut's northeast corner. Call (860) 963–7226.

## NOVEMBER

**Manchester Road Race,** Main Street, Manchester. This 4.7-mile road race—the second oldest in the East—features more than 10,000 runners, some in wonderfully idiosyncratic costumes. It's a Thanksgiving day tradition full of bands, prizes, and lots of good cheer. Call (860) 649–6456.

**Brookfield Craft Center Holiday Exhibition and Sale,** Route 25, Brookfield, usually mid-November to late December. An exhibition of quality American crafts, gifts, and holiday decorations displayed throughout three floors of a restored gristmill. Call (203) 775–4526.

**Festival of Lights,** Constitution Plaza, Hartford, from 4:00 P.M. to midnight daily, late November to early January. Hundreds of thousands of twinkling fairy lights are fashioned into fanciful shapes to celebrate the holiday season. The day after Thanksgiving, the lights go on and the Big Guy (Monsieur Kringle, that is) arrives by helicopter. OK, the helicopter is lame, but the lights are cool.

**Artistry,** Guilford Art Center, 411 Church Street, Guilford, usually November and December. This holiday sale features innovative and unusual crafts from more than 500 of the country's leading artists. Call (203) 453–5947.

## DECEMBER

**Christmas at Mystic Seaport,** Mystic Seaport, 75 Greenmanville Avenue, Mystic. You'll swear you've been transported back to the 1800s as Mystic really goes all out to make the holidays of yesteryear come alive. Don't miss the evening "Lantern Light Tours" (by reservation only). Call (860) 572–5315.

**First Night,** many locations throughout downtown Hartford. A family-friendly (no alcohol) New Year's Eve celebration, live entertainment and foods throughout the afternoon and evening. Early fireworks for the rug rats and midnight fireworks for adults. New Year's Eve. Call (860) 722–9546.

**Stanley-Whitman House Tour,** 37 High Street, Farmington. You'll begin with a stroll along High Street, decorated for the holiday season. then enjoy a light supper of soups, breads, and dessert. Afterwards, you'll take a tour of this historic house, led by costumed guides, enacting mini-dramas connected with Christmas and the history of Farmington. Admission; reservations required. Call (860) 677–9222.

# Indexes

*The Kid Stuff Index appears on pages 227–28.*

## GENERAL INDEX

## KID STUFF INDEX

# About the Authors

Transplanted Midwesterners turned born-again Yankees, David and Deborah Ritchie live in Avon, Connecticut, with their three feline companions, Gremlin, Magpie, and Vlad.

Both the Ritchies have worked as editors, staff writers, and game designers. Today, they are freelance writers who specialize in business and technical writing. Most of their work involves helping clients such as Morgan Stanley Dean Witter, J. P. Morgan Chase and Co., Bayer Pharmaceutical, Pratt & Whitney, British Airways, DuPont Pharmaceuticals, and United Technologies Corporation to develop online documentation systems, Web sites, and intranets. In their spare time, the Ritchies frequently contribute travel, food, and lifestyle articles to several regional and national magazines.

# About the Editors

Transplanted Midwesterners who met at a Milwaukee university way back in the 1950s, Joan and Tom Bross became dedicated New Englanders nearly half a century ago. Their two "home bases" have been Old Lyme on the Connecticut coast and (currently) big-city Boston.

Both Brosses are freelance writers for newspapers as well as magazines such as *National Geographic Traveler*, *Travel Smart*, and *Antique Trader Traveler*. They are long-time contributors for various travel monthlies as well as New England and Canadian guidebooks published in Great Britain. Tom specializes in Germany, Austria, Switzerland, and Finland; Joan has considerable expertise in the field of antique art prints. Tom also writes frequently about San Francisco–area attractions and has contributed to *Historic Traveler*, *Travel America*, and *Yankee Traveler*, as well as Boston's two daily newspapers, the *Globe* and the *Herald*.

Joan and Tom always appreciate hearing from readers. You can contact them c/o Globe Pequot at CTOBP@aol.com.